D0955686

DEATH
BEAT

A COLOMBIAN
JOURNALIST'S LIFE
INSIDE THE
COCAINE WARS

María Jimena Duzán

Translated and edited by Peter Eisner

HarperCollins*Publishers*

A Sylvia
Y a todos los muertos que me inspiraron
y a los vivos que me animaron

HarperCollins books may be purchased for educational, business, or sales promotional use. For information please write: Special Markets Department, HarperCollins Publishers, Inc., 10 East 53rd Street, New York, NY 10022.

FIRST EDITION

Designed by Alma Hochhauser Orenstein

Library of Congress Cataloging-in-Publication Data
Duzán, María Jimena.
[Crónicas que matan. English]
    Death beat : a Colombian journalist's life inside the cocaine wars / María Jimena Duzán ; translated and edited by Peter Eisner.
        p.   cm.
    Includes bibliographical references.
    ISBN 0-06-017057-3
    1. Violence—Colombia. 2. Drug traffic—Colombia. 3. Colombia—History—1974– . 4. Journalists—Colombia—Crimes against. 5. Duzán, María Jimena. I. Eisner, Peter. II. Title.
HN310.Z9V53213 1994
363.4'5'092—dc20   93-36048

94 95 96 97 98 ❖/RRD 10 9 8 7 6 5 4 3 2 1

CONTENTS

THE KIDNAPPING

I looked at the clock. It was high noon. March 2, 1982.

The café in the Hotel Agualongo in Pasto was empty, and a waiter of Indian extraction, who had brought me an espresso, poked his head from behind a swinging door from time to time.

Everything had been like clockwork so far, but I couldn't help being nervous. I was chain smoking, and the coffee ate away at my empty stomach.

As they had instructed me to do, I had taken a plane that morning from Bogotá to the town of Pasto—one of the few regularly scheduled DC-3 flights you can find anywhere in the world. Pasto is in the Andean highlands, on the Colombian border with Ecuador. They told me not to bring anything that looked like a suitcase or might suggest that I had left on a trip. But I did carry a *mochila arhuaca*—a woven shoulder bag—the kind that students wear, a small tape recorder, a toothbrush, and some deodorant. They had promised that I would be staying only four or five days in the camp.

I was to have the newspaper *La Republica* under my arm, and at 12 P.M. sharp, a man would enter the coffee shop of the hotel and say, "Excuse me, are you looking for Pablo?"

I was to answer, "No, for Pedro."

With this man's help, I was to become the first reporter in Colombia to meet Jaime Bateman, the legendary leader of M-19 (short for April 19 Movement), in his jungle hideout.

The risks were considerable. Anything could happen to me. Colombia was beset by political and social protest; the government, which saw M-19 and other guerrilla groups as its number-one enemy, had been harsh and repressive. President Julio Cesar Turbay Ayala was widely charged with trampling civil rights in his campaign to crush the guerrillas, and charges of torture were being reported in the news media.

I was a precocious young reporter, just twenty-four years old. Although I had never been a member of any leftist movement, I knew many people who were. As was the case at many universities in Latin America in the 1970s, all sorts of leftist splinter groups and guerrilla cells—Maoists, Trotskyites, pro-Cubans, and anti-Cubans—were commonplace at the University of Los Andes, where I was studying political science. Although I did not share their ideologies, I was, like many young people, discontent with the traditional political parties, the Liberals and the Conservatives, which had monopolized Colombian political life since the beginning of the century. Neither of these two parties had anything to tell my generation or, at least, so we believed. We simply wandered with uncertainty between a nonviolent Left filled with internal conflicts and the combative leftist guerrillas who had learned well how to capitalize on this discontent.

I often used my column in *El Espectador* to condemn instances of torture that I had seen with my own eyes—not because I was a leftist or a guerrilla, but because I believed that such incidents were an affront to human rights. But the political polarization at the time produced a type of McCarthyism in Colombia, just as it did in other countries in Latin America. M-19, the guerrilla group that set up my interview, had collaborators in both the state-run and private universities. Therefore, as soon as I began criticizing human rights abuses, the military suspected me of being a guerrilla collaborator, specifically a collaborator with M-19.

There was no question that the guerrilla movement was gaining momentum. There had been a number of highly visible and successful operations, and M-19 thought it was scoring important political points.

M-19 was founded in 1972. When I did the interview with Bateman, there were about 1,000 men under arms. The organization started as an urban guerrilla movement, but moved to southern Colombia when pressed in the cities by the army. The organization maintained an appeal among urban young people. From their power bases in the countryside, they were able to commit terrorist acts in the cities. One major attack was the 1985 kidnapping of members of the supreme court at the Palace of Justice. Many leaders of the organization were killed when the army stormed the palace to regain control. The only important member of the organization to survive was Carlos Pizarro, who became commander in chief of the organization in 1987. In August 1988, M-19 kidnapped Alvaro Gomez, a four-time candidate for the presidency and a prominent member of the Conservative party. M-19 decided to abandon armed combat and demobilized in 1991. At that time, 800 men lay down their weapons.

Each of the guerrilla groups had supporters all over the country, and the power centers were divided into sectors. M-19 started as an urban guerrilla force, but later moved into the countryside, controlling an area south of the capital in Tolima and the Cauca Valley.

M-19's first great public action was the takeover of the Dominican Republic Embassy in Bogotá on March 6, 1979. It was a precision-tuned operation, timed just after Bogotá's entire diplomatic corps had arrived for a cocktail party to celebrate Colombian national independence day.

The M-19 unit swooped down on the assemblage and held fifteen ambassadors, including the U.S. ambassador, Diego Ascencio, in a four-month siege. Following protracted negotiations with the Turbay government, M-19 finally let the hostages go. In the process, it received $4 million and won free passage for the guerrillas in the embassy to fly to Cuba on a plane supplied by the government.

Next came an embarrassing arms seizure from the North Canton military barracks. Members of M-19 dug a tunnel from a nearby house right into the basement of the brigade, where the arms were stockpiled. The operation went through without a hitch.

It had already become commonplace for M-19 to hijack dairy trucks to distribute free milk to people in the poor barrios of Bogotá, Medellín, Cali, and other cities. The aim of this tactic was to win the sympathy of the people, and it worked. The people had no love for the military, and many enjoyed watching M-19 operate with seeming impunity. The army was unable to do anything to halt M-19's highly visible, sporadic attacks.

Then M-19 took one other step, which would prove to have broad and deadly consequences. On November 12, 1981, they kidnapped Martha Nieves Ochoa, the sister of Jorge Luis Ochoa, one of the heads of the Medellín cocaine cartel, and demanded a $15 million ransom.

To avenge this direct challenge to one of their own, the Ochoa family joined forces with Pablo Escobar, a onetime street thug turned drug trafficker, and his right-hand man, Carlos Lehder, a German-Colombian national who had been jailed in New York for setting up early cocaine routes with Escobar from Colombia to the United States. Together with other major drug traffickers, they amassed a multimillion-dollar war chest and founded an organization they called MAS—Muerte a Secuestradores—"Death to Kidnappers." The initial strategy was to kill M-19 members and their supporters one by one to force Martha Nieves's release. But MAS quickly evolved into something else: a self-sufficient paramilitary group financed by the drug bosses, which in turn collaborated with the anti-Communist crusade being conducted by the Colombian army. MAS was the first of several such paramilitary operations that formed on the Right, in response to the guerrillas' growing strength and power.

So, with this interview, I would fall right into MAS's accusations. My own opinions even gave me pause: I never agreed with the use of force as a means of changing things. But I had to confess that I felt a deep curiosity to find out about a guerrilla movement like M-19 from the inside. In the end, my reporter's instincts won out.

For security and safety reasons, only three people knew what I was up to. The first was ex-president Carlos Lleras Restrepo, who was now the head of a peace commission convened by the current president, Turbay Ayala, in an overdue attempt to seek a peaceful solution to the guerrilla conflict. Several days earlier, the Turbay government had offered a new amnesty for guerrillas who would lay down their arms. But the amnesty included provisions that critics called unacceptable. FARC (the Colombian Revolutionary Armed Forces) and other guerrilla groups rejected it. M-19's answer was not known, although it was the only guerrilla group that had shown an interest in talking. When I went one afternoon to see Lleras Restrepo to tell him about my trip, he raised my spirits with some words of support: "If I were your age, I wouldn't hesitate to do the interview."

The others who knew about my excursion to see M-19 were Guillermo Cano, the editor and publisher of *El Espectador,* the newspaper where I had worked for six years, and my mother, who was, as always, the first to encourage me in my work, even though she knew and feared the danger it put me in.

I looked at my watch again. It was 12:20. In Bogotá they had assured me that the person would arrive on time. The waiting was getting more and more nerve-racking in the deserted coffee shop.

Then a man came in and sat down next to me. For a moment I was relieved, thinking that my contact had finally arrived. But the man just sat down and asked for coffee. As he drank the coffee, he looked at me out of the corner of his eye, which made me feel even more nervous. I hid the newspaper, as if I were holding evidence that would give me away. With all the newspapers sold at any airport, M-19 had asked me to pick up *La Republica,* which did not circulate widely and was hard to come by. I was lucky enough to meet a man who was carrying one under his arm. I was so relieved to see the newspaper that when I asked him where he had bought it, he took pity on me and handed it over.

I looked at my watch again, while the man next to me put his hand in his coat and pulled out his wallet. I figured he was going to pay the bill and leave. But he took out a small notebook, one of the cheap ones that sells for ten cents, and continued to sit there.

By 2 P.M. nothing had happened. The last plane back to Bogotá would leave at 3 P.M. I had to decide.

Well, I thought, this has gone far enough. There was still enough time to get a taxi back to the airport. I had given it my best shot and could now relax and go home.

The plane to Bogotá was filled with soldiers. "We are in the middle of an operation against an M-19 column that has infiltrated Caquetá," one of the soldiers said as people chatted across the aisle. A chill passed over me. I would have been there, right in the middle of it. I was relieved that the guerrillas hadn't kept their date.

When I got back to my house in Bogotá, a message was waiting for me from my intermediary with the guerrillas. I dialed her number with little enthusiasm. She answered brusquely and said, "We were waiting for you in the hotel restaurant for lunch, but you didn't show up."

The mix-up was absurd. My contact had arrived on time, but went to the restaurant instead of the coffee shop. So we were around the corner from each other the whole time.

After the confusion was cleared up, my intermediary said that they were still waiting for me. But I told her that the stress of going through the whole thing twice was just too much. I asked her to cancel the meeting. Half an hour later, she called me back.

"Impossible. My friends are waiting for you and they can be there for only three days. This time somebody will go with you all the way from here. Don't worry. Nothing's going to happen to you."

It was a question of mind over matter. The prospect of going back to Pasto was frightening, but I wanted the story. I retraced my steps of the day before, this time with a silent chaperone who hardly glanced my way as the vintage plane bounced along from Bogotá to Pasto. My companion on the trip was about twenty-five years old; he looked like a student. This time both of us were carrying *La Republica* under our arms. We never spoke to each other. In Pasto, I took a taxi to the Hotel Agualongo once more, but this time I went straight to the restaurant.

The elegant restaurant was filled with well-dressed businessmen, and I realized that my jeans and boots were not exactly appropriate. I looked for a table in a corner that would give me a good view of the door. In a few moments, my companion from the airplane came in and sat at the opposite end of the room. At about 12:05, a neat, well-dressed young man came in.

"Excuse me, are you looking for Pablo?" he asked.

"No, for Pedro," I said.

We then got down to business. He told me that I could call him Tony, and that my departure was set for the following day before dawn. Meanwhile, I was to stay holed up at a room in the hotel so that no one would see me.

Tony paid for lunch, in dollars rather than pesos, and I saw that he had a wad of American money in his wallet, which surprised me. He took me right to my room and left, saying I should speak with no one. The following morning he called to say that I should order room service for breakfast. He told me that a problem had developed, since the army was in the area around Pasto, and we would have to wait until the following day to leave. The time I spent in that room was terrible: I felt like a prisoner, not knowing what was going on, always afraid the army would find me and think I was collaborating with the guerrillas. I couldn't sleep or rest. Just after midnight of my second day in the hotel room, Tony finally came to get me.

I was to disguise myself, he told me, and he would give me fake documents with an alias because we would have to go through some roadblocks where my documents would be checked.

I pulled back my hair and covered it with a kerchief. I wore glasses and put on the slacks and jacket that Tony gave me, which were not the kind I would normally wear.

We left the hotel at four the next morning. The cold of the Andean mountain air and the accompanying fog had descended upon Pasto, swathing the desolate plaza in mist. Across from the hotel, a Willys jeep was waiting for me. The door opened, and a young blond man greeted me warmly. "Let me introduce you to my wife and my son," he said.

I said good-bye to Tony and got into the jeep. I rode with my new "friends" toward Mocoa, the capital of Putumayo. The trip had to be made on a stretch of road with the ominous name of the Death Triangle, a name it won from the excessive number of drivers who crashed after failing to negotiate one of the treacherous mountain curves as the road cut across the Andes. The trajectory was then downhill into the humid southern plains approaching the Peruvian border.

You really couldn't call this a highway at all. It was built in the 1930s to pursue a war with Peru, and no administration had bothered to do any repairs since then. It was wide enough for only one car. When an oncoming vehicle approached, there was a standoff until one let the other pass. Often cars just slipped off the road and plunged over the side into the valley below. The road was said to have claimed more victims than had all the guerrilla assaults in Putumayo.

Every time we approached a roadblock, my companions had me rehearse my cover story: "My name is Patricia, and I'm traveling with my cousins, the Gomez family; we are going to Mocoa to a ranch we have there. I work as a teacher in Pasto."

A bit later another jeep came along and stopped near us. A dark-complexioned man, about thirty-five years old, got out and greeted the others. "She's the reporter," my driver told the newcomer. He turned to me and said, "This is where we leave you, comrade." Then he and his family drove off.

I got into the jeep with my new chaperone, and we headed off again, bound for Mocoa. We finally got to the village at around

8 A.M., four hours after I had left Pasto. The huge central plaza of the village was covered by immense, shady Icaco trees. Along muddy side streets, peasants who had worked the fields since dawn were returning for breakfast. None of the streets was paved, and only a few buildings had electricity.

Mocoa was a Wild West town—a land without law. Government officials have little sway in places like this; the law of the jungle is what matters here—law controlled by the shifting power of local political bosses, landowners, and guerrillas. There is death and violence in places like this, but the news rarely makes the headlines in Bogotá.

My host took me to the most unlikely place—the regional election headquarters for Luis Carlos Galán, the Liberal party leader and future presidential candidate who would later be murdered at the hands of the drug bosses.

Soon a campesino wearing a ruana against the cold came in and gave me the traditional breakfast in these parts, ACPM (arroz, carne, papas, and maduro)—huge portions of rice, a minimal ration of meat, some potatoes, and some bananas. But I wasn't hungry and just had some rice.

The campesino gave me some advice. "From here on in, every time food is put down in front of you, eat it because you'll never know when you'll eat the next time." The advice didn't change the message I was getting from my stomach, however.

I asked where the toilet was and was led to a putrid outhouse, where the stench of sewage was overpowering. There was no sewage treatment in Mocoa because it would be too expensive; instead of plumbing, there was a hole in the ground.

The lack of sanitation, of course, is a source of life-threatening diseases in places like Mocoa. In Colombia, more people die from tropical illnesses (such as malaria and typhoid) than from direct acts of violence. Interestingly, one of the so-called antisubversion policies adopted in Colombia has been to block the sale of quinine products—the treatment for malaria—in areas where the guerrillas are active. The cruel result is that the peasants of these areas are left without medicine, while the guerrillas get their supplies from underground networks. Mocoa was one such area where the people suffered high levels of chronic malaria.

At around 10 A.M. we left for Orito, one of the first places in Colombia where Texaco found petroleum reserves when it began exploring for oil about half a century ago. On one side of the highway, I could see the impressive Texaco drilling equipment. Along Orito's paved streets there was a fully equipped country club, complete with tennis courts and swimming pools. Across the highway misery abounded. The roadbed had been sinking under the weight of the trucks that hauled out the crude oil. The houses were made of adobe. While Texaco's luxurious country club was bathed in light, across the road a few kerosene lamps flickered dimly in the night. If I had been born here, I thought, I could easily have become a guerrilla.

That evening we slept in an adobe hut of a family whose children had all gone off to join the rebels. My guides woke me up at dawn with a drink of coconut milk. I had time only to get dressed and go out the door. My driver from the previous day was waiting for me. He handed me a pair of rubber boots and introduced me to Manolo, a short, muscular man who looked like a thug, who was to be my guide into the jungle.

Manolo was one of those people you find in Colombia who knows the streets and has learned how to scrounge, scavenge, and steal to survive. Sometimes, he told me, he sold packs of Marlboros he picked up in Ecuador; at other times, he sold coca paste on the Ecuadoran border. He had the resourcefulness of a man who had twice foiled attempts on his life. He carried two bullets lodged near his spinal cord as a reminder. "I was making a deal and got burned," he explained. "The army almost took me out that time."

He had been with the guerrillas since M-19 had extended its operations into this area in the mid-1970s. He gave me the impression that he had gotten involved more to have a job than because he believed in revolution. He knew vastly more about contraband and stealing than he did about Marxism. Years later, Manolo's disfigured corpse was found on the side of the road near Orito.

While he marched ahead, I hacked away at the leaves and twigs in the path, trying to keep up with him. The chattering of the monkeys and the infernal shrieking of the birds were nerve-racking. When we came into a clearing, I saw the first of a series of patches of coca plants that were to become more evident along the fifteen-hour march.

"Some of the campesinos have decided to plant this shit because it helps them get by. They can put together enough money to buy a generator and maybe even a refrigerator. We have a deal with these people, and it works well. They plant the coca leaves, and we [M-19] provide the protection.

"But these are small-timers who have nothing to do with the Medellín boys. Even I go out sometimes to make some spare cash selling coca paste on the border. It helps me put together enough money to live on."

It was drizzling on and off, and the path was getting more and more slippery. When we crossed over a small rise, I couldn't tell if the water dripping over my eyes and down my back came from sweat or from the rain. It was probably both.

"We're almost there," my companion said. "Only about seven hours to go."

We went up a slope, and I grabbed at whatever I could to maintain my balance. This interview was proving more complicated than I had anticipated.

When we came to a stream, Manolo hacked down some banana leaves, wrapped them expertly in a bundle, and lowered the makeshift ladle he had created into the water. "Good work," I said. He shrugged. An unseen bird let out one of those ungodly shrieks, and a chill ran up my mud-encrusted back. "If I get out of this, I swear that I'm going to quit smoking," I promised my suffering insides.

Suddenly, we heard a noise. "Hit the dirt," Manolo ordered.

I went down and found that we were in a swamp. "Great, I thought. This is it."

I had just enough time to grab my shoulder bag. "If they kill us," I thought, "somebody from my family will recognize it."

Then we heard a bird screeching nearby. Manolo got up on his haunches and listened attentively. He put his hands to his mouth and imitated the birdcall.

"False alarm," he said. "We're OK; it's our guys."

All of a sudden, amid the thick underbrush, I could make out the approaching forms of guerrillas in olive drab carrying Israeli Uzis.

It was 7 P.M. A man in a Ché Guevara–style beret lifted me out of the mud. "Welcome, compañera periodista," he said. "We've already put out the news in Bogotá that you've been kidnapped." We had agreed that for my protection, this interview would come across as a kidnapping. Without such a precaution, the government security forces would mark me as a Communist. The result would be a lot more dangerous than trekking through the jungle.

We still had many hours to go before we would reach the guerrilla headquarters.

My clothes were torn and my face was scraped and muddy by the time we approached the camp. My pack was soaked, and I had tied my jean jacket around my waist. I could make out more and more guerrillas amid the trees. We had arrived.

At the nearby river some women guerrillas were just finishing getting washed. It seemed out of place, but they were impeccably dressed. I noted that they wore nail polish and managed to negotiate the mud without getting dirty. I came upon an area that seemed to be the center of activity. A tall man grabbed me by the waist and pulled me over.

"This is the M-19 Hilton," he said with a mixture of sarcasm and good cheer, pointing to a hammock that would be my bed. I immediately recognized him as Jaime Bateman, the leader of M-19.

Bateman was a veteran guerrilla who had left M-19's rival, FARC, seven years earlier. FARC was connected to the Soviet-line Colombian Communist party, which had decided that Bateman was not following party orthodoxy. Always a free spirit, Bateman broke ranks and set out on his own, establishing M-19, the first urban guerrilla movement in Colombia.

FARC in turn sent out a commando team to kill him. But Bateman co-opted his intended assassins and brought them into his new organization. These same men were now serving as his personal bodyguards.

Bateman came from the Caribbean city of Santa Marta and was what is called a *costeño,* which meant that he had a certain joie de vivre that was, in a way, anathema to ideology. He liked to laugh, to party, to drink, and to dance into the night. I can still hear his syrupy Caribbean accent echoing among the trees of the deep jungle rain forest.

"La revolución es como una fiesta," he told me. "The revolution is like a celebration."

Bateman was the only one in the group who had more books than guns. He also carried a Sony tape recorder, along with two tapes: one of salsa music ("so there's always an excuse for a party") and the other, Beethoven's Ninth Symphony, which he jokingly said he used as an antidote against snake bites. One day, it seems, Bateman—who had an intense fear of snakes—stumbled across a rattlesnake. His tape recorder slipped out of his pocket and started playing Beethoven's Ninth when it hit the ground. The snake was charmed and slithered away.

My intention had been to stay at the camp no more than five days, but military operations in the vicinity changed my plans. M-19's answer to the government amnesty was succinct. "No."

I stayed in the jungle for a month.

In line at the airport in Puerto Asis for my trip back to Bogotá, I saw that several people boarding the plane were carrying copies of my newspaper, *El Espectador*. I was still in disguise, fearful the army would be tracking me. But I was jolted to see my picture on the front page with the headline: NO NEWS ON THE MISSING JOURNALIST—MARÍA JIMENA DUZÁN.

I read the story over another passenger's shoulder. My disguise was fine—no one gave me a second glance. I sat down next to a trader who dealt in exotic animals and birds. It was an interminable trip on the old DC-3. When we got to Bogotá, I dashed for a taxi and headed straight for the newspaper office. Rushing to the entrance, I was stopped by a security guard who knew me well.

"It's me, María Jimena," I said, looking around to see if there were any police in the area. He didn't recognize me at first. The guard stared at me hard and then relaxed, finally realizing who I was.

I vaulted up the stairs and ran into the newsroom. Everything stopped. Then my friends surrounded me. Through their hugs and laughter and tears, I saw a look in their eyes that indicated that they had not expected to see me again.

At 11 P.M., the only building with its lights on in the industrial sector of southwest Bogotá was the low modern headquarters of *El Espectador*. At that time of night, just a few reporters who run the night operation are left in the newsroom. They huddle around the night editor handing in late-breaking stories for the close of the city edition.

It was little more than twenty-four hours since I had marched out of M-19's jungle hideout. The day had been long, and I was exhausted. I could still smell a trace of sugar cane, mingled with river water, exuding from every pore.

All day I had been writing the first of a long series of articles about M-19 and the guerrilla wars. Guillermo Cano, the editor in chief, had encouraged me to write quickly, to get it all down on paper. But by 11:30, I was ready to go home. Some friends drove me back to the center of town.

At night Bogotá is almost deserted. There was a dry chill in the air as we drove up Thirtieth Avenue, which was bathed in a vacant fluorescent glow.

I can remember each instant of what followed. I said good-bye to my friends as they dropped me off at the front door of my house. I made a mental note that the military security guards who had been posted there since my disappearance had been pulled back. "It's strange," I thought. "Why aren't they here?"

When I closed the pale green wooden door, I could hear my friends' car driving away in the distance. I started to climb the stairs.

Suddenly I had the hellish feeling of being torn apart, hurled into the air, and slammed to the floor as if a catapult had suddenly seized me. Then all was still.

In the silent aftermath, I found myself at the bottom of the stairs, a cloud of gunpowder wafting about. My mother and sister came running, screaming for help. I regained my senses and took a mental inventory. I was not badly hurt, but I could feel that my back was bleeding, that splinters of wood from the door had dug into me like projectiles.

I looked around. The whole entrance to the house had been ripped apart. The bomb, I was sure, had been timed for my arrival.

I struggled to my feet and went upstairs. A few minutes later the phone rang. I jumped to answer it, hoping that it was Guillermo Cano, my boss, calling to find out what happened. It was not.

"The bomb was set by MAS, bitch," said a man with a deep voice. "The next time, we'll kill you."

I dropped the phone and collapsed into a chair.

I never returned to that apartment. The national police, suspicious that members of the army had something to do with the bomb attack, advised me to go underground. I wrote the series about the guerrillas in hiding. For part of the time, about a month, I stayed at a cousin's house without ever going outside. The police intelligence unit sent me a bodyguard named Hector— a hulking, iron-jawed man, always polite and impeccably dressed.

For a while, Hector stuck so close to me that I could hardly go to the bathroom by myself.

I had never imagined that I would reach the point of having to be accompanied by a bodyguard. I had thought that only business-men or high-ranking government officials would have bodyguards as they went from place to place in their Mercedeses. I, in con-trast, was a twenty-four-year-old reporter with a tiny Renault—a car that barely had room for Hector and me, no less for the machine gun that he put out the window every time we stopped at a light.

When we were not in the car, Hector carried the machine gun in a scratched but fine-quality leather attaché case that flipped open at the touch of a button and, like a kid's transformer toy, became a machine gun. Despite it all, he was more like a compan-ion than a bodyguard. When I went to a meeting or a party, I avoided introducing Hector as my bodyguard. When he accompa-nied me to my friends' homes, he was treated as just another member of the group. Some people thought he was my boyfriend. My friends would offer him a drink, and he would ask for brandy. Although he took a drink, he never forgot about his attaché case, which always rested on his lap.

I thought privately that Hector had been well chosen by the police as the one to protect me. He was cultured and well man-nered and didn't fit my image of an unkempt, rough bodyguard. I also thought that he was not only guarding me but gathering information. When all was said and done, I was still suspected of collaborating with the guerrillas. And who better than Hector could pass as another young person at the parties thrown by my friends? I decided not to hide anything from him. I introduced him to my friends, many of whom were leftists and many of whom weren't. I answered his questions almost naïvely. What I managed to find out about him matched what I had figured: He had infil-trated various guerrilla cells at the National University to spy on them.

I never got used to being protected by the same eyes that were watching me. During those months of seeing Hector's face night and day, I promised myself that this would be the last time I would have a bodyguard.

Like many Colombians, my father, Lucio Duzán, decided to build a new life in Bogotá in the late 1950s, when the Colombian capital served as a refuge for many Liberals who had abandoned their towns and villages to avoid political persecution at the hands of the Conservative-controlled police, during a time called *La Violencia*. As a Liberal, he had defended his village, La Villa de Rosario de Cúcuta, when it was besieged by the Conservatives. The townspeople had even named him sheriff; for quite a while he wandered about with a pistol in his belt, sleeping wherever night found him, with mattresses piled up against the windows to block the gunfire of the Conservative police. He had seen how the police hanged their victims, how they cut the penises off corpses and stuffed them in their mouths. He had seen pregnant women, their breasts full, murdered. He had seen hell.

Things got to the point where he had to leave town or face the almost certain prospect that he would be killed. So one day he escaped to the capital, hoping to revive his love for writing and journalism. In Bogotá, the first thing he did was change his name, as many others did—from Jesus María Galvis to Lucio Duzán—so that the Conservative police would not find him.

The second thing my father did was to adopt the Bohemian lifestyle of a single man on the loose. He was tall, good-looking, and able to mix an intellectual thirst with good whiskey and revelry. He started writing using his new name and pursued a career in Colombian journalism at *El Espectador,* a major daily newspaper in Bogotá run by his close friend Guillermo Cano.

My father told us little about his hapless life during La Violencia, diverting the conversation when we started questioning him; it was my impression that he wanted to erase those years from his memory and thought it was better not to recall them. However, as a memento of the period, he kept the Smith and Wesson revolver he had used when he was the sheriff. It was always in the glove compartment of our car when we drove outside Bogotá on weekends.

My mother's story was much the same. She came from a wealthy, prominent Liberal family, but La Violencia changed their destiny. The Conservatives destroyed her family's ranches and seized their lands. A girl from a family of means, she suddenly had to leave school and get a job.

Since the turn of the century, Colombia had been governed by two parties, the Conservatives and the Liberals. With industrial and postwar changes, the two parties were strengthened and began to represent two distinct philosophies. The Conservative party was of feudal origin and was closely linked to the Catholic church, which had always been an important institution in Colombia. The Liberal party gained its strength in the emerging urban areas, promoting theories of free exchange and the creation of new forms of social organization.

The conflict between Liberals and Conservatives leading to La Violencia was triggered in 1948 with the assassination of Jorge Eliecer Gaitan, a Liberal leader who represented the left flank of his party. A few days before his death, he had been chosen to challenge the ruling Conservatives as the Liberal party's candidate for president.

Gaitan was gunned down in the heart of Bogotá, and his murder outraged his supporters, most of whom were of humble origin. They took to the streets, looting stores and setting fires, intending to burn down the city. My mother, just thirteen at the time, found herself trapped at her school downtown, where the first rioting and fires broke out. She and her classmates were kept in the school for three days and three nights, under orders to stay inside. Communication was impossible; telephones were cut off. My mother knew only what she could see from the window, and it was a sight she would never forget—snipers perched on buildings firing point-blank on people running desperately through the streets. She had never seen death up close.

The rioting spread to the countryside. Neither Bogotá nor the rest of the country would ever be the same again—not only because so many buildings were destroyed, but because the lives of all Colombians had changed forever.

The assassination of Gaitan was the start of a ten-year political war between Conservatives and Liberals. It ended in 1957 with an armistice that created the so-called National Front, by which both sides agreed to alternate power every four years.

No one knows how many people died in La Violencia, but estimates range from 200,000 to 300,000. What is certain is that it was an unspeakably devastating horror. Tens of thousands fled the blood-soaked countryside for the cities. Suddenly Colombia, a primarily rural country, became an urban nation. Today about 70 percent of Colombians live in urban areas.

I was born in December 1957, the year of the armistice. Although the dispute between Liberals and Conservatives had been decided, politics and the Liberal party were also the main course at dinnertime at my house. Like many children of that generation of Liberals besieged by Conservatives, I grew up with macabre stories of murders and violations by the Conservative police. It was no surprise, then, that my brother, sister, and I grew up thinking that the devil himself was a Conservative.

If the agreement to alternate power managed to halt the battle between the Conservatives and Liberals, it also produced political inertia, consolidating the closed bipartite system that slowly became an anachronism. The people of my generation saw no ideological differences between the two parties, which they believed had coalesced into a single power structure. The other Colombia, the Colombia of teeming slums, marked by exile from the land and no escape from poverty, was neither cared about nor heard from. Despite the National Front, new forms of violence were emerging, a product of the social injustice that was not being addressed by the traditional parties and that served as a breeding ground first for the guerrilla movement and then for the drug dealers, both of whom capitalized on the people's discontent.

My father died of lung cancer in 1975 thinking that the worst had already passed. A few days after his death, his loyal friend Guillermo Cano offered me the opportunity to continue writing the column that my father had written for so many years. The proposal moved me, but it seemed inappropriate. I was only sixteen years old and had just returned to Colombia from high school in England. It was not customary for newspaper columns to be inherited, and it did not seem to be the most appropriate way to break into journalism. Nevertheless, I accepted the challenge. It was Guillermo Cano, my guide, my great teacher, who took me by the hand and made a journalist out of me. It seemed like it would be so easy.

On March 18, 1982, while the rest of Colombia voted for a new president, I was still in hiding at my cousin's apartment in the northern hills of Bogotá. From the balcony, I had a lovely view of the city, its six million people scattered below in the undulating countryside nestled in the Andes. The building was adjacent to the backyard of an immense house. It was the home of Belisario Betancur, the Conservative party's presidential candidate, who, by every indication, was about to be elected president in a landslide.

As I looked out beyond the house, I saw Belisario on the patio, standing near a sculpture by Feliza Burstyn, a Colombian artist who had fled the country after the army decided she was a Cuban spy and who had died in exile in Paris.

I was surprised to see him standing there alone—the man who was the object of all the country's attention at that time. Although Belisario was nominally a member of the Conservative party, in many ways he was more liberal than the best-known members of the Liberal party. His most attractive quality was the easy way in which he spoke to people. He had that special ability to personify the common man; you could easily imagine him down at the local *cantina,* listening to music and having a drink with friends. A self-made man who had risen from the streets to reach a position of power, he had the resourcefulness and tenacity that Colombians hold dear.

I went out on the balcony and called to him. He didn't recognize me, so I told him who I was.

He seemed genuinely surprised. "What in the world are you doing around here?" he asked. His tone and bearing already seemed presidential. "I thought you were hiding outside the country. But I'm happy to see you.

"Do not allow yourself to be discouraged or overwhelmed. Keep up the good work." He thrust one fist in the air with a dramatic flourish. It was as if he was taking on energy, emerging from his silent moment on the balcony as we spoke.

After a pause I asked him how he felt on the verge of being the president. "Loneliness," a single word, was his reply.

Shortly after our meeting, the news came over the radio: "Belisario Betancur has been elected president of Colombia."

DRUGS AND POLITICS

Belisario Betancur's election in 1982 was not the only political development that year. For the first time, the drug traffickers had won important electoral victories in Congress and the local legislatures.

Pablo Escobar came to Congress in 1982 as an alternate member of the House of Representatives from Antioquia state, where Medellín is located. He was elected, along with the regular representative, Jairo Ortega, on a nationwide slate controlled by Liberal Senator Alberto Santofimio Botero. In the Colombian system, this alternate membership gave Escobar the status of congressman. It meant that he sat in for Ortega if Ortega was ill, was traveling, or could not otherwise attend sessions. It also meant that he had congressional immunity—that he was exempt from being charged with crimes.

Escobar had become a member of a Liberal party organization in Antioquia called Liberal Renewal and had formed his own philanthropic organization, "Medellín Without Slums," whose objective was to build schools and stadiums in the slum sectors around Medellín.

At the time of the election, Escobar was gaining fame for his wealth and status, but he had not been proved to be a criminal; there were suspicions and allegations, but no convictions or outright evidence, so his standing for election was perhaps not as peculiar as it may seem now, given his reputation as an international archcriminal. Botero, Escobar's political associate, had close relations with the Medellín crowd, although he was never identified with any drug-related activity.

At this time in Colombia, anyone with money and rhetoric could conduct a political campaign, regardless of his or her reputation. With a weak criminal justice system, people were rarely convicted of major crimes. In any case, the entrenched two-party system was awash with corruption and influence peddling by a long-standing wealthy elite. Escobar—and his money—were first welcomed by that elite, but were later rejected when he and his drug-dealing friends turned murderous in response to the government's attempts to suppress them.

Escobar's entry into politics revolutionized election campaigning in the country. Whereas buses and trucks once bounced along local roads to ferry candidates and their supporters, Escobar and company traveled by helicopters and executive jets. They had the money to build elaborate campaign platforms when other candidates spoke from the roofs of cars or from flatbed trucks. They also used fireworks and security cordons—in short, all the trappings of an American political campaign. When Escobar wanted to have a campaign rally, he turned to his friend José Ocampo—Pelusa ("Fuzzy")—who owned Kevin's, a popular discotheque in Medellín, where the cream of the drug-trafficking organizations held an antiextradition forum in April 1983.

Extradition between Colombia and the United States had been approved on November 3, 1980, during the government of Julio Cesar Turbay Ayala. It became law in March 1982.

The proposal was first suggested by Washington, where it was considered a key weapon in the fight against drug trafficking. Besides this agreement, U.S. authorities had proposed a treaty on mutual legal assistance, intended to facilitate the exchange of criminal evidence between the two countries. For obvious reasons, the proposals were kept secret in an attempt to avert both speculation in the news media and possible pressure on the Colombian Congress.

But rumors that Congress was hurrying to approve the treaties came to the attention of the drug traffickers. The mutual-assistance treaty was dropped for lack of support in Congress, but it did approve the extradition treaty. "Actually, the exchange of criminal evidence was more dangerous for the traffickers than the extradition treaty," a member of President Virgilio Barco's government told me.

News coverage of the extradition treaty began only after the accord had been approved in a secret session. At the time, the country was preoccupied with a tumultuous presidential campaign. None of the criticism and debate surrounding the treaty talks in Congress was filtered to the news media. Two months after the treaty was approved, it received a brief mention on a back page of *El Tiempo,* the country's largest newspaper.

Early in the Betancur administration, the U.S. government had sought the extradition of two Colombians—Jesús Mejia Romero and Lucas Gomez van Grieken—who were wanted in the United States, but the president's office had denied the requests. Attorney General Jimenez Gomez ruled that the treaty was unconstitutional on procedural grounds. During the forum at Kevin's, Escobar and Carlos Lehder made fiery speeches in which they called the treaty, among other things, "a violation of national sovereignty."

Colombians first heard Lehder's name linked to drug dealing when his name showed up among the drug traffickers participating in MAS. Slowly, his presence began to be felt, especially in the political arena. Like Escobar, Lehder entered politics by founding his own party, a mixture of leftist populism and rightist, pro-Nazi rhetoric, which he called the National Latin Movement. On March 11, 1983, the same year that Escobar came to Congress as an alternate, Lehder's party managed to win several seats in the Quindio state assembly, as well as in the Armenia city council.

That was the extent of the news about Lehder until July 1983, when he admitted to being a drug dealer in an interview on the Caracol Radio Network, whose broadcasts are heard throughout Colombia as well as in neighboring countries and the United States.

The interview was greeted with outrage; editorials in both *El Espectador* and *El Tiempo* lashed out at him. The incident was a scandalous and impudent admission by Lehder, the newspapers said. And they criticized the role of the news media in giving him a forum for voicing such blatant disregard for the law.

The government reacted to Lehder as if he had issued a direct challenge. The attorney general and the Ministry of Justice named a special prosecutor to investigate Lehder's activities. Yet he stood on safe legal ground: The crimes he mentioned all took place outside Colombia, and his wealth had recently been legitimized by a nationwide amnesty on tax evaders. He could not be prosecuted on any of these grounds.

Following the accusations against Lehder and the recognition that he could not be touched, Felipe Lopez, the editor in chief of *Semana,* a weekly newsmagazine similar to *Time* and *Newsweek,* decided that it was time for a profile on Lehder. He assigned the job to one of his reporters—my sister, Sylvia.

Sylvia spent a week in Armenia on the Lehder story, while Lehder attempted to win her over with his notorious charm. He took her out dancing and sat with her for hours, listening to Beatles music or chatting nonstop about his love of German culture, smoking marijuana the whole time.

Lehder took her to his newspaper, *Quindio Libre.* The newspaper displayed Colombia's coat of arms on the cover, and under the masthead ran the slogan: "This newspaper does not accept advertising from foreign multinationals. We are here to promote Colombian business."

Sylvia came back to Bogotá on Lehder's private plane, rushing into the house after the flight. "Guess who the pilot was?" she asked me. When I didn't answer, she said, "Lehder."

"These guys are completely nuts. They are out in the open about what they are doing," she told me. "He's not even hiding the fact that they are dope dealers."

Three days after Sylvia came back from Armenia, I went to answer the phone.

"Is Sylvia home?" asked a man whose voice I didn't recognize.

"I'm sorry, she isn't in," I said. "Who's calling?"

"Carlos Lehder," he said.

At first I thought it was a practical joke, but it wasn't. It was Lehder. I found it upsetting to hear his voice, since I was remembering the bomb attack carried out by MAS, of which he was a charter member.

The new visibility of the drug bosses was part of their national political strategy. Profiles on the more prominent ones began appearing in all the media. The drug bosses opened their homes to reporters, giving tours of their new estates and talking about their likes and dislikes and their backgrounds. Without saying so, they tacitly admitted the business they were in, as if they were Hollywood stars.

Before Sylvia's interview with Lehder, a colleague at *Semana* had done a profile on Escobar. It was the first and last intimate

interview with Escobar, and it caused a sensation. Under the
headline "The Robin Hood of Medellín," the magazine ran an
extensive interview in which Escobar attributed his immense fortune to a rare sense of what it meant to be a businessman. It
quoted Escobar as saying, "At sixteen, I owned a bicycle rental
business; after a few years wandering around, I got into buying
and selling automobiles and finally ended up selling real estate."

The magazine portrayed Escobar as coming from "humble
extraction, with the desire to use the power given him by an incalculable fortune to be the nation's prime benefactor. Undoubtedly
we'll be hearing more from him." Escobar was a powerful man of
modest origins, working on inner-city developments—that was
the article's theme. Others might have had their suspicions, but
the article settled for the merely ironic.

At that time, the name Escobar meant little to American and
Colombian authorities. Neither government paid much attention
to the activities of the dealers or to the alliance among the death
squads, their supporters in the military, and the drug dealers. In
the United States in the 1980s, all attention was focused on the
Colombian Left, which seemed to pose the greater threat to forces
that still saw communism as the great overriding challenge to
world stability—and U.S. interests. In 1981, Colombia's Nobel
Prize–winning author Gabriel García Márquez was stripped of his
U.S. entry visa because he was a close friend of Fidel Castro,
while Pablo Escobar traveled freely and frequently to the United
States. Many Colombian writers, diplomats, and intellectuals had
their visas canceled, while drug bosses went back and forth with
ease. One of Escobar's last trips in 1982 included a stop in Washington, where he had a photograph taken of him holding his son's
hand in front of the White House.

Escobar had no apparent criminal record because his résumé
had been tampered with, and no one who knew the truth lived to
tell the tale. But it was known that he was the son of a servant
and that he had grown up in Rionegro, a poor town in Antioquia,
near the provincial capital Medellín. Anyone you asked would say
he was a broker in automobile sales and a cattleman on his
father's ranch in Rionegro.

Escobar was indeed involved with automobiles, not as a broker but as a car thief. There was already talk of his connection
with drug dealing, but these were only rumors circulating in certain sectors of Medellín; there was no proof and certainly no

alarm sounded by the government. To the eyes of the closed aristocracy of Medellín, Escobar's extravagant taste and his predilection for the garish made him no more than a nouveau riche with a penchant for giving handouts to the poor, fancying himself a latter-day Robin Hood.

"You should go see for yourself how Pablo Escobar has improved living conditions in the slums around Medellín" was the common refrain one would get from *paisas*—the nickname for people from Medellín. It was true, in fact, that Escobar had built hundreds of homes on property he owned with the goal of relocating about one thousand families from the slums. It was said, however, that his own squad of hit men and assassins received priority for obtaining the new housing.

It was clear that Escobar's operation had a sinister side from the outset. For example, in a classic Mafia tactic, Escobar was reputed to control a network of taxis around town that he bought and gave to the drivers. These taxi drivers formed a perfect information network; anything out of the ordinary would get back to him immediately. As a side operation, he also provided low-cost theft insurance for the fleet. If a taxi was stolen, the driver would receive a free replacement cab while the search for the stolen vehicle went on.

At the time, the most frequent story bandied about Medellín was that when Escobar's application for membership in the Union Club, the most exclusive social club in town, was turned down, he exacted revenge by financing a strike by the club's employees, who walked out and demanded higher wages. Although Escobar did not get into the Union Club, he did have influence in high places and was welcome among the region's real decision makers. He hobnobbed with local Liberal party leaders, and his own social program was backed by no less than the archdiocese of Medellín, led by Cardinal Alfonso Lopez Trujillo, the primate of the Colombian Catholic church.

Lopez Trujillo was Colombia's only cardinal at that time, a prelate with easy access to the Vatican, especially to Pope John Paul II. It was he who took on the task of halting the spread in Colombia of Liberation Theology, an international Catholic movement that emerged in the Latin American church in opposition to Pope Paul VI and the church hierarchy. The movement had actually been born in Medellín at a crucial ecumenical conference in 1976 and was an answer to charges that the church was enriching itself while losing contact with the poor and disenfranchised masses. Among other things, it offered a radical reinterpretation of biblical themes from the perspective of the impoverished and powerless, directly connected religious beliefs to political activism, and was a manifestation of a worldwide movement for human emancipation.

Some adherents of Liberation Theology went to the extreme of establishing links with guerrilla movements; others did not. But that association, coming in the midst of the Cold War, stigmatized the movement's supporters as Marxist priests, and they were rejected by Rome. Neither Pope Paul VI nor John Paul II accepted the movement, but it grew in Latin America—which has the largest concentration of Catholics in the world—as an answer to the great poverty and injustice that was all around.

Liberation Theology flourished in many places, but not in Colombia, where the Catholic church had always been strongly conservative. Despite the long-standing tradition of priests becoming involved in guerrilla movements (as was the case, for example, of Camilo Torres, who fought with the National Liberation Army [ELN] in the mid-1970s and died in a military ambush), Lopez Trujillo and the conservative Colombian church he led were successful in blocking the movement. Priests who went against him were simply banned.

However, the cardinal's moral outrage with Liberation Theology did not extend to the case of Pablo Escobar, who was certainly no proponent of the suspect movement. Just like the army, the cardinal saw communism as immoral and evil, but he seemed to have no objection to Escobar's spreading vast sums of money around the slum, until 1983, when Escobar's drug activities caused him to be expelled from the Congress. From the outset of Escobar's populist campaign in the barrios, two priests from Lopez Trujillo's archdiocese, Elias Lopera Cardenas and Hernan Cuartas, supported Escobar's social activism and sometimes toured with him, delivering fervent homilies for his social causes.

Trujillo never actually spoke out on Escobar's behalf, but he did sanction Escobar's relationship with the archdiocese and certainly never put a halt to the church's support for Escobar's political populism. From 1982 to 1984, when he was forced underground, Escobar legitimately could say that the Catholic church was squarely behind him, in the person of the cardinal who controlled every parish in the country.

Even as Escobar won the right to join the elite at play, his opulent lifestyle did not change the adoration he received from the people in the slums around Medellín who saw him as a role model and an idol. He was their leader and their benefactor.

The first to disclose Escobar's true profession was neither the Colombian government nor the U.S. Drug Enforcement Administration. It was Luis Carlos Galán, a young politician who in 1978, founded a political movement known as the New Liberalism that existed outside his own Liberal party.

One of my first assignments as a journalist was an interview with Galán in 1979. Galán had a fiery way of speaking. There was conviction in his voice as he told me that he was sick of corrupt clubhouse politics, always run by the same group of men who knew how to get elected but knew nothing about good government.

"I propose a different style of government. Those in power have no idea of how to go about running a country. They only know how to win elections," he told me. His plan, he said, was to clean out the bureaucracy. "The Liberal party has been the backbone of the evolution of this country," he said. "But today it must face reforms or cease to exist."

Galán's words seemed to be more than just rhetoric, so I was not surprised by his swift decision to begin investigating Escobar and his Medellín splinter group when the Liberal party announced it was supporting his candidacy for the 1982 presidential election.

The investigation did not take long to confirm the rumors that had been on the street: Since 1975 Colombian customs officials had suspected Escobar of being a drug dealer. Although Escobar had been arrested several times, charges against him had always been dropped. Moreover, the investigation showed a string of drug-related murders during the previous year. The victims were all known to be involved in drug dealing, and Escobar's name was linked to all of them.

The method was obvious; Escobar had simply murdered his way to the top, wiping out potential adversaries one by one. And when he was through, he had it all: It was impossible to sell a nickel bag of cocaine on the street without word getting back to him.

He had a unique way of bringing new people into the business. A rumor was circulated that a heavy load of cocaine was about to be shipped out; anyone who wanted to participate could invest some money in the deal. If the shipment was successful, each investor would share the profits, and if it was lost, Escobar would reimburse the initial investment. The method attracted many investors—above all, those from certain sectors of the upper class who, with no moral considerations, had decided to put their capital to work in this new business that functioned like the stock market.

Meanwhile, Escobar was creating a separate, highly visible identity linked to public services and acts of benevolence. The rhinoceros and hippopotamus at the zoo he built in Puerto Triunfo were already receiving visitors. And his ranch at Napoles was on everyone's list of prime tourist stops. Over the entrance to the ranch was a giant archway with a private plane attached to it. Everyone told the story that the aircraft was hoisted there to commemorate Escobar's first successful cocaine shipment to the United States.

The information Galán gathered was more than enough to confirm the rumors about Escobar, and he decided to repudiate Escobar's support publicly. He chose to do so at a political rally at Rionegro Plaza in Medellín. "I reject the support of certain persons whose fortunes are of questionable origin" were the words he used. He did not name Escobar, nor did he have to. This was Escobar's turf, and the allusion could not have been more direct.

Without knowing it, Galán had just signed his own death sentence. The countdown had begun, and Escobar would exact his revenge eight years later. Galán's repudiation of Escobar and the facts he gathered about Escobar marked the beginning of one of the most violent chapters in Colombian history. They were little reported in the country.

THE PHOTOGRAPH

While Escobar and Lehder were amassing their fortunes and building political power, Guillermo Cano, the editor and publisher of *El Espectador,* along with the rest of the Colombian press, watched and waited.

I had gotten to know Cano and his family well since joining the staff in 1975. The first thing I realized was that Guillermo was no stranger to controversy and danger. In the late 1970s, he had come out against his own party and condemned the torture and abuses of human rights that had characterized the Liberal government of Turbay Ayala. In the 1980s, the newspaper would take on the financial establishment by daring to denounce white-collar crime, mismanagement, and fraud at one of the nation's most important financial conglomerates, Grupo Grancolombiana, whose properties included banks and savings institutions, industrial concerns, and the media. The exercise led to the loss of advertising revenue and the beginning of an economic struggle for the paper that hasn't ended yet.

Building on that contentious economic battle, Guillermo decided to open a new front. The newspaper would report on the growing threat of drug dealing and the criminal enterprise that was swelling around it.

The newspaper had become for me more than just a place to work. It was my family. And Guillermo Cano, despite his diffidence, had taken me under his wing, carefully guiding me through the ins and outs of the craft of journalism.

Family and work had merged for Guillermo from the beginning. Shy more than introverted, and an inveterate, ardent soccer fan, Guillermo had inherited a certain family trait: perseverance under fire. It was evident in his father, Luis Gabriel, whom he had succeeded as publisher, and in his grandfather, Fidel Cano Gutierrez, who founded the newspaper in 1897 on El Codo Avenue in Medellín. Don Gabriel's sons, Fidel and Luis Gabriel, served jail time for daring to publish the news that others sought to hide. Guillermo took over the newspaper when he was thirty years old, and he, too, had to face the threat of official censorship.

The roadblocks were never-ending. Assailants sent by the rival Conservative party burned the newspaper's building to the ground in 1968. That setback was severe, but most painful was the loss of the nation's oldest newspaper archives. Confronted with such a tumultuous, challenging situation, Guillermo had learned to survive with the stoicism of someone simply committed to the written word and the good that solid writing would do for his country. But attitude could not improve his precarious health. At fifty-seven he already had suffered a heart attack; he ate little, and his doctors had warned him to quit smoking, but he kept it up anyway. The ashes of Kool cigarettes burned in the ashtray on his desk, and there was a supply of cigarettes for anyone in the newsroom whose pack had run out.

He was starting to show that characteristic hunched-over posture that comes with old age, but it was as if he also carried the weight of forty years of Colombian politics. His political philosophy as a liberal democrat was forged during La Violencia.

On the morning of September 7, 1983, I saw Guillermo suddenly run through the newspaper's city room. He was heading to the photo library, calling all the while for Luis de Castro—Don Luigi—a veteran reporter who was the newspaper's institutional memory. Guillermo, it was clear, had come up with an idea. He was certain that he had once seen a picture of Escobar printed in his newspaper. He had Don Luigi ask the librarian to pull all the files on people named Escobar.

"Here it is," said Don Luigi, with a cigarette stuck between his teeth, after having flipped through all the files. He held up a pho-

tograph of two prisoners jailed on drug charges in Medellín. One
was Pablo Escobar.

"Just as I thought," Guillermo said, looking at the picture
with growing excitement. "We've got a great story for tomorrow.
Let's get all the space we can on the front page."

The story exploded the next day. Until that moment, all the
talk of Pablo Escobar and drug dealing, including Galán's accusations, was the stuff of tantalizing-yet-unproved rumblings that he
was amassing a fortune as a don of the cocaine dealers in Medellín. Cano and Galán's separate efforts confirmed Escobar's true
pedigree, but until this moment, no one had been able to connect
him directly to actual convictions.

The photograph that Guillermo found was perfect. It had been
taken in June 1976 in the Bellavista jail in Medellín, where Escobar had been jailed on murder and drug-dealing charges. Just
another common criminal, Escobar was captured in Itagüí with
his cousin Gustavo Gaviria. They were carrying thirty-nine kilos
of pure cocaine in eighteen plastic bags, along with $5,000 and
50,000 pesos in cash.

And Guillermo had remembered his face.

Don Luigi was in charge of the ensuing investigation. He confirmed that Escobar had been indicted and that a twisted jurisdic-
tional dispute ensued. Along the way, two key witnesses—both
police agents—were murdered mysteriously. The judge in the case
and the police commander both received death threats. Escobar's
lawyer argued that since the truck was stopped in Pasto, that was
where the case should be handled.

The case went to the Supreme Court, which upheld the appeal,
and the two men were released on bail. They had eluded capture,
and for eight years the case had been forgotten.

After the article in *El Espectador* was published, there was an
uproar. In Medellín the newspaper was being hawked for 1,000
pesos a copy, twenty times the cover price.

The first call that Guillermo received came from the minister
of justice, who told him that he was going to do everything possible to pressure Congress so that Escobar would lose his parliamentary immunity and could be judged in a Colombian court of
law. The investigation of the previous charges would be opened on
the strength of *El Espectador*'s report, and a new charge was
added. Gustavo Zuluaga Serna, a Superior Court justice in Medellín, issued warrants for the arrest of Escobar and Gaviria, charg-

ing them with conspiracy in the murder of the two police investigators in the case.

A few months after that, Zuluaga Serna was promoted to chief criminal court justice in Medellín Superior Court. Two weeks later he was found machine-gunned to death in his car.

Nevertheless, after several weeks of discussions, Colombia's Congress managed to rescind Escobar's congressional immunity so that Escobar could be prosecuted on murder and drug charges. But Guillermo Cano considered it a Pyrrhic victory at best.

He wrote an audacious column about Escobar on Sunday, November 6, 1983, criticizing the government for not going far enough. "For some time now, these sinister men"—as he called the drug traffickers—"have managed to create an empire of immorality, tricking and making fools of the complacent, doling out crumbs and bribes upon them while a cowardly and often entranced populace stood idly by, content with their illusions and entertained by stories of their jet-set lives."

For a few days after the article came out, Escobar tried to follow his normal routine. He made a political appearance that week in Envigado, a stronghold of his supporters. But then Liberal Renewal, the political group through which Escobar came to Congress, expelled him from its ranks. Shortly thereafter, Cardinal Lopez Trujillo ordered his priests to have nothing more to do with Medellín Without Slums.

It was a quick reversal. Escobar had been repudiated by the political class that had helped him climb to prominence, rejected by the same oligarchic circles that welcomed him to their sumptuous feast of power and by the church officials who had so willingly accepted his money.

Shunned by society, Escobar was forced to move his power base underground. After operating freely despite the insinuations and rumors that surrounded him, his fate had been changed forever by a newspaper article.

In March 1984, a month before his death, I saw Rodrigo Lara Bonilla, the minister of justice; he was indignant and frightened. A plot to kill him had just been uncovered, and he was clearly disturbed and nervous. "*El Espectador* is the only ally I have left," he said.

The drug bosses picked their target appropriately. Appointed minister of justice in 1983, Lara Bonilla ordered the seizure of hundreds of private planes involved in drug trafficking; it was he who led the operation against the gigantic drug laboratory at Tranquilandia and conducted criminal investigations of Escobar and other members of the Colombian cocaine cartels. The drug bosses were not about to let him continue, and they set out to destroy his reputation. On August 16, 1983, Escobar's front men called Lara Bonilla to Congress to explain a check for one million pesos given to his congressional campaign (before he was appointed minister of justice). The check was valid and had been accepted by the leadership of his campaign. Evaristo Porras was not known to Lara Bonilla's congressional campaign committee, but he was perhaps the most powerful capo in the southern Colombian Amazon.

The trap sprung on the minister of justice was not only perfect but showed how little the complex brinkmanship of the drug bosses was understood. For the first time, the drug dealers would expose themselves and provide their own names. Congress saw the spectacle of Jairo Ortega, the congressman with whom Escobar served, standing in Congress and denouncing Lara Bonilla to his face for having received money from "Mr. Evaristo Porras, a drug trafficker charged with narcotics violations in Lima." Ortega offered as proof a poor-quality recording in which Porras referred repeatedly to Pablo Escobar "as a person who has become a wealthy man with the profits of his drug money."

Lara Bonilla answered the challenge with a raging flourish. He seized hundreds of planes used by the drug traffickers, he led the investigation that resulted in the discovery and raid of the Tranquilandia laboratory, and became a fervent supporter of the extradition treaty.

If Evaristo Porras was not recognized in Bogotá circles as a drug boss, the same was not the case in Leticia, the Amazonas provincial capital on the banks of the big muddy river in the nation's extreme south. There, Porras was the dominant power broker. At age thirty-four, he already owned twenty businesses, hotels, houses, ranches, several cars and trucks, a luxurious yacht, and three private planes. He controlled the entry of coca paste from Peru and Bolivia and sold it to the large organizations in Medellín, Cali, Pereira, and Bogotá. Since 1982, he had consolidated his own cocaine export network to the United States, France, and Spain via Panama.

The Porras clan was comprised of individuals just like him.

They were tough, hard-nosed men who cut their teeth during La Violencia and who had ventured into this jungle no-man's land many years before.

Porras was a man who did not mince words. He was used to enjoying himself, and his whims were law. Once, for example, he kidnapped three prostitutes from Leticia who worked in a bordello known as the Godfather. He held them for three days, submitting them to a series of degrading acts and sexual aberrations, like forcing gun butts and bottlenecks into their vaginas and rectums. When the women were finally set free, they had to leave town, under threat of being killed.

Porras liked being involved in politics. In 1985 he founded a political movement called the Liberal House of Amazonas, which won enough votes in 1986 to hold several seats on the local council. Porras was accused of being the intellectual author of so-called Operation Cleanup, in which seventy vagrants who were wandering about Leticia were murdered.

The only person in Leticia who stood up to Porras was veteran journalist Roberto Camacho Prada, *El Espectador*'s correspondent in Leticia and president of the local chamber of commerce. When the story circulated about the check sent to Lara Bonilla, Camacho Prada took on a singular and mismatched battle against Porras. He wrote reports in *El Espectador* about the drug-trafficking organization led by Porras, but he didn't stop there. In 1985 he decided to make a sworn statement about Porras before the minister of justice that was used to open an investigation of drug trafficking in the Amazonas region.

On July 16, 1986, Camacho Prada was murdered with three newspaper boys in broad daylight in the middle of Leticia. A survivor of the attack told a police investigator that Porras had ordered the killing. Later, the policeman was also killed.

Back in 1983, after the bribe allegation before Congress, and with the stakes rising dangerously all the time, Lara Bonilla launched a battle to protect his good name. Many of those who supported his attempt to fight drug trafficking backed away from him. Suddenly, he found himself alone. Once he was an advocate; now he was a suspect with a criminal investigation pending against him because of Porras. The situation had gotten to the point that whenever he prepared for a trip, he went through his bags dozens of times, fearing that someone had slipped in some cocaine to incriminate him.

On April 23, 1984, Lara Bonilla, still serving as Colombian minister of justice, was assassinated on a street in northern Bogotá.

News of Lara Bonilla's murder reached me during the Festival of the Legend of Vallenata. This festival, one of the most important musical events in the Caribbean coastal region of Colombia, inspired Gabriel García Márquez to write *One Hundred Years of Solitude*. Word of the killing was like a bolt of lightning; it tore me apart.

Some friends and I had just been talking about how the festival had changed because of the onslaught of the drug dealers. In earlier years, the king of the festival, the center of attention, sang his songs at the homes of the local aristocracy and dedicated them to former presidents. Now the celebrations were held behind the shuttered doors of the drug traffickers, where the whiskey and the dollars flowed freely.

I remember one person in particular at the festival that year. He was well dressed and distinguished looking, but he had a prominent gold tooth when he smiled. I noticed him one morning as my friends and I gathered for breakfast at a table beneath a large mango tree. I mentioned that I had a craving for shrimp cocktail like the one served at the Fisherman's Club in Cartagena. Immediately, and with a flourish, the stranger said, "Let me invite you to Cartagena. We can be back in two hours." I thought it was a joke.

"We couldn't do it without a plane," I said, trying to back out tactfully.

"Precisely so," he said. "My plane is waiting outside."

I found out later that he was a prosperous merchant in ether, one of the main chemicals used in making cocaine.

With word of the justice minister's death, all Colombia was in turmoil. His assassination showed that the drug dealers would stop at nothing. It was a watershed, a crucial public killing that commanded attention, even after so many unknown innocents had been killed in the countryside. Against his will, President Betancur saw himself finally obliged to start using the extradition treaty with the United States.

Evaristo Porras was arrested by DAS (the Colombia Department of Administrative Security) in Cartagena in November 1986 on drug-trafficking charges. Two months later, he staged a mysterious prison break. He was extradited back to Colombia the same year by the government of Ecuador, but he was released after serving an eighteen-month jail sentence. No one else was ever arrested or convicted in the Lara Bonilla case.

In June 1984, Colombian ex-president Alfonso Lopez Michelsen was in his suite in the Hotel Cesar Park Marriott in Panama City. The night before, he had arrived as an election observer in Panama.

At the time, Panama had become a refuge for Colombian traffickers. They felt safe from the application of the controversial extradition treaty, invoked by Betancur after Lara Bonilla's death. In Betancur's declaration of all-out war on drug trafficking, he had extradited Hernan Botero, the owner of a soccer team, on charges of being a money launderer.

In leg irons and handcuffs, Botero was shown on national television upon his arrival in the United States. The image produced indignation at home.

The drug bosses took advantage of this nationalistic reaction. A few days after Botero was extradited, they issued a communiqué that said, in part: "We repudiate the harsh treatment to which our fellow Colombians are being submitted in U.S. courts. We prefer a tomb in Colombia to a jail in the United States." That saying became their motto.

The communiqué was signed "The Extraditables," who described themselves as the armed unit of the drug dealers. It said that they were prepared to take any steps they deemed necessary against those who would counsel an international solution, that is, extradition to face U.S. justice.

The telephone rang in the opulent Marriott suite in Panama City. It was Santiago Londoño White, Lopez Michelsen's political ally and fund-raiser. Londoño White had come to know members of the Medellín cartel while they were still living in the open, not yet accused of any crimes. "There's a group of Extraditables here who want to talk to you," he told Lopez Michelsen.

"And what could they want to say to me that they could not also say in writing to the president?" he asked.

"They are meeting in Panama and want to make an offer to the Betancur government. And they think you're the right person to bring the proposal back home without letting it out to the press."

Lopez Michelsen thought long and hard about the proposal. He accepted a meeting with the drug bosses, well aware that two months after the assassination of Lara Bonilla the country was in no mood for tea and crumpets with the authors of the deed.

Two days later, at around noon, the telephone rang in his suite. Londoño White was there with Lopez Michelsen, and he answered. "It's all set, the meeting will be right here in the hotel on the seventeenth floor," said a voice.

A few minutes later, the two men went to the meeting. The door was opened, and a ruddy, dark-skinned man, whom Lopez Michelsen had never seen before, stood there. This, he found out later, was José Gonzalo Rodriguez Gacha. Rodriguez Gacha was silent throughout the meeting. Also in the room were Pablo Escobar, Jorge Luis Ochoa, and Jorge's brother Fabio Ochoa, top leaders of the Medellín cartel. Lopez Michelsen sat down and listened.

"They always talked about the same thing," the former president told me, recalling the meeting. "They said they were victims of persecution, that the security forces had trampled in their garden." The meeting lasted two and a half hours, with Pablo Escobar doing most of the talking.

The former president said the drug bosses were frightened by the government's reaction after Lara Bonilla's death. "They said that they had nothing to do with the murder of Lara Bonilla because, according to them, justice was forcing him to testify," apparently referring to the court case involving Porras's campaign contribution. "They said that way they could hurt him more than by killing him," Lopez Michelsen added.

"It is a lie to say that they asked for an end to extradition," he stated. "They neither spoke about extradition at the Panama meeting nor did they propose paying the country's foreign debt," as had been reported of the meeting. "That was fiction."

This was not the first time that a dialogue of this type had taken place between officials and the drug bosses. A month earlier, the Colombian attorney general, Carlos Jimenez Gomez, had the first contact, apparently meeting with Pablo Escobar. But that earlier contact never was reported in the newspapers. There was a mention of it in the magazine *Semana,* but it mostly passed unnoticed.

After the Panama meeting, Lopez Michelsen called President Betancur and told him about it. Betancur asked Lopez Michelsen to prepare a report on the meeting. In turn, Jimenez Gomez held another meeting with Escobar in Panama.

The negotiations would not have had much impact had it not been for Juan Manuel Santos, the assistant publisher of the newspaper *El Tiempo,* who found out about them after one of Betancur's cabinet ministers spoke too freely at a party. Santos was indignant. He decided to check out the story with the best possible source: Lopez Michelsen himself.

It was a brief telephone conversation.

"Mr. President, can you tell me if that meeting in Panama was at the Hilton Hotel?" he asked, getting right to the point.

"No, it was at the Marriott," the former president said.

That was how Santos confirmed the negotiations. He decided to publish the story in the newspaper the following day. The report made national and international headlines.

The revelation that a dialogue was taking place with the Extraditables just two months after the assassination of Lara Bonilla was, to say the least, embarrassing to the Betancur government. What was worse was that two days later word came of the assassination in Medellín of Judge Tulio Manuel Castro Gil, who was investigating Lara Bonilla's murder.

In response to the story, Betancur chose to lie, to cover up. When asked by reporters on national television if there had been talks, he stated that these conversations had not been condoned by him, but were unofficial, outside the government; he also instructed his spokesmen to say the same thing. He was trying to provide a clear signal that he was not giving in to the drug interests. His decision was to begin enforcing the extradition treaty for real. From that moment until the end of his term in July 1986, there were sixteen extraditions. The final extradition was Carlos Lehder, who was tried in 1987 in Jacksonville, Florida, and sentenced on July 20, 1988, to life in prison on a drug and conspiracy conviction.

AN ATTACK ON THE PALACE
OF JUSTICE

In truth, if a poll had been taken in 1985 about the greatest problem facing Colombia, drug trafficking would not have been mentioned as a destabilizing factor. The answer would have been the threat of guerrilla insurgency. But in one of the great ironies of Colombian history, the guerrillas now found themselves working with the drug interests.

On November 6, 1985, a forty-two-member squadron from M-19—my hosts in 1982—seized the Palace of Justice in Bogotá. The plan was to take the Supreme Court justices hostage and to present an "armed indictment." M-19 wanted the court to take three specific steps: declare a government cease-fire accord constitutional; investigate the president for human rights abuses, charge him with malfeasance in office, and force new elections as a result of these actions; and, finally, to reject explicitly the extradition treaty with the United States.

Politics in Colombia surely made strange bedfellows. It was clear that the drug traffickers would do anything, even link up with the guerrillas, to achieve their goal, which was to safeguard their ability to operate freely, just like any other international business. M-19 shared a common cause with the drug dealers—anti-Communist fervor in Colombia and in the United States made it just as likely that they could be a target of extradition. Neither side could bear the prospect of being captured and shipped out of the country to the United States. It was obvious, M-19 members told me some time later, that the extradition treaty was just as big a threat for them as it was for the drug traffickers.

There was always a subtle interplay between the government's efforts to suppress the guerrillas and its attitude toward the drug dealers. When efforts against one waxed more important, those toward the other waned. The debate over which was the "real" enemy continued in Washington as well as in Bogotá. Should the United States be fighting Communists (as Oliver North maintained—leading the country down the road to the Iran-Contra scandals) or should it be fighting drugs (as President Bush would publicly claim it was, and aggressively)? Just as U.S. officials were able to look the other way when the men they declared "the moral equivalent of the founding fathers" were discovered to be dealing drugs, the Colombian military didn't hesitate to link up with the drug dealers to fight the guerrillas. It was primarily the citizens of Colombia who were trying to do something effective about the drug trade.

No guerrillas were ever extradited under the terms of the treaty, but guerrilla leaders had every reason to believe that the precedent of extraditing drug dealers could easily lead an enthusiastic government official to go after them in the same way—and, after all, Washington saw the Communists as the greater threat from the outset.

By acting as the spearhead of the Palace of Justice attack and striking out for their mutual interests, M-19 was also paying off an old debt it had with the Extraditables for the kidnapping of Martha Nieves Ochoa in 1981.

Ivan Marino Ospina was now the leader of M-19—Jaime Bateman, my host at the guerrilla camp, had been killed in a private plane crash on the Colombian-Panamanian border. Ospina had taken the first steps toward mending fences with the cartel by ardently taking up its antiextradition cause. Just before he met with President Betancur in Mexico for peace talks, he issued a declaration: "For every Colombian extradited, an American citizen in Colombia will be assassinated." This was to be a token of solidarity with the Extraditables.

At the same time, the Supreme Court was expecting threats and actions to come from the drug bosses of Medellín, not from the guerrillas. Since June 1985, several members of the court had been receiving anonymous threats intended to pressure them to rule against the extradition treaty.

"Hello, you miserable wretch," one written threat said. "We are writing to you not to ask, but rather to demand your support for our position. In this regard, we will accept neither your resignation, nor your abstention, nor feigned illness, nor suspicious or sudden leaves of absence. Anything less than a vote in our favor will be taken as a vote against us, as well as a declaration of war against us. From our jail cells, we will order your execution and we will shower blood and bullets down upon all those you hold dear." The threats came in telephone calls as well from people identified as Colombians sought in the United States on drug charges and therefore liable for extradition should the measure be declared legal.

The mechanism of the extradition treaty required that each request transmitted by the U.S. government would have to be reviewed by the Colombian Supreme Court. Meanwhile, the law passed by the Colombian Congress approving the measure was being questioned in three separate suits. So the decision of the court was expected at any moment, both on the overall treaty and on the legality of the law on extradition.

For months, no fewer than sixty police stood guard at the Palace of Justice. There was no reason to slacken security: During October, new rumors were circulating about the possibility that M-19, not the drug cartel, would make a move on the justices. The rumors had even appeared in *El Siglo,* one of the country's major newspapers.

But as was the case of the bombing of my house, despite all the advance warning, on the day of M-19's attack on the Palace of Justice, the police contingent was not there. The takeover lasted three days. Betancur rejected negotiations, even though the appeal for talks was made by the chief justice, Alfonso Reyes Echandia, from inside the building.

On the second day of the siege, smoke could be seen pouring out of the building. Rather than negotiate, the military and the police launched an apocalyptic assault. It is not known whether the fire was caused by the assault or whether the fire was set. But the flames destroyed everything, including the files of the pending extradition cases and testimony about torture allegedly conducted by members of the armed forces. Ninety-five people, including twelve justices—half the Supreme Court—were killed.

On November 12, 1985, with the ruins of the Palace of Justice still smoldering, a volcano that had lain dormant for 200 years erupted with all the ferocity that only nature can muster, sending a torrent of mud down on the helpless town of Armero. More than 20,000 people were buried.

I went to Armero directly from the siege at the Palace of Justice. The vision of destruction there was indeed infernal. I saw pieces of limbs scattered in the mud and an imploring hand frozen on the caked surface of the ooze. I saw the bodies of children asphyxiated where they slept, families torn apart, and survivors who did not know what happened to their missing loved ones. For a time, I forgot about being a reporter and pitched in with the relief effort. I stopped filing stories and helped people find their missing children or rescue survivors still caught in the mud.

That week in November 1985 was one of the most wrenching and unforgettable times I've experienced. It seemed as if Colombia and Colombians were being punished by God.

The tragedy was made worse by the feeble relief efforts of the government, a fact that the drug dealers seized on to build popular support. The drug barons said that the government was criminally negligent in this natural catastrophe and that officials could have prevented much of the loss of life by evacuating people when scientists warned of the impending eruption.

The dual catastrophes within a week of each other were too much for a country that was suffering greatly from a serious economic problem that was partly a consequence of the worldwide recession. Many countries were simply closing their doors to Colombia's principal exports—coffee and flowers. The result was that the price of these products went down, production dropped, and unemployment rose precipitously. The decision to open up the economy and liberalize the financial system made it easier to import products from overseas. This action made the situation worse because there was less call for Colombian goods at home.

The accelerated devaluation of the peso that the country had suffered since 1982 had increased proportionally in 1985 so that the dollar debts of public and private companies were growing astronomically. Financial institutions that were already on the brink of ruin because of speculation and foolhardy decisions were destroyed.

Agricultural products were also severely affected. Cotton and beef were no longer exported, and coffee and sugar exports decreased considerably.

But if the river of mud in Armero was sweeping everyone else away, the drug traffickers were firmly anchored and went about their business. When the government barely responded to the tragedy of Armero, a tough and powerful young emerald dealer went personally to help the victims. It was the first time that Colombians had heard of José Gonzalo Rodriguez Gacha, later discovered to be Escobar's key partner in drug exports to the United States. Carlos Lehder sent planes, dropping drug money from the air over Armero.

Slowly, carefully, surely, the drug cartel had penetrated our economy. Billions of drug dollars served as a sort of cushion to avoid an even sharper economic crisis in the country. One economist ventured to say that the Colombian drug bosses brought $1.5 billion into the country every year, about 4 percent of the gross domestic product.

Drug dealing was a gigantic business whose dimensions now rivaled the structure of the Colombian coffee-exporting business. It was that enormous economic power which tried to propel itself into legality, first clandestinely and later in an aboveboard campaign for political power.

The drug Mafia began to make a grand show of its riches. Its members acquired luxurious homes, antique automobiles, and flashy, custom-built off-road vehicles. Thanks to legal loopholes, they laundered part of their capital in the nation's financial institutions; they bought ranches and lands, hotels and businesses. And they bought soccer teams in a country that would do anything for a winner.

At his perch in the newsroom, Guillermo Cano was writing with a sense of foreboding. Able as ever to scrutinize the reality of events without having to go to cocktail parties where there were sure to be juicy bits of gossip, he was one of the first people to warn about the capacity of the drug money to detonate internal conflicts and to corrupt the nation's already weak institutions. His premonitions not only hit the mark, but resulted in his murder.

On the morning of December 17, 1986, a gesture by Guillermo Cano moved his wife, Ana Maria, deeply. Before he left home for the newspaper, he embraced his oldest granddaughter, Adelaida, aged five, with the tenderness and anxiety of a grandfather who was giving a final hug to his very life.

He was obviously nervous the entire day as he walked around the newsroom. And he called his wife several times during the day, which was out of character for him.

The recent assassination of the magistrate Hernando Baquero Bordo on July 31, 1986, just a few days before the court was to issue a ruling on the legality of the extradition treaty between Colombia and the United States, led to an even more tense situation. In 1979 Baquero Bordo had been one of three officials in the attorney general's office who had been sent to Washington to agree to the terms of an extradition treaty, along with Virgilio Barco, who was then Colombian ambassador to the United States.

At about 6 P.M. Guillermo said good-bye to his oldest son, Juan Guillermo, in the newsroom, and they exchanged a brief glance. And while the image of his father receded, Juan Guillermo was recalling the report of a driver for the newspaper who had noticed someone on a white motorcycle. The report had reached his father, but as usual Guillermo paid no special attention to it.

As was his routine for more than thirty years, Guillermo Cano left his office at 6:45 P.M., after having given one of the few interviews he could accept—he hated being the object of news reports. The interview was about the annual journalism awards.

The reporters asked him if he was afraid, and he answered with the same words he had used when a bomb exploded in my house. "You have to keep going . . . in the business we're in, we just have to learn that every day we leave home the possibility exists that we may not come back."

It was his turn.

At 7 P.M. on December 17, 1986, Colombia radio reported that "two assassins on a motorcycle, no more than twenty years old, posted at the newspaper exit, fired on the car of the publisher of *El Espectador,* who apparently was gravely wounded." Cano was taken from the car and quickly driven to the nearest hospital. He died en route.

After the murder of Guillermo, his older brother, Luis Gabriel, became publisher. Luis Gabriel, who had been business manager of the newspaper, had a patriarchal air; he was a humble man, but commanded the same respect and prestige afforded Guillermo. In the newsroom there were three managing editors: Guillermo's sons, thirty-four-year-old Juan Guillermo and thirty-one-year-old Fernando, and Jose Salgar, one of the deans of Colombian journalism.

The four men arrived at the newspaper office every day surrounded by bodyguards and wearing bulletproof vests; with this entourage, they seemed more like ministers of state than newspaper editors. Protection measures had been reinforced considerably for everyone at the newspaper, not only for the bosses. It was easy to confuse plainclothes security men with reporters in the newsroom. As one key precaution, we were encouraged to vary our routes and schedules in arriving and leaving the office each day.

The morning of Tuesday, January 13, 1987, I decided to take the Circular Bypass, a lovely parkway that cuts across the city from north to south at the foot of the hills that surround Bogotá. When it was sunny, I liked to go that way to gaze at the trees and shimmering mountains. It was also the quickest route across town, and I had a special reason for wanting to get to the office early.

The night before, my housekeeper, Empera, told me, "There's a man outside who wants to talk to you. He says it's urgent." I went into the vestibule of the apartment building and peered through the blinds. It was Ramiro (not his real name), an old acquaintance of Lebanese descent, whom I knew for his dark sense of humor and his ability to straddle the diverse social classes of Bogotá; as a lawyer, he was equally at home among ministers and thieves. He told me he was in too much of a hurry to come in and went right to the point. He had come, he told me, as a messenger of the Ochoa family, the Medellín drug traffickers.

"The Ochoas had nothing to do with the murder of Don Guillermo Cano and want his family to know that. I'm their lawyer and I'm working on the extradition problem with them. It may be true that Pablo Escobar is a violent man, but the Ochoas are not murderers; they do not have private armies at their disposal.

"I know them well and I told them I would do everything possible to find someone from *El Espectador* who was willing to do an interview with them. You're the only person I know at the newspaper. The idea would be for you to go with me to meet with them the day after tomorrow. I will have a private plane waiting."

This was, needless to say, a shocking offer. Not even a month after Guillermo's death, some of the country's most notorious drug dealers expected me to talk with them. This time the personal danger and the chances of getting caught in a precarious political situation outweighed the story. I was not interested, and I doubted that the Canos would agree to such a meeting. I tried to put Ramiro off the best way I could, telling him that it would be up to the management of the newspaper.

"Listen," he said, insisting. "The Ochoas are desperate. They feel persecuted. Their children can't go to school anymore; the family is separated and in hiding. It's really an extraordinary situation."

"I'm so very sorry," I said tersely, and I think a note of sarcasm crept through.

"The Medellín cartel is nothing like it is portrayed—there is no King Arthur and no round table," the lawyer told me. "Each member is independent. At times and in certain enterprises they join forces. But in other cases, like in the killing of Guillermo Cano or the justice minister, the Ochoas were not at all involved."

"I can tell you this from the outset," I replied. "I really don't think the Cano family wants to hear the Ochoa family's defense."

"Just deliver the message; that's all I ask," the lawyer said.

There was some truth in what he had said. It was simplistic to treat the Medellín cartel like another Hollywood version of a Mafia family, complete with rigid codes and ancestral-based bureaucracy. The large drug dealers in Medellín and Cali and the smaller cartel operations were largely autonomous. They kept separate books, and their methods of operation were distinct. Most of the time, they worked independently, but they joined forces when a lucrative business deal required additional players.

But that didn't change the basic point. I wanted no part of the interview. It was not the first time that someone had put forth this image of the Ochoas as fine, respectable people, misunderstood and persecuted unfairly by the authorities. The family patriarch, Don Fabio Ochoa, was a folksy sort of fellow, a wealthy rancher and an ardent horsemen, well known in international equestrian circles.

Don Fabio's sons—Juan David, Jorge Luis, and Fabio, Jr.— were sophisticated, well-educated young men, but they were also sought by Interpol, and the United States named them in a 1987 indictment for drug trafficking. Juan David, the oldest, was apparently the least involved in the smuggling operation. Jorge Luis, often said to be the mastermind of the family operation, was an intimate of Pablo Escobar. He also had been jailed in Spain in 1984 on drug-trafficking charges. But, in a case that outraged U.S. authorities and poisoned the United States' image of Colombian justice, he had been extradited from Madrid in 1986 to Colombia, rather than to the United States, and promptly set free by a judge. The event brought strong condemnation from the Reagan administration. Fabio, Jr., was implicated in the killing of Barry Seal, a onetime trafficker for the cartel who turned state's evidence in the United States. Seal was murdered at a Salvation Army halfway house in Baton Rouge, Louisiana, on February 19, 1987.

Unlike Pablo Escobar, who was shunned by the upper class, the Ochoa brothers were born to a prosperous family whose members were well connected in the highest social circles. The Ochoas did, however, introduce Escobar around town, helping him win respectability. After 1983, when Escobar was, for all intents and purposes, living a clandestine life underground, the Ochoas were more visible, occasionally appearing at public events. They kept in touch with Bogotá's political and business circles. They often lobbied in the news media to improve their image, trying to differentiate themselves and their "peaceful ways" from the more violent tactics of Escobar and Rodriguez Gacha. So it was no surprise to hear this argument from Ramiro, their lawyer. And it was also not unusual for the likes of the Ochoas and journalists like me to know the same people. Perhaps the situation is like that in other, larger countries, where a president's son, for example, can be implicated in a major banking scandal or where major industrialists court favors from presidents, senators, and congressmen and invite them to spend weekends at their palatial estates and to cruise on their private yachts.

While driving to work on January 13, 1987, the morning after Ramiro's visit, I felt unsettled. I knew I still wanted no part of the interview. Already the normal caravan of motorcades and cars with security guards was careening through the city streets. It was the guards' job to protect judges, ministers, and political leaders; I could see them looking out of their armored windshields, sizing me up as I maneuvered around them in my little Renault. All the security apparatus—the sounds of car engines running at high speed, of motorcycles, of horns honking insistently, and of sirens—followed me as I drove to the office. It was nightmarish; a permanent aura of violence hung over the city and the country.

When I got to the newsroom, the level of tension was even worse than that of the street. I went right to Fernando Cano's office. Thin and gentle, Fernando seemed to have inherited not only his father's stoic manner but a premature hunch, perhaps from stooping over galley proofs so much of the time. At thirty-one, he carried the family name proudly. He was over six feet tall and had more gray hair than one would expect of a person his age. He was married to María Isabel Cassas, who had also been a philosophy major in college, and they had three daughters.

I told Fernando about the Ochoas' proposal, and he immediately called a meeting in the boardroom, attend by all three managing editors, as well as Fernando's uncle, Luis Gabriel, and mother, Ana Maria, who handled the publisher's role and business administration of the paper. The reaction was much the same as I had predicted to the Ochoas' lawyer the night before. Within a few hours, they had put together a draft version of an editorial that would reject any form of dialogue with the drug dealers. Salgar brought me a copy.

"This is what we have agreed to say. Look it over for me," he said.

I had just started reading it when Fernando raced frantically into the city room, a news story from the wire service fluttering behind him. "There's been an attack on Enrique Parejo in Budapest," he said. "Let's get working on it."

Enrique Parejo was the Colombian ambassador to Hungary, sent to that post in an attempt to protect him from reprisals by the drug bosses. Parejo had taken over as minister of justice after Lara Bonilla was assassinated in 1984. It was he who had signed the first drug extradition orders, and it was under his orders that Colombia resumed spraying coca plantations with the chemical glyphosate. The decision to resume spraying came under pressure from Washington—Colombia had suspended the spraying program upon hearing reports of the chemical's threat to the health of the people in that area.

At the end of the Betancur administration, Parejo, like other prominent politicians leaving the government, needed to find some place to lay low for a time. The theory at the foreign ministry was that it would be safer to place people in Eastern Europe because the state security controls would make it more difficult for would-be assassins to operate. That theory proved to be wrong.

According to the wire-service account, a young man came to the front door of the Colombian embassy in Hungary, and security was so lax that the ambassador himself answered. The man swiftly pulled a revolver out of the pocket of his overcoat and shot

Parejo point-blank in the face. The report said that Parejo was in critical condition.

"Now it's no longer safe outside the country either," Fernando said, as I made futile attempts to call the embassy for more information. "These guys go out and kill people wherever they want to."

Amazingly, Parejo survived the attack. Three bullets lodged in the bones of his face and did not penetrate his brain. Today he has a severe speech impairment, but is otherwise healthy. The assailant was later identified as a twenty-two-year-old Colombian, part of a three-member assassination team sent by Pablo Escobar from Medellín. All three men were captured by Interpol in Europe and sent back to Colombia in 1988, but were released for lack of evidence. At the time of the attack, however, no one knew exactly who was responsible, but it was certainly no time to think even remotely of talking to any member of the Medellín cartel.

Within moments of the report about Parejo, Ramiro, my visitor of the night before, was on the phone. He was either a good actor or unaware of the attack.

"Ready for our little trip?" he asked.

"There's just been an attack on Parejo in Budapest," I told him tersely. "I don't think we have anything else to discuss." I hung up.

On January 14, two days after Ramiro's visit, all the print media in Colombia issued a joint declaration, timed to appear on the front pages of their newspapers. It was an act of unprecedented solidarity, and we saw it as having historical significance:

The news media believe that the nation and its government are confronting an open war declared on them by the drug Mafia. Faced with this war, the news media have taken a valiant stance, and have paid a high price in blood. But they view with astonishment that neither the actions of the government nor the reaction of the various segments of society correspond with the danger the nation faces—the threat that the country will be totally dominated by drug dealers. The attack on the former minister of justice added to the recent murder of Guillermo Cano obliges us to form a united media front—newspapers, magazines, radio, and television—to confront this declaration of war on Colombia. For that reason, we have agreed to be vigilant, to demand that the government, the nation's political parties, and Colombian society as a whole unite in solidarity toward the development of effective solutions to win this war begun by the drug dealers.

The idea of creating a common news front against the drug dealers had been brewing since my friend and colleague Enrique Santos Calderón had raised the idea a few months earlier. Enrique's family owns *El Tiempo,* the nation's largest-circulation newspaper and *El Espectador*'s rival in Bogotá. There was competition between the papers, but that did not mar our long-standing, close friendship.

In addition to being one of the widest read, most controversial columnists in the mainstream Bogotá press, Enrique also participated in the leftist movement, founding *Alternativa,* a contentious magazine that won the prestigious support of his friend Gabriel García Márquez. In its pages he criticized administrative and military corruption, as well as the rise of the drug cartels. Such stories brought numerous lawsuits and threats, making him the target of one of the first attacks by drug traffickers on a journalist. In December 1976 a bomb partially destroyed the offices of *Alternativa.* The following day another bomb blew up in the garage of Enrique's house, minutes after he and his wife arrived home; miraculously, both were uninjured.

In 1980, disenchanted with the revolutionary left, Enrique returned to his family's influential newspaper where he continued with his column. Of those long-gone days of revolutionary ideals, all that remained was a brace of friends and their occasional nostalgic get-togethers. What concerned Enrique was not so much the dynamic and economic potency of the drug traffickers, but their ambitions for political power. And what disturbed him most was the chilling arrogance of the new drug barons and their attempt to subjugate institutions, intimidate an entire society, and silence all critics. This was all the more true following the first assassination of a journalist by the cartels in 1986: Echavarria Barrientos, deputy publisher of *Diario Occidente,* was killed three months before the assassination of Guillermo Cano.

For that reason, on the day of Guillermo Cano's murder, Enrique organized, in the space of a few hours, the celebrated Day of Silence. On Friday, December 19, 1986, all news media in Colombia maintained twenty-four hours of silence in a desperate but eloquent protest of the brutal annihilation of a journalist. No one objected to the economic consequences of the protest.

The blackout sought to demonstrate to the public the seriousness of what had taken place and the outrage felt by journalists. On the Day of Silence, a group of journalists from different newspapers conducted a mass march through the center of Bogotá, an act that dramatically underlined the degree of indignation and fear that the murder of Cano awakened. This united protest, followed by the joint statement in January, was a step toward the most intriguing experiment in professional solidarity ever conducted in the history of Latin American journalism—a steering committee of all the communications media in Colombia. We called it "the Kremlin," but it was really a journalistic front dedicated to fighting drug terrorism.

There was already a tradition at *El Espectador* and *El Tiempo* that stories involving the drug trade were to carry no bylines, being tagged instead as prepared by "the investigative team." The theory behind this cover formula was that if the entire newspaper was to be held responsible, no individual would be threatened. This theory proved ineffective, however, because in time everyone knew the names of the reporters who handled the stories. The whole concept of investigative reporting in Colombia owed something to the atmosphere created by the Watergate scandal in the United States; in both cases, journalists became well-known personalities. We soon learned, however, that our brand of high-profile investigative reporting would face dangers far beyond anything experienced by Bob Woodward and Carl Bernstein. It was true that at times we were able to investigate corrupt officials, who were removed from public office in due course. But the price for doing so was high. Reporters were forced to maintain a low profile as they continued their investigations; often they went into hiding. There were increasing death threats, and many stopped working entirely or fled the country.

This was the case for many of my colleagues, not only at *El Espectador* but at other large newspapers, at radio and television stations in Bogotá, and at papers in smaller towns and cities around the country, where reporters were less visible and thereby less protected than we were in Bogotá. It was always wrenching when reporters from other parts of the country would call in to offer us information and then ask our help to protect them. But we were powerless to offer much help; we were also under constant threat, safeguarded only by the fact that the murder of a reporter in Bogotá would not go unnoticed.

Beyond all the other obstacles, we were having difficulty obtaining access to official documents. Although Colombia has a law that is the rough equivalent of the U.S. Freedom of Information Act, it was not effective in getting us the material we needed. The bureaucracy involved was daunting, and obstacles were always thrown in our way. Thus, we were forced into using our ingenuity to get the facts we reported.

We developed, for example, "Deep Throat" sources among civil servants in Congress who were disgusted with the corruption around them. We also cultivated guerrilla informants or brave neighbors near ranches where cocaine laboratories and stockpiles were hidden; we sought out (or were sought out by) mysterious ex-police agents and investigators, some motivated by moral outrage and some by vendettas against drug bosses who had crossed them.

To confirm a report in the course of our investigations, we could touch base with everybody in the circuit: our best insider drug source, our guerrilla contact, and our stealthy official contact. The risks were enormous; when the identities of these informants were uncovered, the informants were mercilessly killed by the drug bosses and their allies. The process became more complicated still when our work began to have an impact on the dons of the drug-trafficking world. We unmasked drug traffickers' control of soccer teams and revealed the alliance between the drug bosses and political figures and the corruption inspired by drug money in the army.

But the cover formula was shattered by Cano's murder. Not only was the editor killed for the investigative team's stories, but the drug bosses had decided to hold everyone at the newspaper responsible. So in the wake of the assassination, all the journalists at *El Espectador* found ourselves fearing for our lives and at the same time vehemently outraged by the attempt to halt our work. Our investigations were yielding important information about the expanding network controlled by the drug bosses. But there was no safe way to publish what we had. We were afraid.

In a series of conversations among the leading journalists in the country, it was decided that the only way for reporters and their publications to be more or less protected as they conducted these types of investigations was for all the news media to publish and broadcast the same drug reports at the same time. The identities of the individual media outlet and individual reporter were to be kept secret.

This decision was not taken lightly. After decades of intense competition among the major newspapers for advertising revenue and for readers, as well as professional jealousy among the journalists, how easy would it be to work together? It would be akin to the U.S. television networks, along with the *Los Angeles Times, New York Times,* and *Washington Post,* sharing information and publishing the same stories on an appointed date.

How easy would it be to arbitrate the various points of view that made up the national news media? Those of us in Bogotá also ran the risk of antagonizing the media outside the capital, which always accused us of having an imperious attitude, charging that we cared only about officialdom and too little about the realities of the rest of the country. It was absurd, in a sense, that we were choosing to defend freedom of the press by slicing away part of its essence, the individual drives and rivalries that give newspaper reporting its vigor. But we had come to the conclusion that scoring a scoop was often lethal; standing alone, we stood a good chance of being picked off one by one.

We agreed that the only ones to know the source of our unified reports would be the seven-member steering committee, whose members were Fernando Cano, Enrique Santos, Antonio Caballero, Fabio Castillo, Mauricio Gomez, Andrés Pastrana, and me, representing the major newspapers and magazines in Bogotá. We nicknamed the committee "the Kremlin," and I was appointed the group's assistant coordinator.

The first meetings were held at my house in an atmosphere of secrecy and great care. Since the arrangements were made by telephone and everyone assumed that the lines were tapped, we used some silly code phrases that probably didn't fool anyone— statements like "Something's shaking at my place" or "Gorbachev has a meeting at the Kremlin" when we wanted to be more exotic. This was hardly enough to keep news of the meetings quiet.

Each committee member traveled with a brace of bodyguards, and the whole neighborhood could see immediately that whatever was happening was more than a socialite's tea party. The neighbors were already far too suspicious to fall for a ruse like that. This was not an innocent part of town. Luis Carlos Galán, the leader of the New Liberal party, lived next door. He was packing his bags for a six-month fellowship in England at Oxford University to get a respite from the death threats for a while. His bodyguards alone—there usually were eight—were enough to attract attention.

Across the street was the administrative office of Coca-Cola. It was also highly guarded, not because there was a fear of attack by the drug Mafia, but because Coca-Cola seemed the perfect target for attack by the guerrilla groups.

Meanwhile, living in the penthouse of my building were relatives of President Virgilio Barco. Often Carolina, Barco's wife, stopped by to visit them, multiplying considerably the number of bodyguards and automatic weapons already in the vicinity.

Everyone was on edge at the Kremlin meetings at my place. One night, for example, as one of the supposedly secret sessions at my home was breaking up, Felipe Santos, Enrique's cousin, who had left the meeting just a few minutes earlier, telephoned me.

"María Ji, I'm calling because I saw a suspicious white van parked outside the building when I left. I just got home, but it was worrying me. I think we should move these meetings around from now on."

I was frightened. Fernando Cano was just leaving when the call came in. "You're sure it was a white van?" he asked. "That's what he said," I replied. Fernando relaxed and chuckled a bit. "Call him back and tell him to calm down. It's my new bodyguards."

Despite the false alarm, we did decide to vary the meeting places. We had become so worried about safety that we were confusing our protectors with supposed assailants.

We had some notable successes in the course of our eight-month cooperative effort. In all, we published five special reports, which was quite an accomplishment considering that with each report we had to negotiate an agreement among all the nation's news media. We also decided to drop advertising from businesses or organizations that were presumed to be fronts for the drug Mafia. And we forced the cancellation of a bicycle race sponsored by a radio station that was linked to the Cali cartel. That was no small matter because in Colombia, as in Europe, bicycle racing is a major sport.

There was so much enthusiasm that the Kremlin group began to consider the idea of doing an exposé on drug trafficking in the United States. We had information about what happened when Colombian cocaine arrived in the United States; there were American drug dealers too, but their activities were often submerged in reports of Colombia's drug cartels. We even had the investigative team chosen and primed to leave for the United States. The project never got off the ground; it was too expensive and time-consuming for our available resources, although I continue to think that more reporting is needed on the United States' connection to Colombia's cocaine cartels.

In our haste to publish something quickly in the days after Cano's death, we made what was probably a tactical error. We decided to publish a four-part *Miami Herald* series about the drug rings. Although the series gave us a chance to keep the drug traffickers' names and deeds in the newspaper, the effect was not all that great. It was a good series for the United States, but in Colombia the material had already been reported.

The second joint report was by Colombian journalists, and it was just as strong and uncompromising as we wanted it to be. It was a minutely detailed report on the hit-squad murder of the former chief of the national antinarcotics police unit, Colonel Jaime Ramirez.

Ramirez was killed on November 17, 1986, on a highway en route from his brother's ranch to Bogotá, the only day that he let down his guard and gave his security detail the day off. Ramirez had led one of the most important victories in the fight against the drug dealers—the discovery and dismantling of the Tranquilandia drug laboratories in the southern Colombian jungle. In that raid, a joint United States–Colombian drug task force seized what was a record at the time—nine tons of pure cocaine. Basing our information on Ramirez's personal diaries, we journalists were able to show that the assassination was not only planned by Pablo Escobar, but that Ramirez was fully aware of the plot, which involved corrupt members of his own police force. But he also believed that the contract on his life had been canceled.

Despite the fact that our report named members of the military and civilian security forces who were involved, the story did not provoke the least reaction. There was not so much as a denial; the government and the police maintained utter silence. The drug bosses, known to lash out aggressively at unflattering portrayals in the press, also were silent. To this day, I can't explain the lack of response. On the one hand, I think that the public had been so overloaded with information about death and violence surrounding drug dealing that people had become almost impervious to further accounts of violence. On the other hand, I think that neither the government nor the public knew how to respond when an entire industry essentially took up the cudgel in what should have been a governmental investigation. The silence was testimony to the sad reality that the machinery of government was severely impaired.

But the Kremlin group kept up the pressure. The third report sought to offer new, clear evidence on the assassination of Minister of Justice Lara Bonilla in April 1984. The idea was to time this report with the impending trial (in absentia) of Pablo Escobar and José Gonzalo Rodriguez Gacha as the intellectual authorities of the murder. The report was issued as planned, but the trial was suspended two days before its scheduled opening, apparently because of judicial intimidation, and never held. To this day, the murder of the Colombian justice minister has gone unpunished.

For many reasons, the media's common front began to show rifts. Fear and disagreement caused the split. As Juan Gomez Martinez, the publisher of *El Colombiano,* noted, "We are in the lion's cage and the situation here in Medellín is quite different from that in Bogotá." Later, as mayor of Medellín, following a kidnapping attempt against him, Gomez would begin to support the concept of dialogue with the drug dealers to bring a halt to the drug-terrorist violence in his own backyard.

Meanwhile, television and radio participants in our united pool were having increasing difficulty finding reporters who were willing to go on the air and describe our reports for fear of being identified. To allay such fears, or at least to lower the heat for a while, the Kremlin decided to change the pace in its fourth report.

In that report, we took up a theme little discussed to date— the use of crack in the United States and the use in Colombia of *basuco*—a highly toxic drug produced from the poisonous residues of coca paste, gasoline, and kerosene. Basuco was cheap and accessible, and its use was reaching alarming proportions among the poor, the unemployed, and the street children of the nation's cities. Like crack, which is also smoked, basuco causes irreversible damage to brain cells and produces convulsions, lung spasms, and death. Although its use never reached the level of crack use in the United States, the number of basuco cases admitted to hospitals in Bogotá tripled in the two-year period from 1986 to 1988.

By focusing on the prevention of drug use, we kept the commitment to joint publication intact. Nevertheless, the atmosphere at the Kremlin meetings made it obvious that our collaborative effort was drawing to a close.

Things became more complicated still when we broached the subject of our fifth report—the Cali cartel. Because the Medellín traffickers were the more violent of the two cartels, they had always received greater attention; Cali's operations were less bloody, more businesslike, therefore less obviously "newsworthy." In addition, the members of the Cali cartel were (and still are) part of the traditional wealthy business class, owners of major businesses and even media outlets in Cali and thus had seemed untouchable.

But there were truly alarming developments in Cali that needed to be reported. In the course of our investigation, we found that well-known businessmen and an array of current and former government officials were linked in some way to the leading Cali drug boss, Gilberto Rodriguez Orejuela. After President Betancur's decision to apply the extradition treaty with the United States, it was learned that Rodriguez Orejuela had been sought in the United States since 1979 on charges of trafficking in cocaine. In 1991 he was charged in a U.S. federal money-laundering indictment.

The Kremlin lasted only a few more weeks. The tensions among the various media became more and more pronounced the closer we came to writing about the Cali cartel. Because of the fear of reprisals, representatives of many of the media outlets that joined our original group of seven stopped coming to the meetings. Nobody wanted to be the first to point the finger at the Cali dealers, whose lawyers were always ready to threaten lawsuits and to lobby with publishers against reporters' efforts to "defame innocent businessmen." Suddenly, those of us who were left in the Kremlin realized we were a minority. We could have kept at it, but the effort seemed to outweigh the risk. The last meeting, an awkward and sad affair, was at my house, as usual. We spoke and laughed, arriving at the conclusion that considering the diversity of the news media, we had at least been able to show the drug traffickers that reporters in Colombia refused to be gagged. With or without a common front, the stories would keep coming.

EL RAUDAL

In El Raudal, a village on the shores of the majestic Rio Guayabero, the production of coca paste is a cottage industry. It begins on the back porch of a farmhouse, where sun-dried coca leaves are ground up and mixed with ethyl ether, acetone, hydrochloric acid, and paint thinner. The resulting precipitate is a gummy residue—coca base.

By the mid-1980s, growing coca had become the principal source of local income; coca-leaf plantations were springing up all around, and farmers saw their economic problems dissolve in a bath of easy drug money. Traditional crops in the region—corn and beans—were rotting in the fields; there was no market and little infrastructure to handle this produce. But with coca leaf, the drug dealers took care of everything. Moreover, the leaf could be harvested three times a year, and there seemed to be an unlimited number of buyers; the demand always exceeded the harvest.

Most of the plantations were a few acres each. The economy of the plant was evident. Two hundred grams of coca leaf, derived from two plants, become a gram of cocaine.

Everyone benefited in this process. Before 1980, El Raudal was a poor river settlement, a collection of humble thatched-roof huts and general stores where provisions were sold. In contrast, in the first half of the 1980s, peasants were buying Betamax video recorders, which had become status symbols in the jungle. Per capita there were more jewelry stores in El Raudal, population 500, than in Hong Kong. Everyone sought to buy gold jewelry, and nothing less than 24 carats would do. Gold jewelry was not only considered a good investment, it was also the symbol of wealth and prosperity. It was common to see men wearing heavy gold or emerald rings, as well as gold medallions, chains, and bracelets; the women and children also wore gold—rings on all their fingers, earrings, and chains. "Be careful with anyone not wearing gold chains around here," a beautiful young widow warned me. She boasted of having had more husbands than Zsa Zsa Gabor.

All the clothing in El Raudal was purchased in Miami and smuggled in as contraband. Brands like Banana Republic and Pierre Cardin were sold alongside gear that was supposedly army regulation only, a further sign that the military was participating in the local economic boom. There were now cement houses—another sign of prosperity—and each house had its own electric generator. Electric appliances were also commonplace in these houses in the middle of the jungle.

There was only one way to get to El Raudal—in a sailing skiff on the river. The skiffs were old but well-maintained boats. The seats were lined with colored cloth that had little yellow arrows on the borders. The steering house generally was covered with velour, and the prow inevitably had on it an image of the Virgin. Each boat had a powerful sound system, with speakers strategically placed up and down it. The skiffs of Guayabero were to the region what convertibles are to the French Riviera or what gondolas are to Venice. They were not only for transporting people; they were a lifeline, especially for the transport of the chemicals needed to make cocaine—above all kerosene and ether. Shippers had to pay a steep tax to the army so they and their cargo would not be detained.

The Guayabero region, like many others, had in recent years been more or less taken over by FARC—the pro-Soviet guerrilla group that was the oldest and most ideologically orthodox rebel organization in the country. The guerrilla-controlled zones were like miniature republics, complete with roadblocks marking the crossing between government- and guerrilla-held territory. The guerrillas filled their coffers, and the army prospered by levying a tax on the peasants for importing the chemicals needed in these independent republics.

"We cannot oppose the needs of a population that has found in coca its best and only form of subsisting in the damned jungle," one commander told me, somewhat apologetically, I thought. Like many guerrilla commanders, he had been educated at Patrice Lumumba University in Moscow.

Once a boat left Puerto Arturo, the change was startling. There was a guerrilla checkpoint located a mere ten minutes away. Immediately one began to see signs along the Guayabero's banks declaring entry into "Liberated Territory." Some signs contained slogans supporting the Sandinista revolution, others lauded the great accomplishments of the FARC fighters, and still others proclaimed the grand objectives of armed struggle. There were quotations from Salvadoran guerrilla commanders and from Augusto Sandino, the inspiration for the Nicaraguan revolution. And on each placard was the figure of Jacobo Arenas, FARC's political boss.

But the bonanza was short-lived. By 1986 the peasants were complaining about being squeezed from both sides. As one coca grower told me, "We used to make out with a lot of money because a kilo of coca got to be worth 500,000 pesos, but now it doesn't pay. With all that you sometimes have to pay the army to let the ether barrels get in, and with the taxes we pay to FARC, we're in bad shape. Not only are prices down, but the death squads are killing our people. They figure that because we live in an area controlled by FARC, we must be Communists."

I met this farmer in December 1986 in San José del Guaviare where he was participating in a march by 40,000 coca growers protesting their plight. It was one of the largest peasant protests in years. Down the Guayabero they had come, organizing a demonstration to challenge the abuses by these rightist death squads and to seek relief from the economic crisis provoked by the suddenly plummeting price of coca leaf.

San José was a typical southern jungle town. Located on a plateau along the Guaviare River, it was a major center for the cocaine business. I had flown there from Bogotá with a number of government officials to view the scope of the drug business. Other than a week-long trip through the jungle, flying was the best way to get to the region. We circled in toward the scruffy landing strip that pretended to be the main airport for the town, which was the capital of the jungle-park region. "This is a miserable excuse for an airport all right, but it's second only to Bogotá in air traffic. There's a plane landing every minute . . . all loaded with cocaine," one of the officials said.

"What's that big building over there?" I asked as we taxied to a stop. "Oh, that. They call it the Drug Enforcement Administration," the official said, chuckling. "That's where the antinarcotics police live. They just sent a couple of hundred more as reinforcements. You know, they go out on raids, they do house-to-house searches, and all that. Funny thing, though, they don't do too well. No guns, no cocaine . . . and they never catch any crooks. That, by the way, is lucky for them. There's no jail here, and they wouldn't know where to put the people if they caught them. And anyway, the judges aren't in such great shape either. They all wear guns.

"It's the law of the jungle . . . the law of the pistol."

Calamar, another town that depended on the coca economy, was also falling on hard times. The currency exchange in the Calamar area was governed by the price of coca paste. In a region that had prospered in the boom years, there was now no electricity or water, and the local airport, the third busiest in Colombia, after Bogotá and San José de Guaviare, was reducing its operations. With falling coca prices, fewer shipments of coca were leaving the area.

Despite this sudden economic downturn, Calamar was still capitalizing on its reputation as a jungle hot spot. Its discotheques were as well apportioned as those of Bogotá, Medellín, or Cali. The bars were made of fine hardwoods and the decorations were lush and lewd. The drinking glasses were crystal—a great luxury in the jungle—and the bartenders filled them generously with contraband Scotch whiskey brought in at premium prices.

Calamar was also renowned for having the most popular, fanciest bordello in the region. Its proprietor was "honored" not only for being the owner of such a respectable establishment but for being a renowned public citizen. The prostitutes of Calamar were a legend unto themselves. Men traveled from all over the area, paying up to $200 for two hours of recreation in a country where people who work for the minimum wage don't make that much in a month. These women were not only the most sought-after whores in southern Colombia, they were the richest.

A few weeks before my first visit the prostitutes had caused a scandal that was still a frequent topic of conversation. Hearing that the army was about to occupy the Guaviare region—FARC had been operating there uncontested—the prostitutes staged an antimilitary protest march on the paved highway that links Calamar with San José del Guaviare. They were fully regaled in their most opulent jewelry and finest gowns, and violinists accompanied them as they set out on the road, warning, "If the army comes into town, we'll take all our money out of the bank." Since these women were important patrons of the Bank of San José del Guaviare (such was the scale of their wealth), their demonstration convinced local businessmen to lobby the army, and the military maneuvers were canceled.

Calamar was an important wholesale coca clearinghouse where FARC made money by collecting taxes on coca-leaf proceeds. But the guerrillas were also in charge of protecting drug-processing laboratories in the vicinity, precisely because of the lack of government control. Calamar was strategically located close to the border with Peru, the largest producer of coca, and not far from Colombia's coca fields.

One day I was taken to the infirmary in Calamar, where I was treated for injuries from a fall. The local FARC squad commander came walking in with three young blond men, obviously foreigners. "We don't want hippies or drug addicts around here nor the dregs of capitalism," he said, spouting Marxist rhetoric. The three had long hair and a stoned look in their eyes. The town was not that big, and I had seen them earlier sitting around playing Beatles music on the street, when someone had whispered jokingly to me, "They're probably DEA agents." They were kept in jail for several days and then were ordered by the police to leave the region.

By 1987 the joint operating agreement between FARC and the drug bosses was falling apart. In 1984 two FARC commando teams raided one of the laboratories they supposedly were guarding and stole a vast supply of weaponry, along with $700,000 and 216 kilos of cocaine, worth more than $4 million in the United States. For the members of the cocaine cartel, that raid was akin to a declaration of war.

In 1984 the Betancur government had negotiated a peace accord with FARC. As a first step in military demobilization and before they would enter civilian life by participating in elections, the organization had created a political wing—the Patriotic Union. The Patriotic Union's first candidate for president was Jacobo Arenas, one of the best-known guerrilla leaders in the country— and FARC's political commander.

Taking advantage of the truce, I went to see Arenas in September 1986 at his guerrilla headquarters, known as Casa

Verde, in an area called La Uribe on the eastern rib of the Andes. Under the terms of the peace accord that established pacification zones not subject to military control, FARC was allowed to keep its main headquarters at La Uribe. Casa Verde was more like a country club than a guerrilla headquarters, and was visited by ex-presidents, government emissaries, leaders of other guerrilla organizations, and an array of Colombian journalists and foreign correspondents. My visit there lasted a month.

FARC had established an elaborate infrastructure in its thirty years of existence. The camp had solar-energy panels, the commanders were bivouacked in cement buildings, and the troops slept in huge field tents. Communications were sophisticated; once the truce was signed, FARC installed a hot-line microwave telephone circuit with which they could contact advisers at the presidential palace and order new supplies from the capital. At the center of the camp was a small school where the commanders taught Colombian history. Attached to the building was a huge meeting hall where there were social events, video presentations about Simón Bolívar, and "cultural committee" shows of the works of Bertolt Brecht. The paths made of crushed stone and the environmentally designed bathrooms, built alongside mountain streams, were set low enough to wash away liquid runoff but high enough to clear frequent flood waters that could wash them away. There was a soccer field, which was sometimes used for volleyball too.

In their comfortable homes the guerrilla chieftains entertained their guests with extravagant pleasures hauled into camp by mule trains from Bogotá. They reminded me of the feudal Colombian landowners at the turn of the century who imported grand pianos from Paris and shipped them all the way up the Magdalena River. In this case, the mule trains were trekking across the entire eastern mountain range.

I knew the route all too well because I made the staggering trip myself, accompanied by several heavily laden mules. We crossed the blustery peak of Sumapaz by the same route that Bolívar followed on his campaign to liberate the continent a century ago; we traversed teeming rivers where one of the pack animals was torn to pieces as it was swept away in the swirling current. Only when we arrived at Casa Verde after eight days on horseback, exhausted after having taken tender care of the remaining mules, did I discover the truth: While I supposed that they were carrying supplies for the guerrillas, in reality their heavy cargo was nothing more than a shipment of fine cognac, a gift that a friend was sending to Jacobo Arenas.

With about four thousand fighters divided into twenty-four battalions, FARC had come to be the most prominent guerrilla force on the continent, controlling 40 percent of the nation's territory—more than any other rebel group. The zones over which FARC had jurisdiction were part of the vast Colombian hinterlands forgotten by the government in its dizzying drive toward urban development in the 1960s. While Colombian authorities built suburbs and major highways between cities, they ignored vast sections of the country; much of rural Colombia is isolated by hilly, trackless terrain. In the 1980s and 1990s it was easier to travel to Miami from any Colombian city than it was to reach the southern part of the country. In that no-man's-land the vacuum left by a government whose presence was never felt was slowly filled by a new power structure established by the guerrillas.

By 1986 Colombia had the dubious distinction of having more guerrilla groups than any other country, each one controlling a strategic sector of the country. After FARC, the most important groups were the Maoist-oriented Popular Liberation Army (EPL) and M-19, a nationalist movement that distanced itself from both Moscow and Beijing. These two were the first to enter talks that led to the demobilization of their forces. Of the three, only M-19 began as an urban guerrilla force; the others were rural-based organizations. Another new guerrilla organization, the National Liberation Army (ELN), had also cropped up. The original leaders of that organization were wiped out in a 1975 military raid, but surviving members had regrouped, thanks to an influx of extortion money paid by the Dutch company Mannesman to avoid ambushes as it built a new oil pipeline from Caño Limón in the east across the mountains to the Caribbean.

Malcolm Deas, a professor at St. Anthony's College at Oxford University, once remarked that Colombian guerrilla movements could be set up easily in anyone's backyard but that none had any prospect of victory. Rather, each was locked in a perpetual stalemate—perhaps they could maintain support in the countryside, but they were no match for the government in the cities. The best they could do was launch occasional raids and steal and extort the money they needed for food and supplies in the areas under their control.

Such was the case with FARC, which had become quite a regional power in the south and southwest sections of the country where it was uncontested by the government. There FARC controlled everything from alcohol sales to marriage licenses. It also managed land distribution, built medical facilities, authorized the construction of primary schools, and provided other services. It had taken on the trappings, in short, of a regional government.

In return for these services, FARC, like all governments, set up a tax system for the citizens under its rule. Tax liability varied according to the needs and requirements of individual battalion commanders. "Look, you won't find any thievery around here. . . . You can go out at night peacefully and stroll about without worrying who will come up to you," a local commander told me one evening, with all the pride of a small-town politician. What he said was true.

Nevertheless, the cantonization of the country into what were akin to independent republics was not all peace and harmony. There was a darker side to the story. At night, while the well-cared-for citizens slept, "disciplinary committees" hit the streets on their accustomed rounds, paying special attention to the few large landowners left in their areas. They pressured the landowners for more and more protection money. Those who refused were branded government collaborators and army spies, and their punishment could easily come the following morning before a firing squad in the town square. Peasants who refused to give sanctuary to the guerrillas knew they risked being buried alive just to remind them who was the law; guerrillas who deserted the ranks were hunted down and shot.

In April 1991, a peasant led the army to a common grave at FARC's central command headquarters at Casa Verde. About 450 guerrillas were found buried there, most bearing single bullet wounds in their heads, the sign they had been executed. One peasant witness said they had been killed in a "cleansing operation" to rid the ranks of army informants.

The guerrilla's control tactics might be barbaric, but they were no different from the "justice" meted out by the drug-financed death squads in areas under the army's control.

There was a certain coexistence between the army and the rebels. The guerrillas knew they could not outgun the army and rarely took the troops on directly. And local military commanders, answering to a bureaucracy in Bogotá that was out of touch with the goings-on in the countryside, didn't bother to attack the areas controlled by the guerrillas. No commander wanted to pick a fight in which he was certain to suffer losses. So the FARC guerrillas were able to maintain uncontested control over 40 percent of Colombia's total land area.

But financing the guerrilla movement took large sums of money—too much to be raised from robbery and protection payments alone. So the guerrillas also kidnapped wealthy ranchers and held them for large ransoms. Sometimes the same rancher would be kidnapped two or three times even though he was faithfully paying his "taxes" to the guerrillas. The money that FARC made in such ventures was often invested in the Bogotá stock market; financiers asked no questions about the source of the funds they managed. Sometimes, FARC found itself the victim of funding scams through just the type of capitalist system its doctrine abhorred.

In the drive for funds FARC also found a new source of income, perhaps the most important source it ever had. It began to allow drug dealers onto land it controlled to promote the development of coca plantations. By 1980, 80 percent of the coca-leaf production in southern Colombia was in areas controlled by FARC. In return for allowing this new, illicit agricultural industry to prosper, the guerrilla command collected tithes—15 to 25 percent of the profits from sales in the form of a direct tax on each coca seller.

For FARC it was good business. For the farmers of southern Colombia it was a windfall. They had always dealt in contraband—at first animal skins and more recently marijuana. They had been growing marijuana from seeds that American drug dealers had brought to them in the early 1970s. Recently, however, the marijuana market had been in a decline, with increasing production in the United States and elsewhere taking away the Colombians' share of the market. Then some respectable-looking gentlemen came to the farmers of San José del Guaviare with a new idea: "Plant these seeds; leave everything else to us." They were dealing in a new hybrid strain of coca they thought would be better adapted to the jungle plain than was the traditional mountain-grown crop. Despite the high-tech approach, however, this strain of coca was never as profitable as that grown in the Peruvian Andes and Bolivia.

All the while Colombian drug bosses were consolidating their control of the market. By 1985 they had a monopoly: from the farms of Peru and Bolivia to the Colombian laboratories to a distribution network that shipped their refined product to eager consumers in the United States and Europe. The more they depended on Peruvian and Bolivian production, the less interested the Colombian traffickers were in what happened in Guaviare.

So, paradoxically, the Colombian coca boom of the 1980s brought about a drop in coca prices in the Colombian jungle. Suddenly the immense sums of money and the prosperity that came with it were gone, and poverty and deprivation returned.

FARC's two leaders were Jacobo Arenas and Manuel Marulanda Velez, the latter known universally by his nom de guerre, Tirofijo, or "Sureshot." Tirofijo was of peasant extraction and spoke little. The guerrillas under his command were dealt with strictly; they had to be clean shaven and wear their hair in a short-cropped, military style. "Whoever sold the idea that guerrillas have to be long-hairs with Ché Guevara beards?" he asked me one day, outside his house at the guerrilla camp in La Uribe. He had just hung a big sign on the door of the house that read, "Cursing Not Permitted." The truce with the government, however, had caused a change in his austere lifestyle. He complained about getting a potbelly as a result of easy living: "Before the truce I could hardly eat at all; now they have me on a diet."

Arenas was a tall, dark-skinned man with a mustache—the stereotype of a guerrilla commander. He wore military fatigues with a Lenin insignia on one lapel; black boots; thick, black-framed glasses; and a camouflage jacket that hid an expanding waistline. When I met him in 1985 he was in his sixties and had a clear, crisp way of speaking in a cadence held over from his younger days as a labor union leader. He seemed to be a vain man; he dyed his hair to hide the gray and wore a neckerchief to cover his double chin. Jacobo was addicted to board games and not above cheating if it was necessary to steal victory from defeat. Despite his devotion to Marxism, he considered himself close to a member of the Colombian establishment: ex-president Alfonso Lopez Michelsen. The two men had worked together in a dissident wing of the Liberal party in the 1950s. With the truce, Jacobo said that the first thing he wanted to do upon arriving in Bogotá was to have a cup of tea with Lopez Michelson.

Jacobo loved horses. His favorite of at least seven Alazan

horses he had was named Rayo. When I was there he had a girl-friend named Olga, twenty years his junior, the most recent in a long line of admiring women. Often the two of them would take an afternoon ride in the surrounding hills and valleys, "his mountains," as he called them. I must say that the image of Arenas seemed to me much more in keeping with the life of a wealthy patrician inspecting his fiefdom than of a guerrilla leader who sought to change the system through armed struggle.

I once asked him about his contradictory relations with the Colombian drug bosses whose goals and principles diverged so much from those espoused by the Left. A glass of cognac in hand, he replied, "The drug-dealing problem is a problem for the bourgeoisie. This is a fight we won't get involved with. What does matter to the country are the rightist militias who are killing leftists with the immunity bestowed upon them by certain military authorities."

During the month I spent in La Uribe, the guerrilla organization kept advertising the impending return of Arenas to Bogotá as a candidate of the Patriotic Union, which he controlled. Jacobo Arenas had not been to Bogotá in thirty years, and vain as he was, he prepared a triumphal arrival speech, which he rehearsed with Olga. Six months before the elections, however, Arenas withdrew from the race, explaining, "My life is in imminent danger. FARC intelligence has told me that there is a plot to kill me as soon as I get to Bogotá. So I've decided to remove my name from consideration."

Arenas died of a heart attack in August 1990 at age sixty-five—a natural death in keeping with his bourgeois life of repose after decades of guerrilla fighting. FARC did not demobilize as he had hoped. And Casa Verde did not last much longer than he did. The army seized control of the stronghold in a surprise attack on Casa Verde on December 9, 1990, driving out guerrilla leaders and killing 120 FARC fighters.

The new candidate of the nascent Patriotic Union was Jaime Pardo Leal, a warm, down-to-earth person who I came to know well. He had an unbuttoned look to him. His suits were always disheveled and hanging, and he never did anything to straighten them out. He had a nervous twitch. But none of this was an impediment to his successful oratory style, which had been warmly received since his days as a law student at the National University.

Pardo Leal was considered a respected jurist by many; those

who knew him called him an honest, well-informed, competent man. But he was a member of the Colombian Communist party, and that fact was all the army needed to know. His charges against the death squads were dismissed as nothing more than an "international Communist conspiracy to cast aspersions on the Colombian armed forces and their campaign against subversion."

Nevertheless, Jaime kept up his denunciation of human rights violations because he believed that the people had a right to know. His high profile only served to increase the number of death threats against him. The threats came in mock obituaries announcing his burial and in menacing telephone calls to his office. But they only pushed him further in his denunciations. In February 1987, at the burial of one of the members of the party, Pardo Leal had gone even further in his criticism saying, "The drug dealers are financing the Colombian right-wing militias."

This charge was published on the front page of every newspaper in Colombia. I remember it well because that day I had lunch with a friend, and as we scanned the front page, the same words came to our lips simultaneously: They are going to kill this man.

On October 18, 1987, a Sunday, Pardo Leal's federal police bodyguards had taken the day off. Someone must have known that they would. Pardo Leal was attacked on the highway as he returned to Bogotá from his ranch in La Mesa in Cundinamarca State. He and his driver were killed in a hail of bullets. Police files showed that his three assassins made a clean and quick getaway and were promptly paid for their services by representatives of Rodriguez Gacha. While Pardo Leal's body was en route to the mortuary, the three were already receiving their 3-million-peso reward for having carried out their mission.

Significantly, the official investigation into the murder of Pardo Leal did not point to the larger conspiracy involving the armed forces in concert with the drug bosses. Rather, it simply stated the obvious, that "the assassination of Jaime Pardo Leal was committed by drug traffickers and emerald smugglers." There was no mention of corruption inside the police and military and these groups' probable links to the crime. Two years later, in the judicial inquest into the murder of Pardo Leal, Rodriguez Gacha, named in the indictment as the mastermind, was absolved, and no member of the armed forces was named. Four years after Pardo Leal's death, security sources showed me documents proving that the assassins were indeed at the service of Rodriguez Gacha and the paramilitary bands.

As brazen as the death squads were, their link to the drug bosses was not the major preoccupation of President Virgilio Barco, the Liberal party's standard bearer who was elected in 1986. An engineer from the province of Santander, Barco was not given to public speaking, but he won the affection of the electorate. He swept into office with one of the largest pluralities in Colombian history.

Submerged in a domestic political agenda, Barco was working on a plan to redistribute wealth to the neediest sections of the country. The program involved development projects in rural Colombia and measures to ease poverty in the major metropolitan areas. Every time there was an assassination of note or a particularly heinous massacre, the president quickly went on television to point out how many additional kilometers of highways had been built by his administration and gave an unending string of statistics about the number of bridges being built and the number of wells and pumps being installed in slum districts.

Unlike his predecessor Belisario Betancur, Barco had good relations with the army. Together they had formulated a plan to negotiate peace with the guerrillas under the catchphrase, "A hand extended and a firm wrist."

Internationally, the battle against the cocaine dealers was subordinated to the battle against communism. In Nicaragua, the battle on the Costa Rican border against the Sandinistas was being financed with drug money. The U.S. ambassador to Costa Rica, Lewis A. Tambs, had just arrived there from a stint as ambassador to Colombia. Before his departure from Colombia in November 1985, he had brought into vogue the exaggerated notion of a "narco-guerrilla" alliance in which Cuba was supporting the leftist guerrillas and financing their efforts by selling drugs in the United States. The only truth in this idea was that originally some FARC guerrilla units had protected the cultivation of coca in the south and provided security for some laboratories run by the drug bosses. But as time went on, FARC was being cut out and replaced by rightist militias who were just as willing, if not more so, to finance their anti-Communist efforts with the wages of the cocaine trade. However, the idea of godless Communists and ghastly drug dealers plotting together fit better into the

ideological makeup of the Reagan administration. The connection
stuck but was never submitted to the test of reality.

The United States' analysis also found enthusiastic adherents
among Colombia's military. The chief of staff agreed wholeheart-
edly that the violence gripping Colombia was the work of a drug
alliance with the Left. But more than one military chief knew that
the Barbula Battalion in the Middle Magdalena Valley was working with the militias and the drug dealers. It simply was not
politic for them to say so. Barco similarly rejected the idea of an
independent rightist militia movement linked to drug trafficking.
In 1988 he referred to the question of the rightist militias as "a
semantic problem."

By 1986, in stark contrast to the Reagan myth, it was becoming evident that a sinister new force was at work: the alliance
between drug dealers and right-wing paramilitary groups. This
alliance was responsible for the bombings around Bogotá aimed
at supposed leftist targets and guerrilla sympathizers. In every
case I investigated, I found links to corrupt members of the
Colombian military and police. Initially their alliance was
defended as an effort to combat leftist guerrillas and the Communist onslaught. As such, it won favor from rightists at home
and abroad, notably members of the fervently anti-Communist
Reagan administration. Apparently, it was acceptable to use
drug money if it was used by the proper side. From the outset,
the United States overlooked charges of human rights abuses
leveled against the police and the army in what it saw as a holy
war against Cuban-backed communism. Moreover, the Reagan
and Bush administrations were endorsing the military by providing millions of dollars for the army to fight the drug war.

What took the form of an anti-Communist front quickly
revealed its true character: This was a witch-hunt against anyone
to the left of center. These death squads were not fighting guerrillas on the battlefield but assassinating civilians in hit-and-run
attacks. They lashed out at those who defied them or got in their
way—judges, journalists, and any police and military personnel
who they could not evade or co-opt. By 1989 this rightist alliance
with the drug bosses, which evoked fear at home and was little
understood abroad, was responsible for killing 40,000 Colombians
since 1987, among them three presidential candidates. Everyone
had a friend or relative who had fallen victim to bombs or bullets.
One was my sister, Sylvia.

But in 1986 the dimensions of this alliance were unknown, and there were other ominous political developments. The Patriotic Union, FARC's political arm, had managed to receive 4 percent of the popular vote in that year's presidential elections. In the ensuing year, 500 members of the Patriotic Union were murdered. The government had no answer to the searing question of who was responsible for the killings. There were no suspects in any of the crimes. It was evident that a menacing force, immune to government action, was at work.

The death squads began issuing lists of their intended victims. The names were sent to newspaper offices around the country, provoking panic at first, then a sort of badge of courage for those who had made it to the lists without flinching. Although we started to take the threats for granted, many of those marked for death were, in fact, murdered. Human rights groups were organizing demonstrations to pressure the government for answers and for civil guarantees. In August 1987 alone, twenty-five people were murdered in Medellín. Among them was Hector Abad Gomez, a prominent member of the Liberal party and president of the Antioquia State Committee on Human Rights. Abad Gomez was also a professor at the University of Antioquia, the province of which Medellín is the capital. About twenty fellow professors and a number of journalists, whose names had appeared on the death list along with Abad Gomez, fled into exile following his murder. Some are still in exile today.

THE EXTRADITABLES

Violence was on the rise in the country, but it was not apparent in Bogotá. In the cities the traditional parties still issued promises of "greater efficiency" and "new security measures." The cities were awash with campaign posters, and the newspapers crammed their pages with each new political nuance, each new debate.

The emerging favorite in the 1988 election for mayor of Bogotá was Andrés Pastrana of the Conservative party. Pastrana's father, Misael Pastrana, had been president of Colombia from 1970 to 1974. Andrés, aged thirty-three, was part of the inherited ruling class of the country. On the one hand, he seemed to be quite serious—he was always immaculately dressed, and I never saw him without a tie. He was a cultivated man, very charming and intelligent. A well-informed man of action, he was always willing to put forth a strategy to deal with the country's problems. On the other hand, he had a distinct informality, was jovial, and seemed younger than he was. Andrés was trained in law, though he never practiced. In his ten years as a television journalist, he had gained a reputation for integrity and sharp reporting.

He was a natural choice for our Kremlin group; in the months after Guillermo Cano's assassination, we saw each other frequently at our clandestine after-hours meetings, which were held mostly at my house but sometimes at a neighborhood bar called

Chispas—Sparks—where he always was first to report the latest jokes and gossip.

That all changed when he shifted from journalism to politics. He was a child of the Conservative party, and he surprised none of his reporter friends when he announced his candidacy for mayor of Bogotá in August 1987. From then on, he no longer showed up at our get-togethers. Instead we saw him giving interviews, making news instead of reporting it. He was featured in all the opinion polls and became the favorite, even though Bogotá was traditionally a Liberal stronghold. Andrés had a special charm that translated well in public. We forgave him the transgression of leaving the journalistic fold to side with the politicians.

On the evening of January 18, 1988, at around 7:30, after a meeting with his political finance committee, Andrés returned to his downtown political headquarters. That night an interview he had recorded with Margarita Vidal, one of the nation's best-known television reporters (perhaps the Barbara Walters of Colombian television) was to be broadcast. Andrés knew firsthand the power of television—he wanted to watch the show carefully with some trusted advisers. He canceled the evening's political activities and sat with two friends in front of the television set, offering them whiskey as they waited for the broadcast to begin. On that evening, he later recalled, he went onto the veranda of the courtyard where his office was located and called down to his secretary, Gloria, for some more ice. Someone came running up the stairs with the newest campaign paraphernalia, and Andrés went to talk about it for a moment in the adjacent campaign press office. The campaign gimmick he was shown was a pair of sunglasses emblazoned with his name and his campaign slogan: Words AND Action. Then the phone rang; after he answered it, he went back to his office, sat behind his desk, and chatted amiably for a few minutes with his two friends.

Suddenly two young well-dressed men forced their way into the room, each carrying a large revolver. One of them quickly handcuffed Andrés and placed a gun to his head while the other closed the door, aiming his gun at Andrés's two friends.

"We're from M-19. We've come for Andrés Pastrana. . . . We have a message for him to send to the government. Everybody shut up," said the man who had handcuffed Andrés, forcing the mayoral candidate roughly to his feet.

One of the friends, frightened and unable to speak, began to shift back and forth nervously on both feet. "We said don't move!" shouted the other kidnapper, who had positioned himself in front of the door, aiming his weapon at the face of the nervous man.

It was Andrés who reacted to break the rising tension.

"Take it easy, take it easy," he said. "I'll be back soon," he said, hoping his words would lower the adrenaline rising in the assailants, who began to drag him out of the room. The men took Andrés out of the office and down the stairs, while the employees stood there, helpless. Though the idea seems absurd, Andrés was comforted by the idea that his captors were from M-19 and not drug dealers, as he first feared when the men stormed into his office. He knew that M-19 had a track record of capturing journalists and others, using them as a conduit for their messages to the government, and invariably releasing them unharmed after a few days. My own experience in their camp six years earlier was proof of that strategy.

When they got to the street, the captors became agitated as they found themselves in the middle of rush hour with people and cars racing all about them. Many passersby walked right in front of them and could even see the handcuffs the men had put on Andrés.

One of Andrés's bodyguards started to approach them.

"Hurry, the cops are coming," said one kidnapper, behind the wheel of the getaway car parked at the curb.

"Kill the son of a bitch!" shouted another, looking at the bodyguard staring at them.

"Don't shoot!" screamed Andrés. "Don't do anything! Why should you kill him? I told you I would go quietly," he begged.

The kidnappers pushed him into the backseat and sat on either side of him. The driver very nervously pulled out into traffic.

Right away, Andrés could see the men were totally confused . . . and lost.

"It's not this way, go that way," said one.

"Shut up, asshole, it's this way!" said another. "I told you this bastard was going to be trouble. This is what we get for taking the contract."

Andrés learned from these snippets that the men were not guerrillas themselves but had been hired by others—something that gave him an uneasy feeling. That was not the way the guerrillas usually operated.

After a few minutes of curses and insults, the car turned onto a darkened side street. The kidnappers forced Andrés out of the car.

"OK, into the trunk," shouted one.

"The trunk? But how will I breathe?" Andrés asked. They pushed him in. It was dark and a rank odor made him feel like vomiting. He began to sweat and could hear the ticking of his watch and the sound of his own heart beating in an infernal rhythm. He tried controlling his breath as best he could, taking little gulps of air when he had to. But the car was bumping over pothole-marked streets and he couldn't establish a rhythm. Every jolt was jarring.

It seemed incredible, but faced with few alternatives, Andrés felt relaxed, even relieved. "Shit, if I ever get to be mayor, I promise here and now to pave every pothole in Bogotá," he said in an internal dialogue that gave him a stifled chuckle in the midst of this horror. Suddenly the others opened an air hole from the passenger compartment, and he could breathe a bit better. Andrés felt better and began to speak:

"Where are we going?" he asked.

"Shut up and breathe," one of the captors snarled.

Suddenly Andrés felt the car brake.

"Damn, there's cops up ahead," the driver said. "Close up the space in the backseat and everybody shut up." Andrés could hear the men getting their guns ready. He closed his eyes and shuddered, fearing the worst. It was very possible that they were approaching a military roadblock. If they were stopped, there would be shooting—and the trunk was sure to be hit.

The minutes passed by like an eternity. Andrés was no longer paying attention to time; he could only feel, from one instant to the next, that the shooting had not yet started.

But nothing happened. They kept driving and after a while, the kidnappers pulled the car over and opened the trunk. Andrés found himself on a darkened street. The kidnappers led him into a house and up the stairs into a sparsely furnished room. Two of the men stayed with him and the other stood guard outside. The room had a bed, a radio, and a television.

"Can I go to the bathroom?" he asked.

"Si, señor," one of the men answered. He took the handcuffs off of Andrés. The two men led him to the toilet, and he had to urinate with them standing next to him.

"Okay, so tell me, when do I see your boss?" he asked.

"Tomorrow, sir," was the reply. Again, his kidnapper addressed him as *sir*. He was favorably impressed with the respect his captors seemed to be showing him.

"We'll be taking you to a place where they'll pick you up and then we'll bring you back home," one of the men said.

All in all, Andrés thought, they were treating him fairly well. The fact that they had plans for him was comforting: There would be a tomorrow. They brought him coffee and turned on the television just when his interview with Margarita Vidal was going on the air.

So he sat there watching himself on television with two different companions from those with whom he had planned to watch the show.

After the interview the news came on. Andrés was amazed to find that there was no word about him. It was unbelievable. This was his own family's station at which, until recently, he had been the anchorman. (Andrés found out later that the news director was holding back on word of his capture, hoping for a last-minute scoop. The news director fully expected the harried reporter-turned-politician to come running into the studio with a first-person account of his seizure and release by M-19.)

Andrés's captors switched the channel, and a rival reporter broke in with a late bulletin: *"El Noticiero Nacional* has just learned that Andrés Pastrana has been found unharmed and is en route to his campaign headquarters." As Andrés watched the report from captivity, many of his friends, including me, were trying to telephone his office to say how relieved we were that he was safe. The report sounded so authoritative that his captors began to argue with one another about how they could prove that the man they had in custody was really Andrés Pastrana.

One of the men took off his new shoes, complaining about blisters. They both had shiny weapons and fine clothing. Guerrillas did not have the money for such luxuries.

At around 4 A.M., as near as he could tell, one of the kidnappers woke him up.

"Get ready, sir," he said. "We're going for a helicopter ride. You're going to see the boss."

Andrés shuddered at these words: M-19 didn't have helicopters.

"Where did the helicopter come from?" he asked.

"We stole a couple from the druggies," one of the men answered. Andrés didn't like the answer.

The helicopter arrived, and he was led blindfolded and handcuffed outside and onto the plane. When they landed, he could tell by the wind and the air that they were no longer in Bogotá. The men forced him once more into the trunk of a car. After a while, the car stopped, and he was led into a building where he climbed a flight of stairs. His captors took off the blindfold and the handcuffs. Now he was in a room with a small bed and a television set that otherwise looked like a jail cell. Every half hour, one of the guards came back, pointed a gun at him, and left. His ulcer seemed to be boiling with pain. He needed his stomach medicine.

His captors were professionals. They brought in food, but all the implements were safe—no sharp edges. There was nothing to help him escape or that he could fashion into a weapon. After lunch they brought in a bucket of water and a toothbrush. A bit later, they gave him some newspapers—*El Mundo* and *El Colombiano,* Medellín's two dailies. He was in Medellín, home of the cocaine cartel!

Suddenly he heard voices, and a guard came in and blindfolded him once more. Another man came into the room, and Andrés heard a new voice. "Good evening," the stranger said, speaking in a refined manner.

Andrés was numb with fear. The voice was disconcerting. He remembered thinking that if he was going to die, he wanted to see the people who were going to kill him.

"Tell me something, please," he said. "Tell me that you are who I think you are . . . that you're really not M-19."

"We are . . . the Extraditables . . . and we belong to the Pabón Jatter brothers' command. . . . You probably remember the brothers. Your television station showed them shackled and handcuffed when they were sent to the United States, treated as if they were dogs."

"What are you planning to do with me?" Andrés asked.

"We want you to pressure the government to nullify the extradition orders against the Ochoa family, Pablo Escobar, and Gonzalo Rodriguez Gacha."

Andrés was sweating heavily. Everything that had happened had been intended to scare him. They were not going to kill him, not this time anyway. He calmed down a bit.

"Listen, you've got the wrong person. I'm in the Conservative party, the opposition. How can we influence the government, let alone put pressure on the Council of State?" The Council of State was a kind of Appellate Court, hearing cases involving decrees by the executive branch. It was an avowedly independent judicial body, even higher than the Supreme Court.

"Andrés, you're going to talk to your family and give them the message," the man with the refined voice said. "After that, we'll see. . . ."

The drug bosses had adopted the name the Extraditables as a way of expressing their indignation at the government's decision to send Colombians who were wanted on drug-trafficking charges to the United States. Their motto was "Better a grave in Colombia than a jail cell in the United States."

On December 12, 1986, the Colombian Supreme Court, seriously intimidated by the acts of the Extraditables, had ruled the extradition law unconstitutional on procedural grounds. Extradition fell into judicial limbo. However, on December 31, 1987, Jorge Luis Ochoa was suddenly let out of jail after having been rearrested on November 21 on old charges of bull smuggling and breaking parole after he was extradited from Spain to Colombia in 1986; the intent was to hold him until a way could be found to extradite him to the United States. There was a furious response from Washington. The Barco government felt obligated to reactivate extradition, citing the Montevideo Convention, which declares that the executive branch has the right to order extraditions. The Extraditables, obviously, were worried.

On January 5, 1988, thirteen days before Pastrana's kidnapping, Minister of Justice Enrique Low Murtra issued warrants for the arrest and extradition of five members of the Medellín cartel.

Since the Supreme Court decided it had no jurisdiction in the case, lawyers for the cartel members appealed the minister's decree before the Council of State on January 18, the same day Pastrana was kidnapped. If the government's orders were upheld, it would signal the resumption of extraditions to the United States.

Sometime around one in the morning, Andrés was forced out of his room and taken to what seemed to be some sort of vehicle equipped with a cellular telephone. His guards told him to call his parents' house. As he dialed, he said a silent prayer that they would answer. The telephone was far from the rest of the house and would often ring without anybody hearing it. Finally, the maid picked up the receiver.

"It's me, Andrés, put my father on the phone right away."

His father came on the line quickly.

"It's me. I'm okay. Don't worry."

"What a comfort to hear you and to know that you're all right. Don't worry, everything is going to be okay."

Andrés immediately began to tell his father what the Extraditables wanted. One additional demand was that no one should reveal it was the cartel that had kidnapped him.

After giving Andrés time to speak with the rest of the family, his father again came on the line.

"Andrés, my boy, everything will work out. Nora and the children are staying with us. This may take a while, and you have to be prepared for that. As far as the election, don't worry about that at all. It's not the only opportunity you're going to have. There will be others."

Andrés had not yet signed the necessary documents to run for mayor, and the deadline was only a week away. He doubted he would be freed by then. So, for all practical purposes, the campaign was over. Yet, as he said good-bye to his father and gave his captors the phone, with tears in his eyes, he told himself over and over again: "I will be mayor. I know that I will be mayor."

His guards brought him back to his cell and began talking more freely with him. They removed the blindfold and gave him something to drink. For two hours they spoke, recording their own conversation. The surprising thing was that the hooded man who was so well spoken seemed to be a lawyer; he knew every detail of the extradition process. Andrés himself was a lawyer, but he often got lost in the machinations of international law they were discussing. It seemed surreal.

Kidnapped and held captive by men who had never heard of a law they wouldn't break, he was having a rational conversation with a representative of the drug bosses about the intricacies of the Constitution and the legalities of extradition. The amazing thing about the drug bosses was that although they used tactics of kidnapping and assassination without qualm, they had a fixation about fighting their case on legal grounds. They employed legal minds to research loopholes in the Constitution for each extradition order. It seemed senseless: Why participate so fervently in the system they were trying to subvert?

Andrés listened and listened to the man's distinctive voice, and his mind drifted. Who is this man? he asked himself. Pablo Escobar? One of the Ochoas? Probably not. Was he one of the lawyers who secretly work for them? Andrés never found out. Before he left, the hooded man gave Andrés a book by Jeffrey Archer, *A Question of Honor.* He also gave him a notebook to write in.

For two days Andrés wrote in that notebook as if his life depended on it. His captors now allowed him to take showers, brought him a sweatshirt, and found the pills that he needed for his ulcer. Finally, the Extraditables sent a list of demands to Andrés's father. They asked him to use all his political capital to pressure the Ministry of Justice to reverse its decision in favor of extradition. Strangely enough, the demands have never been published, but the kidnappers did not link any specific act to the liberation of Andrés.

On Thursday, as was becoming routine, Andrés turned on the radio when he woke up and heard the newscaster say that the station was about to switch to a live communiqué from the Pastrana family. Suddenly he heard the voice of his brother, Juan Carlos.

"The Pastrana family announces that Andrés Pastrana is being held by the Extraditables. . . ."

The following day, the story appeared in *El Tiempo* under a six-column headline, which read: THE MAFIA HAS ANDRÉS PASTRANA.

Andrés couldn't believe it. He was no more than a spectator in his own kidnapping. It was like a war of the communiqués that he listened to via television and radio from the solitude of a jail cell.

The following day the Extraditables sent a communiqué to my newspaper, *El Espectador,* declaring all-out war on the government. The ten-point declaration acknowledged the kidnapping of Andrés and expressed "indignation that the headlines of the newspapers in the nation's capital say that Mr. Pastrana Arango is in the hands of the Mafia, since the Extraditables do not belong to the Mafia of the upper class and the politicians, nor to the bankers' Mafia nor to the tremulous financial institutions who squeeze the modest savings of most Colombians, nor to the Mafia of the fictitious multimillion-dollar exporting business, nor to the fraudulent contract Mafia, nor to the Mafia of the cement business and other monopolies. Nor for that matter to the news media Mafia which traffics in the right of respect of families and individuals. . . ."

The communiqué went on to propose acceptable mediators—prominent politicians, journalists, and businessmen—to negotiate Andrés's release. It concluded with the warning: "Mr. Andrés Pastrana receives and will receive proper treatment and his life will be protected as long as the terms of understanding are not severed with those who would disturb the peace by extraditing Colombian citizens; we declare unconditional war on those who we judge to be traitors and who are selling out national sovereignty."

The Sunday following his kidnapping, after having passed a week in captivity, Andrés felt defeated. For the first time since he was seized, he had lost hope. No one came to see him that day. At night on the 8:30 television news, he was surprised to see his brother again on the air. This time Juan Carlos read a communiqué denying any form of agreement between the Pastrana family and the Extraditables and proposed Enrique Santos Calderón as mediator, citing "the balanced handling of national affairs he has shown throughout his career as a journalist."

That Sunday Enrique was at his family's country home, about sixty miles from Bogotá. Andrés's father telephoned him, telling him that the family had chosen him as the person best suited to carry out such a difficult task. Enrique asked Pastrana if it would be possible to share the responsibility with others noted by the Extraditables in their list of conditions, but Pastrana said no. "You are the man we trust to save Andrés's life."

Back in Bogotá, Enrique asked what concessions the Pastrana family was willing to make. "None that harm the authority of the state or its legal precepts," was Pastrana's pointed reply.

The following day, while Enrique analyzed the possible outcomes, a report on Caracol Radio brought more bad news. Attorney General Carlos Mauro Hoyos had just been kidnapped in Medellín. Two of his bodyguards were killed trying to thwart the attack.

"How the fuck am I going to negotiate with these guys after

they have just finished kidnapping the attorney general?" Santos asked, turning to his wife.

Paradoxically, the attorney general did not support extradition. He had opposed the Ministry of Justice's January 5, 1988, arrest and extradition warrants against the Medellín cartel bosses. Hoyos agreed with the Supreme Court ruling that a new extradition proposal should be submitted to Congress. It was no secret that if such a plan were sent to the legislative body, it would be rejected.

It was well known that Attorney General Hoyos traveled every weekend to Antioquia to spend time with his fiancée at his ranch at El Retiro. "Nothing's going to happen to me on my own turf," he would tell his friends.

That weekend, before leaving for Medellín, he called former president Pastrana, a man he hardly knew, to mention that they had found a way for Andrés to register as a candidate for mayor from captivity. He would tell Pastrana about it in person on Monday in Bogotá. The appointment was set for 4:30 P.M.

The next morning, when Hoyos arrived at the airport road in Medellín on his way to catch a plane back to Bogotá, his limousine was cut off by three carloads of assailants who exchanged gunfire with his bodyguard and chauffeur, both of whom were killed. Severely wounded, Hoyos was dragged from the backseat and placed in a van.

Meanwhile, in Medellín Andrés went to the gate and saw the kidnappers huddled intently around the radio. "Make way, get ready, that guy is on his way here," one of them said to Andrés in a triumphant tone. Andrés remembered that long night listening to the voice of the man who was an expert on extradition. The man had told him that they planned one more kidnapping besides his own and that it would be the attorney general because Hoyos was in favor of extradition.

Andrés paced back and forth. It was 11 A.M. Suddenly he heard a noise and someone running toward the room. One of the kidnappers came in, put the handcuffs on him, and left quickly, locking him in behind the heavy steel door. Andrés waited without knowing what was going on outside. Five minutes later, the door opened again, and the same man raced in, carrying an Uzi machine gun in one hand and two assault rifles over his shoulder.

"It looks like the police have found us," he said. "I'm sorry, but you're my life insurance." And he put the gun to Andrés's head, leading him out of the room to the second-floor patio.

"Who's in there?" came a voice from outside.

"Don't shoot. . . . It's me, Andrés Pastrana."

"Let him go, you're surrounded," answered the voice from outside.

"If you shoot, I'll kill him," the kidnapper replied.

The kidnapper led Andrés to the garage and told him to get into the car. He did, but there were no keys in the ignition.

"Take it easy, take it easy, let me go out. I'll tell them not to shoot," said Andrés as calmly as he could.

"I'm coming out," he called to the police outside. "Don't shoot; I'm opening the door. Be careful, don't shoot." Andrés opened the front door slowly and saw where he was for the first time. The house was surrounded by barbed wire; it looked like a prison camp. And the police were not in sight.

The kidnapper was frightened, though, and didn't let him move. "Asshole," he said. "This place is full of cops. Shit, how do I get out of here?"

"Listen," Andrés said, a gun forced against his throat. "Hey, take it easy. Why don't we try to talk to them?"

As if they were listening, a voice came from between two bushes: "I'm coming in . . . don't shoot. I don't have a gun. I'm Patrolman Ramirez, don't shoot."

The policeman approached them slowly, taking deliberate, measured steps. He was no more than twenty-five years old. The kidnapper tensed up more, and Andrés felt the gun pressing against him even tighter. "Don't come any closer," he screamed. "I'll fucking blow both of you away."

"Let him go!" the policeman shouted. "Take me instead—cool it. I'll go with you. Let him go. Nothing will happen to you; just take off his handcuffs and let him come out!"

"Do it, man," Andrés said, trying to be soothing and assuring. The kidnapper had little choice.

The policeman kept coming closer and closer until he was right in front of them. The kidnapper took off the handcuffs and told Andrés to put them on the policeman. Andrés did as he was told, and in the confusion was left with the keys. He ran for his life, and the kidnapper ran off with his new hostage.

As Andrés ran, he saw no sign of life. When he finally got to the woods, it was painfully clear that what seemed to be a massive police rescue operation had been a ruse. There had been four policemen, and now there were three. The policemen had chanced by the house on a routine patrol when a neighbor said that something suspicious was going on in the area.

"Let's get the hell out of here while our luck holds out," one of the cops said. They ran down a paved street until a jeep came into view. "Don't worry, sir, it's one of ours."

As the jeep approached, Ramirez came diving toward them out of the bushes, still handcuffed, and alone. He had dodged the kidnapper, who was preoccupied more with getting away than with messing around with the wrong hostage. They all got into the jeep and sped off.

The first person to see Andrés was a reporter he knew from *El Mundo*, the Medellín newspaper, who had been sent down to cover the Hoyos kidnapping. Andrés almost knocked her down with the strength of his embrace. He was crying for joy, but the celebration was brief. Ramirez said they had to move quickly to safety, lest the kidnappers come after them.

At the town hall, Andrés was well guarded and better received. The mayor embraced him warmly and took him to his office, where he gave Andrés a Coke. Andrés reached for the telephone to call his family just as a call was patched through. He recognized the voice of his old friend Juan Gossain, whose first words were: "Andrés, you're on the air. Guess who else is on the phone. . . ."

I remember it well, sitting in the office at *El Espectador,* shedding a tear as Andrés spoke on that national radio hookup with his father and the rest of his family. Most surprising was President Barco, who also came on the line. Barco usually did not radiate warmth, but on the radio, he did, congratulating Andrés and offering him the use of the presidential plane to fly back to Bogotá.

The kidnapping of Andrés Pastrana had become a nationwide event. It had been repudiated by every sector of the country, across the political spectrum. Pope John Paul II had prayed for his release, and the prime minister of Spain, Adolfo Suarez, had offered to negotiate his release. Hours later, at El Dorado Airport in Bogotá, Andrés received a tumultuous welcome from thousands of people who had come to celebrate at least one happy ending in a country where tragedy was commonplace. The reception was led by Cesar Gaviria, the interior minister at the time, who would be elected president in 1990, after replacing Luis Carlos Galán, another victim of assassination, as the Liberal party candidate for president.

Andrés sat huddled with Nora and their two children in the car on the way home from the airport when the news came over the car radio: "The beaten and handcuffed body of the attorney general of Colombia has been found in a garbage dump in Medellín. It is believed that he was seriously wounded in the kidnapping and his assailants decided to finish him off."

Two months later, on March 23, 1988, Andrés Pastrana was elected mayor of Bogotá. The same week the Council of State suspended the arrest warrants for the extradition of the Medellín five. The cartel had succeeded in intimidating the Colombian government, winning an important round in its attempts to operate its multibillion-dollar cocaine business.

The drug bosses had won the legal battle. Opposition Conservatives would never admit that the kidnapping of Andrés Pastrana had any effect on their position on extradition. Nevertheless, before the kidnapping they had supported extradition, whereas afterward they were inexorably opposed to it. Their opposition came at a time when President Barco, a Liberal, was promoting extradition with a fervor never before seen. Barco did so at considerable political cost. The measure had little popular support; many Colombians simply saw extradition as a loss of national respect and sovereignty.

Leading Conservatives also became the first to speak openly of negotiations with the drug bosses. Among the most prominent proponents of such a dialogue was Juan Gomez Martinez, the mayor of Medellín, who during his earlier tenure as director of the Medellín newspaper *El Colombiano* had been highly critical of an attempt by ex-president Alfonso Lopez Michelson to negotiate peace with the Medellín cartel. At that time, Gomez Martinez condemned the cocaine trade, lashing out at the Medellín cartel as the "masters of vice."

From the beginning of 1988 to the end of 1989, the period of greatest violence from the drug wars, more than 40,000 people were killed. Few were members of the Conservative party. The violence was directed mainly at parties of the Left and members of the Liberal party, including Liberal judges, politicians, political candidates, and Attorney General Hoyos. Hoyos was an unassuming man whose death was hardly noticed because it came at the same time as Andrés Pastrana's highly publicized release. There was so much violence that even with the death of someone as important as Hoyos, few people understood how serious the threat had become.

The day Andrés was released, perhaps the only person who understood where the drug traffickers' violence was leading was Minister of Justice Enrique Low Murtra. Andrés's kidnapping and the subsequent flurry over events revealed the key role that Low Murtra had played in the extradition dealings.

The tortuous road that extradition followed in Colombia reflected the tremendous contradictions that the measure produced among Colombians. Despite the pressures from Washington for Betancur to apply the law, during the first two years of his tenure he did no such thing, arguing that it was an instrument that eroded the country's sovereignty.

In Colombia, where nationalism evaporates easily in profound regional rifts, extradition became a national issue. In the eyes of those Colombians who knew little about Washington's antidrug strategy, the U.S. treatment of the problem had unjustly converted Colombia into a nation of hoodlums and drug dealers. "Instead of trying to extradite Colombians, they should first try to catch the bosses. Or can it be that there are no American drug bosses?" This was the general reaction from people on the street. The day that the Reagan administration ordered economic sanctions against Colombia for the release of Ochoa, that conviction was evident; it was as if extradition would designate Colombia the only culprit in the drug problem. In that context, extradition became an unpopular symbol of oppression, which in turn exacerbated a latent nationalism that Colombians hadn't recognized they felt. The drug dealers ably exploited this perception in the early 1980s; they lobbied against extradition and successfully employed those nationalistic arguments, which touched a nerve in Colombia, not only in intellectual circles but among the majority of the middle and lower classes.

Unlike his predecessor, Barco was a convinced supporter of extradition from the beginning of his government. His obsession with this legal recourse was something that only his closest aides knew of. The arguments raised in opposition to extradition mattered little. Many analysts remarked, for example, that the measure, conceived as a means of capturing the dons of the drug trade, was being used instead to extradite small-time dealers. Given its inability to halt the flow of narcotics to the United States, the price of this policy was the unwarranted loss of lives.

Often Barco's interest in reviving extradition in Colombia seemed to be the product of pressure exerted in Washington. However, those who were closest to the president knew that bowing to such pressure would not have been in keeping with his personality.

Impenetrable and distant, Barco was above all a person who would not allow himself to be pressured. And when he thought an attempt was being made, he reacted with the fury of a Panzer division. The country's political class tried to pressure him, and they found themselves facing an iron-willed man who would not even take their phone calls. Ex-presidents, who were accustomed to serving as oracles for the current leader, found that Barco not only did not consult them, but wouldn't even invite them to the palace for lunch. Journalists, accustomed to having their articles enjoy a certain resonance in the palace, were ignored by Barco with disdain. In revenge for this arrogance toward the news media, we journalists adopted an image of Barco that had little to do with reality.

Barco was treated as an absentee president—incapable, shaky, indecisive, and controlled by a group of young aides; his tendency to talk little became a stigma that forged the image of him as senile to the point where his rare public appearances were seized upon by his political enemies who circulated rumors that claimed he was in poor health.

Only one of the things said about Barco was true. A politician described it this way: The government of Barco was a government not of policies but of obsessions. And extradition was one of these obsessions, which the president pursued to a degree that was equal to or greater than Washington's interest because he had domestic reasons for doing so.

Since December 1986, while the country was still mourning the murder of Guillermo Cano, President Barco, bemoaning Guillermo's death, had set forth his diagnosis of the drug problem with some of his aides:

We're in for a really serious mess. Drug trafficking has had three phases in Colombia. The first phase was the "amusement." It was the period of the grand orgy with the drug dealers when everybody was in bed with them and nobody paid any attention. That was the phase of generalized tolerance when the violence was only registered in internal squabbling among them. The second phase was the "discovery" period when drug bosses no longer could depend on that more-or-less peaceful coexistence and instead began to use violence as a means to defend their business. That was when they first recognized an enemy they did not have before: New Liberalism. And that was when they killed Justice Minister Rodrigo Lara Bonilla. The third phase began when the drug bosses wanted to take over the state. That is the period when I happened to become president. We are facing the greatest enemy that Colombian democracy has ever encountered, and if we falter, they're going to wipe us out. I am not going to let these gentlemen take control of the state, nor will I let them break our democracy.

When he was named justice minister in August 1986, Low Murtra already had unbeatable credentials for the post. He had been a magistrate of the Supreme Court, a member of the Council of State, and one of the few survivors of the siege on the Palace of Justice by M-19 in 1985.

Barco needed someone as justice minister who was an expert on the Supreme Court's legal position on extradition. And Low Murtra was not only well versed in the law, he also knew how to deal with a distinctive Colombian characteristic that surprised many foreigners: Columbia's great legal tradition and the intensity with which justices debate various interpretations of the law.

In Colombia, every decree and every law is the subject of judicial debate. "Before decrees and laws are even issued there is already a constitutional lawyer somewhere in Colombia ready to challenge it," a law professor at the University of Los Andes told me. Despite this predilection, court sentences are upheld and respected by the executive branch with unusual reverence, given the constant threat that the powerful will exact revenge with virtual impunity on those who bring them to justice.

So when the Supreme Court declared the extradition law unconstitutional four months after President Barco took office, it did not unsettle Low Murtra, who, accustomed to legal disputes, dedicated himself, along with his aides, to studying various legal formulas and shaking the dust from treaties that no one knew existed, with the aim of reviving extradition. But while the government was gearing up, so too were the Extraditables. Advised by skilled attorneys, the drug dealers came to know so much of the legal contortions that surround extradition that they had become veritable constitutional experts, prepared to litigate any judicial angle that the executive branch might present. That was the situation in November 1987 when Low Murtra was advised that Jorge Luis Ochoa had been arrested.

Upon hearing the news, the U.S. government immediately presented an extradition request to the Colombian government. President Barco and Low Murtra made it known that they indeed intended to extradite Ochoa even though the Supreme Court had declared extradition unconstitutional. Low Murtra and his aides, knowing they were fighting against the clock, redoubled their efforts to find a legal formula that would enable them to carry out the extradition. The task was not easy because they were dealing with high-level legal strategies. In the midst of such legal machinations, Low Murtra was informed by telephone on December 24 that a judge had set Ochoa free. His reaction was vehement. He immediately called a news conference at his house. "Those who have aided in the liberation of Jorge Luis Ochoa will be investigated," he said sternly, explaining that the judge who freed Ochoa had not coordinated with or been endorsed by the government. However, the liberation of Ochoa brought home how far the drug bosses had been able to penetrate the judicial branch. The Colombian press was severe and swift in criticizing the government for having bungled the affair. Low Murtra received much of the blame.

They following day a photograph of Low Murtra was published in Colombian papers and in many newspapers around the world. It showed him seated on an oversized couch, wearing no tie or shoes and with his shirt open at the collar. With his prominent bald head and his worried, weary expression, he was the image of fatigue and impotence. The photograph depicted the difficult times the Barco government was going through. One U.S. newspaper captioned the photo "Low Murtra, the Colombian justice minister responsible for the liberation of drug dealer Jorge Luis Ochoa."

Washington received the news with great indignation, blaming the Barco government for Ochoa's release. U.S. Attorney General Edwin Meese, from the comfortable confines of his Washington office, said, "Colombia had deceived the United States" and that the Ochoa case was a "shocking blow to international law enforcement."

On January 5, 1988, seeking to demonstrate to the United States that he would take decisive action, Barco instructed Low Murtra to issue an arrest warrant for the extradition of the five leaders of the Medellín cartel, based this time on international law governed by the Montevideo Convention. His tone firm and solemn, Low Murtra made the announcement on television. The drug bosses had managed to create much sympathy for their cause across Colombia, and the very act of defending extradition could cost him his life. It took backbone to stand before a national television audience and announce, come what may, that the Barco administration intended to keep fighting. But he was bolstered by indignation that Washington should actually blame his government—and, by extension, him as justice minister—implying that it was in collusion with the drug dealers. The mere thought was outrageous to him and it gave him strength to speak out boldly.

Even this announcement was not enough for Washington. The day that Low Murtra was announcing the arrest warrants, the Reagan administration decided to adopt retaliatory measures against Colombian exports and against Colombian tourists traveling to the United States. Colombian indignation was great. Even supporters of extradition, like *El Espectador,* published an editorial condemning the arrogant stance of the Reagan administration. But the fury of President Barco was greater still. Through his foreign minister, he called for an urgent meeting of the Organization of American States to protest this "punishment" of Colombia. A resolution rejecting the retaliatory measures imposed by the United States quickly won support from all the nations in the Organization of American States. Astutely, the Reagan administration abstained from voting; after an interchange of letters between the presidents, the United States decided on June 17 to suspend the retaliation.

At this point Barco decided to drop publicly the theme of extradition, while Low Murtra and his aides continued working clandestinely on an unassailable formula. By the end of June 1988, the policy was already edited and refined, but it would not be applied until a year later, just moments before another momentous murder.

For Low Murtra, the year 1988 had been trying and complicated. He had been able to maintain the secrecy of his search for a formula to revive extradition. But the amount of notoriety he received in the press converted him into one of the most fervent supporters of extradition; the threats on his life grew more and more alarming every day. Low Murtra was sent out of the country in July 1988 to become ambassador to Switzerland.

In May 1991, back in Colombia a few weeks before Pablo Escobar surrendered to Colombian authorities, Low Murtra was assassinated. The *Wall Street Journal* saw fit to run the story on page one: "A martyred Colombian hero to whom the world owes a debt."

The truth is that Low Murtra was not even a hero in his own country. When his assassination was reported, many Colombians were surprised that a person so threatened would return to Colombia. But we were even more surprised when we found out that after all he had done in the service of his country, Colombia had forgotten him. He met death at the entrance to the University of La Salle, the only place where he had managed to find a job. No bodyguards were accompanying him when he was gunned down.

Extradition was the tool of choice to unleash "the war for democracy." But Barco's call to arms did not find many devotees among the great majority of Colombians. This was a country where murder could be carried out with impunity, both before and after the rise of the drug traffickers; a country that lacked a tradition of tolerance for ideas opposed to one's own; a country where in the previous ten years many politicians had been the main figures in scandals in their own departments, diverting public funds for their private uses. That country, beaten down and mistreated, could not understand Barco's call "to defend the institutions." A worker in Bogotá told me, "I do know what institutions are. But I do know that what we don't have is very much democracy. I had my little plot of land in the country, and La Violencia forced me out of there and I came to Bogotá. Now I have nothing, and the little I earn when I manage to get work doesn't give me enough to feed my family."

In professional and intellectual circles and in the economic and political spheres, Barco's call to defend democracy had more meaning. But that was not enough. Despite the conviction of his speeches, his rallying cry did not rouse the nation. There was a feeling that Barco lacked leadership and that the government's decisions were not implemented. Besides, his withdrawn and unapproachable character had made him more political enemies than he could deal with. His contacts with the news media were frigid; he had bad relations with the Conservative party, the second largest party in the country; and the never-ending assassinations of leaders on the Left had caused a tense relationship with the Patriotic Union. Support for his programs wavered even in his own party. To top it off, his insistence on extradition had forced a confrontation with the Supreme Court. This lack of political leadership made his campaign to save democracy even less likely to win support, even though it was obvious that if there was no reaction, whatever democracy Colombia had would vanish.

VIAFARA'S HELL

The power plant shuts down at 11 P.M. in Puerto Boyacá, bathing the town in shifting shadows of gas lanterns and occasional car lights.

The shouts and screams would start soon after the lights went out. Bands of vigilantes, known as "self-defense squads," would begin their rounds in search of guerrilla collaborators. The shrieks and cries were interspersed with the staccato sounds of gunfire. No one dared to go out at night. The streets were deserted and houses were shuttered. And for the past month, the bodies of murdered peasants were again floating down the Magdalena river. The smell of rotting flesh in the night air made it impossible to sleep.

The night of January 29, 1984, Diego Viafara heard the sound of a vehicle pulling up to his house. He had just enough time to call to his wife, telling her to grab their daughter and hide.

Four hooded men broke down the door and dragged him out of the house. He was blindfolded and thrown into the back of a camper van. Soon he could hear the sounds of the river. He must be near the banks of the Magdalena. He knew nothing else.

After a while, the van stopped. The men dragged him out and brought him into a hut where the smell of coffee was strong. Despite the blindfold, he could see shadows, bathed in moonlight, of people standing around him. The men walked him to an armchair, let him sit down, and took off the blindfold.

He was surrounded.

"Who are you?" demanded one of the kidnappers, jabbing the barrel of his rifle into Viafara's shoulder.

"I'm Diego Viafara. I've lived here for a few months with my wife and daughter."

"Liar. You are M-19," said one of his captors, spitting out each word.

At first Viafara would admit nothing. But to his dismay, his captors already knew much about him. It was true; Diego Viafara had been a member of M-19. He was a doctor with a guerrilla contingent in Cali under the command of Rosenberg Pabón, an important rebel leader. He said he had studied medicine at Patrice Lumumba University in Moscow, an institution dedicated to sponsoring leftists from Third World countries. Upon returning to Colombia in 1979 he immediately joined M-19, providing health and first-aid services to peasants and rebels in M-19 territory.

In mid-1981 he moved with other rebels to the Magdalena Medio river valley to link up with FARC. But FARC was operating on the run, and it took him months to establish contact. All the while he was being tracked by rightist self-defense squads.

When these squads' periodic harassment became more menacing, he sought refuge in a Catholic church. But even the church walls were not enough to protect him for long. The local parish priest counseled Viafara to take advantage of an amnesty declared by the government of President Belisario Betancur in 1983. "Turn yourself in, hand in your weapons, and all will be forgiven," the priest told him. On December 29, 1983, he did so. Feeling a new sense of protection, he emerged from hiding and went to live in a small house in Puerto Boyacá.

Puerto Boyacá is nestled in the Magdalena river valley, a jungle region located in central-western Colombia where the tributaries of the Magdalena join, creating a web of marshlands and small islets in one of the loveliest and richest ecosystems in the country. The majestic and impenetrable jungle vegetation makes access nearly impossible; as in other mountainous and jungle sections of Colombia, the government's presence and control is almost nil.

The development of the region reflects the problems that many rural sections of Colombia suffered in the 1960s with the growth of the guerrilla movements. One of the great problems of Magdalena Medio was that it hardly had been part of Colombia since 1929, when oil was discovered and the entire region was sold to Texaco. The United States–owned oil company had land and subsoil rights, and there was little official Colombian presence. Things began to change in the 1950s when shifting migrations within the country brought squatters and violence. Texaco fought these squatters' occupation of its lands for a time, and then finally sold the territory back to Colombia in 1959. Yet the government's presence was sporadic and usually came in the form of repression via the army—officials sent troops to protect wealthy landowners who were given rights to the best land against peasant farmers who had no legal right to the land they tilled. The peasants had no choice but to flee inland, where the soil was inferior and where they could grow only enough to barely survive. The constant repression of the peasants was the social cauldron in which guerrilla organizations like FARC were able to establish themselves. The guerrillas were often the only organized presence the rural poor ever saw in these parts. In the beginning the guerrillas were well received because the peasants saw them as a buffer against the landowners and the army. The guerrillas also protected the peasants from cattle rustlers who frequented the jungle wilderness.

But soon FARC's tactics changed. Its increasingly repressive rule was creating anger among the populace the guerrillas were ostensibly there to protect. From the start the guerrillas had extorted protection money from cattlemen and ranchers, but when these larger landowners fled the region, the guerrillas demanded tithes from the middle class and the poor peasant landowners. In reaction to the abuses of FARC, the peasants of Magdalena Medio turned to the only institution they could—the Colombian army—which in 1981 began organizing self-defense militias comprised of peasants in the region.

At first these groups were simply armed militias out to protect their own lands. They carried rifles that were supplied legally by the army. In December 1983, President Betancur's amnesty for the guerrillas and his peace accord gave the rebels the right to form a political party and run for office. The measure, according to polls, was approved by 80 percent of Colombians. But two groups were opposed to it: the Colombian military and the landed gentry, including those of Puerto Boyacá.

In Puerto Boyacá news of the amnesty was immediately dismissed by regional power brokers who saw the guerrillas as

Communists who had to be stamped out. From that point on, patrols of rightist militiamen regularly prowled for guerrillas and were prepared to deal harshly with those who sympathized with the amnesty.

Viafara had been captured by such a group.

"Fucking liar. Let's see if we can't make you confess, you son of a bitch," one of Viafara's captors screamed. As they began to twist his arm out of its socket, Viafara felt excruciating pain. He began to sputter, "I was in M-19, but I'm not anymore. I promise, I promise."

"We're going to kill you," his captor said. Viafara heard three shots and grimaced, shutting his eyes tightly; his heart racing, he wondered with resignation what death would feel like.

There was silence. And when he opened his eyes, the only sound was the cackling of his tormentors.

"Not this time," a voice said. "But you will tell us who your friends are. Guerrillas are not welcome here in Puerto Boyacá. We kill them."

"I have no friends here," Viafara said. "I came here to start over. Look, I'm a doctor. I want to help people. Can I work for you?"

Before daybreak, Viafara was back home. He saw his wife and his daughter, thanking heaven and unable to believe that he was still alive. He understood that it all had been a test—that to stay alive and to protect his family, he would have to show that his guerrilla past was dead and buried. He would have to work with the men who had tormented him.

A month went by and nothing happened. But each night Viafara went to bed with the fear of being spirited away again, at any moment, by the same captors who, acting on some whim or misstep, might not spare him a second time. He could not sleep, he could not rest, and he scarcely left his house. In the fifth week they came for him, again barging through the door and dragging him away blindfolded to the same hut along the river. This time he stayed with them for five years.

Despite their public posture, the self-defense groups were engaging in activities that were far more dangerous. In 1984, when Viafara was brought into the organization, these groups were already becoming a private army at the service of the wealthy ranchers of the region. The ranchers in turn were in the process of establishing the Colombian Cattlemen's Association of

Magdalena Medio. The association became the legal facade under which the private militia would garner political and military might. Seen from a distance, the "nonprofit" association was a benign entity dedicated to providing social welfare to the people of the valley.

However, the cattlemen's association also was the bulkhead for the creation of a private army organization whose aim was to wipe out the guerrillas in the name of anticommunism. At first the cattlemen and farmers contributed money to the group for guns that were purchased clandestinely from the army. Later they contributed in a more substantial way, sending their children and ranch hands as recruits for military training.

The first training site was at a camp dubbed El Tecal in Puerto Boyacá. Organized by the cattlemen's association in mid-1984, the militia units began a crude and disorganized fight against FARC battalions based in the valley. But they quickly went beyond the guerrilla encounters, turning their attention to anyone they suspected of collaborating with the guerrillas. The militias diverted attention from their actions by blaming the killings on MAS, the death squad formed by the drug traffickers. In that way, they figured, they would be able to keep the social welfare image of their organization unblemished. Moreover, they had strong support from the Colombian army, which shared the landowners' desire to counteract the power of the guerrillas.

At times the militias seemed to be an extension of the military. Militia recruits played football with their counterparts in the armed forces. And they were allies in the battle to stop the guerrillas; it was common for the antiguerrilla units of the army's Barbula Battalion, under the command of Major Velandia, to send out patrols in the region with members of the self-defense groups. This campaign was, in the words of the militias, a crusade "to reclaim democracy in the Medio Magdalena valley from the hands of international communism."

The militias controlled military roadblocks, confiscated peasants' food shipments—saying that these shipments were being sent to feed the guerrillas—and established a new pseudo-government structure by setting up checkpoints and demanding that travelers identify themselves in an effort to detect guerrilla collaborators. Although it has never been established how many innocent peasants were killed in 1984, decaying bodies, all murder victims, began appearing by the dozens along the banks of the river. Few were ever identified, and none of the crimes was ever punished.

By 1985 the violence reached such a magnitude that it could no longer be ignored in Bogotá. Something had to be done. Attorney General Carlos Jimenez Gomez, under the government of President Betancur, announced that he would investigate charges by human rights groups of a nascent dirty war. Despite his release of a report implicating key members of the military in a conspiracy to aid and arm the private militias, no action was taken. There was widespread sentiment among influential landowners and businessmen that what was going on in Magdalena Medio was justified. "The peace model in Magdalena Medio" was considered a success, thanks to the self-defense groups. These groups had, after all, achieved the goal of dislodging the FARC guerrillas; kidnappings and extortion by the guerrillas ceased. And many other parts of the country that were plagued by guerrillas had already begun to seek the services of the militias.

Viafara was placed under the tutelage of Henry de Jesús Pérez, the chief of military operations for the self-defense groups of the Magdalena Medio region. Pérez was a tough, tightly drawn figure of a man and one of the wealthiest landowners in the valley.

In mid-1985 Pérez told Viafara to prepare for a trip to the southern part of the country to establish a traveling health program. By this time, as was their goal, the militias were reaching out to other parts of the country. In the guise of public action, they really were seeking to establish an anti-Communist guerrilla network throughout the country.

What Viafara found surprised him. In Guaviare, the region to which he was sent, there was a full training camp with wooden barracks, a giant kitchen, and signs everywhere with antiguerrilla slogans. "Communists need not apply," read one such sign. The camp had a vast stockpile of automatic weapons, including imported AK-47s, hand grenades, and rifles. After a time, Viafara also realized the real reason he was needed in Guaviare. The camp was protecting a cocaine laboratory. There had been recent skirmishes with the FARC guerrillas, and the militias needed doctors under Viafara to treat the wounded. As the fighting spread and increased in intensity, Viafara found himself making more frequent visits to the south, treating the wounded in makeshift tent hospitals and carrying away the dead. He despaired of his life as a paramilitary medic, but he couldn't figure out how to escape.

"Four times they repeated that they were going to kill me," Viafara told us. "They shot at me, but the bullets glanced by me. It was hell."

It took five years in the field, working for the drug bosses and their military consorts, before Viafara summoned the strength to bolt. When he walked into the city room of *El Espectador* on February 17, 1989, he was nervous and sweating. He wanted protection; he wanted to talk.

His testimony would reveal the scope of a crime organization with still-untraced tentacles around the globe. His memory of details and his position as the doctor in the militia organizations brought information so unique and precise that it was still being tapped two years after his arrival at the newspaper.

"I'm not doing it for money; I'm doing it because my conscience won't leave me alone. That's why I've come to *El Espectador*. I want to tell everything I've seen for the past five years in the Magdalena Medio valley. You've got to understand, I'm not doing this for the money. I just want the attorney general's office to protect me. I need help. . . . When they find out I'm gone, they'll try to kill me—and my wife and daughter."

Fernando Cano and Ignacio Gomez, one of my partners on the newspaper's investigative team, were the first to meet with Viafara, who was chain smoking and crushing the butts in a large ashtray that he held close to him; he had already gone through half a pack of cigarettes and five cups of coffee in the short time he had been in the office. Viafara's hands were cold and trembling, and his handshake was that of a worker; his hands were calloused, not smooth like one associates with the hands of a physician. Viafara was scarcely five feet five and was probably not even forty years old. He had a dark complexion and wore a blue aviator's jacket. His left eyelid was swollen.

Fernando offered him a shot of whiskey. He declined. They brought him lunch, but he left it untouched. All he wanted to do was talk.

The scope of Viafara's information was astonishing. At first he didn't want to speak until he made contact with the attorney general. But Fernando scolded and conned him into opening up: "Listen, let's talk a bit to find out if what you have to say is really important. If it is, I'll call the attorney general right away."

This statement upset Viafara, but he started talking anyway. At first he had little to say; he was feeling out the turf. But little by little the conversation became more fluid. Most striking was his photographic memory. He began to provide intimate details of where and how the militia training was conducted, where the cocaine laboratories were, who took care of finances, who the bosses were, and who was responsible for which massacres. It soon became obvious that Viafara was speaking from experience. And it became equally evident that it would be necessary for him to be placed immediately under heavy security. Viafara's information not only provided the first detailed look at the militia apparatus, but it revealed the names of corrupt members of the military, policemen, and politicians who were involved.

Viafara witnessed the formation of a squad of murderers-for-hire whose allegiance was to a band of increasingly wealthy drug dealers. By 1988 the scale of bloodshed was reaching unimaginable heights. Every time there was to be an attack, Viafara was well aware of it. It was his job to examine the members of the hit teams to certify that they were not stoned on basuco. And then he would send them on their way, knowing that these men would soon be murdering peasants for their presumed collaboration with guerrillas and that they would be dumping the bodies in common graves or chopping off lifeless limbs and tossing the torsos into the currents of the Magdalena river. The horror rose within him; the sickness caught in his throat. He would watch these same men march back from their missions, muscles quivering and adrenaline flowing after having killed a medical examiner or an ex-mayor whose crime had been to refuse to collaborate with them.

Viafara also revealed that the militia organizations were receiving their training via a network of foreign mercenaries, mostly from Britain and Israel. These mercenaries would introduce a dangerous element of violence in Colombia—training in the kind of terrorism never before seen, providing the drug bosses with a degree of sophistication that had never been contemplated, with a level of impunity that threatened the integrity of the Colombian state.

While Viafara was speaking to Ignacio Gomez, Fernando left the meeting room and went to his office, somewhat nervous from the import of what he had been hearing, and finally called the attorney general. Horacio Serpa, a committed, veteran Liberal politician, immediately realized the significance of Viafara's testimony. He had spent twenty years in Magdalena Medio and had seen the violence firsthand; ten members of his own political group had been murdered by the death squads. Serpa sent an aide to talk with Viafara. That interview lasted several hours more, confirming for the government what we already knew: This man's testimony was the key to entering the depths of the drug organization.

"We have to get him out of here, with protection, if possible," the envoy said. "If you use bodyguards, don't let anyone know who I am," said Viafara, who knew well the penetration of the drug cartels. "Take it easy, man, they won't know who you are. You're in good hands," Fernando Cano replied. Soon Viafara and Serpa's aide were on their way to the attorney general's office with Cano's personal security detail.

Shaken by Viafara's revelations, we agreed to hold back all the information that Viafara had given us. Two days after Viafara entered official custody, the attorney general called Fernando: "I just want to tell you that Viafara's testimony is monumentally important. I'm sending him over to General Maza (Maza Márquez, the head of DAS, Colombia's equivalent of the FBI), so he can hear what Viafara has to say. This is a bombshell."

Several days later Fernando received another call, this time from Maza Márquez himself. The general said he was debriefing Viafara, confirming the enormous importance of the information. He asked Fernando to withhold publication of any report about Viafara, saying that the government was working on a case based on Viafara's information. He wanted to avoid any chance of a leak.

"What about Viafara's family? What's going to happen to them?" Fernando asked.

"We're working on it. We've got a rescue mission under way in Puerto Boyacá to try to get them out," the general said. "I'll let you know what happens."

The information obtained from Viafara was so momentous that Maza Márquez called in the U.S. Drug Enforcement Administration (DEA). U.S. officials were contributing satellite photographs and AWACS spy-plane intercepts of communications over the area. All the intelligence they gathered confirmed the material provided by Viafara. The DEA suggested that the only way to protect Viafara and guarantee the flow of information

was to take him out of the country under the auspices of the
United States and place him in the U.S. Witness Protection Program. Within a week of his appearance at *El Espectador,* Viafara, without knowing what had happened to his wife and
daughter, was spirited away on a plane to Miami and then to a
secret location with a new identity. Ever since then he has wandered from state to state, without money, sleeping in the open or
in abandoned cars.

"The only thing I want is to be able to go back to Colombia,"
he told a Colombian diplomat. "Here, the DEA promised me lots of
money, but the truth is that I'm dying of hunger." Homesick, feeling betrayed, he appeared at the presidential summit in San
Antonio, Texas, in February 1993, where he attempted to speak.
His wife and child were never located and are presumed still to be
somewhere in Magdalena Medio.

El Espectador broke Viafara's story on April 6, 1989, as soon
as Viafara got safely to the United States. The series started a
chain of reports on corruption and paramilitary activity that
rocked the country.

The relationship of the militias in Magdalena Medio with the
drug organization began in early 1985. Following the decision by
the Betancur government to use the extradition treaty—after the
assassination of Minister of Justice Rodrigo Lara Bonilla—much
of the narcotics hierarchy left in a stampede to seek refuge in
Panama and waited for things to cool off. Such was the case with
Pablo Escobar and the Ochoa family, who were welcome in
Panama, which was under the control of General Manuel Antonio
Noriega. At that time, Noriega was still an asset to the Central
Intelligence Agency, and John Lawn, head of the DEA, was send-
ing him letters lauding his successes in the fight against drug
trafficking.

Not everyone left the country, however. Drug dealers who
were less known at the time took the opportunity to establish
themselves in the hinterlands of Colombia, seeking refuge where
the terrain made access and detection doubtful. It was not difficult to hide out in the jungle regions of the south and central
parts of the country, trackless zones where they could establish
their cocaine-processing laboratories with little trouble. That was
the case with José Gonzalo Rodriguez Gacha.

Rodriguez Gacha, the onetime street hustler, had by the end

of the 1980s come to be the single force to be reckoned with in drug-dealing circles. He used his militias and his money to create a machine that was far more dangerous than the threat of selling noxious drugs. Ultimately, he had political aspirations; he sought no less than to bend the Colombian state to his will.

Rodriguez Gacha was born in the village of Veraguas, a town not far from Pacho, and as a boy, it is reported, he shined shoes to make change. Of medium stature, he was the son of a peasant family in a region where family and tradition are all-important. He never advanced beyond primary school. Instead, like many others his age, he went off in search of his fortune; in the case of most of the young men of this region, that meant going to work in the mines of Muzo, where some of the world's most valuable emeralds have been found.

Rodriguez Gacha eventually rose to be second in command to Gilberto Molina, King of the Emeralds, entering the nether world of illicit emerald smuggling. He had chosen a good patron. Molina had seized control of mining activities by forcing out or killing other mining families, and a peace enforced by violence reigned in the zone. He had even been awarded the government contract for processing emeralds. He enjoyed excellent relations with the Conservative party and he supported its candidates from Cundinamarca and Boyacá in state and national elections. Nevertheless, Rodriguez Gacha decided to leave the emerald mines at Muzo and go out on his own. He chose the Guajira coast, where many Young Turks were heading in the 1970s, a dangerous region that was flourishing because of a bonanza marijuana trade—*marimba* they called it. Rodriguez Gacha soon began to amass a considerable fortune, making contacts that would later grow in importance. He hooked up, for example, with Pablo Escobar, another young man in search of a fortune, as well as others who would later join them in the Medellín cocaine trade.

But within a short time the market for marijuana crashed. Prices dropped as more and more marijuana was being produced in the United States. Soon the marijuana growers shifted their attention from marijuana to a much more lucrative product, one that was more compact and worth many times its weight in "Colombian gold." If he earned hundreds of thousands in the marijuana trade, Rodriguez Gacha was making many millions soon after he began selling cocaine.

His wealth brought independence and an infrastructure that

enabled him to return to Pacho, where he built a headquarters and became one of the principal employers and benefactors in the region. He joined up once more with Gilberto Molina. It was a time of planning and building. Little by little, Rodriguez Gacha created one of the largest criminal enterprises in history. He adapted the infrastructure of the illicit emerald trade, with its laborers, foremen, enforcers, and chiefs, into an extensive narcotics network. He bought up extensive pieces of land in well-positioned sections of the country, where he set up laboratories and built airstrips. He also brought in men who specialized in transporting the drugs along all sections of the circuit, from plantations in Peru and Bolivia to the laboratories and onward to markets outside the country.

His thirst for power brought him into conflict with Molina, his old friend and patron. The final break came following the kidnapping of Andrés Pastrana. Molina was vocal in his opposition to the kidnapping and enraged that it was carried out regardless of his protest. Rodriguez Gacha ordered him killed. In January 1989 several of Rodriguez Gacha's men, wearing military uniforms, appeared suddenly at one of the many ranches owned by Molina. Molina was giving one of his well-known, extravagant parties where the drinks were abundant. There were music and dancing, entertainment, and beautiful women. Rodriguez Gacha's men came as honored guests, dancing and eating with the rest. Without warning, they stopped and mowed down twenty people, including Molina.

Rodriguez Gacha set up his first laboratories in 1982 in Guaviare, one of Colombia's comparatively small coca-planting areas. The coca plantations were protected by FARC militia units.

At first Rodriguez Gacha sought to avoid conflict with FARC. He accepted the same rules that the guerrillas imposed on other large landowners: The guerrillas would protect his enterprise—in this case, the cocaine-processing laboratory; in return, he would pay them a levy to guarantee the security of the laboratories.

It was an agreement governed by the monetary interests of the moment. It worked because both sides made money on the deal. And the arrangement would collapse not because of ideological antagonism, but for the same reasons that led to the creation of self-defense militias in Magdalena Medio: The FARC guerrillas, in the view of Rodriguez Gacha and his Medellín colleagues, overstepped their bounds.

By 1986 Magdalena Medio had become Rodriguez Gacha's operation center, from which he directed his entire cocaine production and shipping business. It also was the major area for recruiting his private army of assassins who guarded his laboratories, ranches, and clandestine airstrips. The main laboratory was La Azulita in Putumayo, on the Ecuadoran border. At the outset the complex was controlled by the rival Cali cartel and protected by FARC guerrillas. But Cali lost it in a raid by Medellín militiamen, who killed six guerrillas and seized $10 million in cash and an adjacent airstrip.

Under Pablo Escobar and Rodriguez Gacha, the processing center at Putumayo prospered. It contained four laboratories, each with twenty microwave ovens to speed up the process by which raw coca base is crystallized into pure cocaine. By the mid-1980s, La Azulita was producing about two metric tons of refined cocaine per week. (At a street price of $20,000 per kilo, that meant that La Azulita, far from being the largest cocaine laboratory, shipped $40 million in cocaine at retail prices a week, or $2 billion a year.)

The chemicals, mostly ether and acetone, without which cocaine hydrochloride could not be made, were readily imported from Ecuador in fifty-five-gallon drums by a sixty-foot riverboat that made weekly trips up the San Miguel river. The raw coca base came from throughout the coca-growing region. Peru is by far the largest grower of coca, Bolivia is second, and Colombia is a distant third. But the laboratories were receiving consignments of dried leaf and base from all three countries. Power was supplied by huge electric generators. At any given time, the facility housed thirty to forty workers who served as cocaine cooks under the supervision of the most important and esteemed people in any cocaine operation, the house chemists. The chemists were there to ensure quality control and to keep the processing plant operating at peak efficiency.

La Azulita was guarded by one hundred militia patrolmen who were trained in Magdalena Medio under the command of a retired army sergeant. The cartel always feared a guerrilla counterattack. Late in 1987 the guerrillas did attack, but failed to dislodge the Medellín drug operation. Viafara said that fifty guerrillas and ten members of the drug dealers' army died in the counteroffensive, which was never reported to and thus perhaps never even known by the Colombian government.

Farther to the north was the processing center at Caquetá owned by Rodriguez Gacha and Pérez. The center, on a ranch known as El Recreo, was really a central receiving base for other laboratory shipments. Another seventy to one hundred men from Magdalena Medio guarded this regional shipping point.

By 1988, however, El Recreo was abandoned for fear it was too well known. The drug bosses were already working on an even more sophisticated replacement. They called it New Tranquilandia, and it was at the same site where officials working with the DEA had dismantled the Tranquilandia laboratories four years earlier.

The earlier raid on Tranquilandia had been the most important one to date. The Colombian–United States team seized nine tons of cocaine, a record at the time, and the police were astonished at the sophisticated network of processing centers with air-conditioned housing, electronic equipment, and airstrips. The raid was a result of tips from informants and high-tech sleuthing by the United States. Super-secret U.S. military satellites, controlled by the National Security Agency, pinpointed the location of the laboratory by marking a barrel of chemicals shipped by a Pennsylvania chemical company to Colombia, which informants said would end up at Tranquilandia. The ensuing raid was heralded as a major success in the war on drugs, though in truth it did nothing to stop the cocaine enterprises.

The new laboratories were to operate under the cover of a cattle ranch, complete with modern breeding techniques, veterinarians, and an aggressive sales program. The cattle were merely a front. About one hundred of the wranglers at the ranch were militiamen who had been sent to guard the new laboratories by the drug bosses from their training sites in Magdalena Medio.

Planes loaded with bags of cocaine, marked with brand names such as Colombian Coffee, El Centavo, and La Reina to identify their producers, were routed from the new site to collection centers in Putumayo, Yari, and Puerto Boyacá and then to a staging point at an airstrip at Puerto Escondido, a ranch owned by Rodriguez Gacha and Escobar on the Caribbean coast. At the airstrip, called El Martillo, teams of traffickers fitted airplanes for the journey to the United States. The planes would arrive at around 6 P.M. They were filled with fuel, the pilots were given their flight plans, and the bags of cocaine were loaded on the planes. The pilots also brought with them graphic artists who were ready to change each plane's tail number and other markings along the way and then change them back on the return trip.

The location and size of the processing plants varied considerably. The drug bosses, receiving a constant flow of military information on police antinarcotics efforts, could quickly move their cocaine stocks and switch venues if a raid was imminent. Little cocaine was ever lost; when it was, the drug dealers wrote off the loss as part of the price of doing business.

By 1987 Rodriguez Gacha had consolidated his supremacy over the self-defense militias of Magdalena Medio, converting them into a private army that he could deploy throughout the country to protect cocaine laboratories and, increasingly, to wage an anti-Communist crusade.

At the outset, these militias received all the training and weapons they needed from their army benefactors. But as the alliance with the wealthy landowners and the drug bosses grew, that training was not sufficient. So members of the cartel increased their contributions, and two new training centers were formed, code-named Zero-One and Fifty. The centers were well stocked but always prepared to break camp and move if a police raid was imminent. This time the pretense of self-defense was evaporating; it was evident that the training would produce the dreaded *sicarios*—professional assassins who traveled around the country and occasionally overseas to do the bloody bidding of the drug bosses.

Viafara witnessed all this in his role as health director. Some of the new recruits he examined, who were usually teenagers, were obviously high on basuco; others were covered with scars usually marking an array of knife wounds that they displayed like badges of honor. Others, hungry and malnourished, confessed to having eaten gunpowder, which they said gave them energy and made them high.

Prospective militiamen were brought before a panel of high-ranking members of the cattlemen's association. They were asked such questions as "Have you been personally affected by guerrilla activities?" "Would you know what to do if you were captured by authorities?" and "Are you capable of killing your father, mother, or brother if they were proved to be guerrillas?"

Of course the answers to such questions would invariably be yes. But Viafara knew that many of these aspiring zealots really had no ideology; they were in it for the good money they expected to earn. They sought to provide for their families and to become famous, with their names in the newspaper like Pablo Escobar and Rodriguez Gacha. Most of them had a history of crime in one of the many crime gangs in Medellín, in the slums, or in the Mafia of the emerald mines.

Once they were accepted, these young men were chosen, according to their education and skills, to be planners or managers, technicians, or foot soldiers of the drug war. Basic training was much like that in the regular army, with an emphasis on special operations. The recruits learned camouflage techniques, personal defense tactics, communication, and counterintelligence.

There were four branches of the security apparatus, each with separate courses of study. First were the so-called patrolmen, who guarded against guerrilla incursions in the countryside. They disguised themselves as cowboys and day workers on farms, where the drug bosses installed laboratories, and had orders to kill any unidentified person who stumbled upon the laboratories or warehouses. When in the field they wore blue or olive-drab uniforms similar to those used by the Department of Prisons and the National Police. Like all members of their organization, they had false documents obtained from local registries in Magdalena Medio. These men earned about $200 a month.

Next were the bodyguards who protected individual cartel chieftains and leaders of the self-defense commands. They earned about $300 a month.

Third were the technical workers at the cocaine laboratories who mixed the chemicals and produced the finished cocaine hydrochloride product under the supervision of the chief chemist at each laboratory. These men were chosen from the cream of the patrolmen's group. They earned $400 to $500 a month, more than the average salary of a captain in the Colombian army at that time.

Last were the "elite commandos," by far the most highly trained in all aspects of warfare. These special forces would carry out attacks against members of the leftist Patriotic Union and other representatives of the government or political parties who opposed the drug bosses. They were the best paid, with a monthly salary of $4,000 to $6,000.

Members of the elite commandos carried out their death raids under the names of other organizations to give false leads to the police. In addition to MAS, they used such colorful names as the Smurfs, the Orphans, the Cats, or Black Hand. Sometimes they left sayings on their victims' bodies like "This guy won't have anything else to say" or "For being a snitch."

Militia training lasted thirty to sixty days, after which the commandos went out on missions designated by the organization. The men had an array of weapons at their disposal—FAL rifles, Israeli Galils, and Soviet Bloc and American armaments—all available in the international legal and illegal arms bazaar.

Viafara provided details on the daily routine of these training courses. This was training for true believers, training steeped in military esprit de corps. The trainees were taught that they were foot soldiers in a holy war to defend Colombian democracy against the onslaught of communism. In reality, the teaching was a subterfuge for training professional assassins to defend the interests of the drug bosses.

The daily routine of the training school and in the paramilitary bases began with reveille at dawn, followed by physical training. Time was set aside for singing spirited, patriotic hymns and prayer, along with military formation and the order of the day. One song that Viafara could remember went like this:

> *I have a comrade*
> *I'll never find another as true*
> *He is constant at my side*
> *Marching at the same pace and*
> *Toward the same goal*
> *A bullet fired at him or at me is one*
> *If it strikes him, it has struck me as*
>   *well.*

And they would recite the motto of the organization:

> Our motto is to defend our children, our home, our possessions, our lands and we will succeed. . . . We are a self-defense group and we are fighting for the defense of honor and the good of the people of Colombia. We fight against the Communist party, the FARC, and the subversive groups in Colombia. . . .

From these ranks came the men who would be responsible for thousands of deaths in a wave of violence that challenged the heart of the Colombian government.

When Viafara met Rodriguez Gacha for the first time in Colombia's southern plains of Yari at the end of 1985, relations with FARC had been broken because of the guerrilla raid the previous year on the cartel's drug laboratory. Rodriguez Gacha, of course, was furious. For him there had to be an immediate and total break with the guerrillas. He wanted the rightist militias to take control not only at the laboratories, but also in his growing land holdings in the south. It was certainly a beneficial deal for the militias in Magdalena Medio. Rodriguez Gacha guaranteed them large amounts of money for this burgeoning paramilitary enterprise.

As important as Rodriguez Gacha was, he had a shadowy partner in his multibillion-dollar operation. The partner was a secretive international financier, identified as a brain trust behind the operations. The police never learned his name; they knew him only by the code name 28.

Sometimes addressed as Pascual, other times as Alejandro, 28 was in his early thirties, about six foot two, thin, dark, and elegantly dressed; he was married to a woman named Clara, with whom he had a two-year-old daughter. It was his task to coordinate drug shipments overseas and to work with Rodriguez Gacha on establishing quantities and prices. His authority spanned all facets of the operation. He determined the number of aircraft necessary to keep the operation moving efficiently, designated foreign airstrips where the airplanes were to land, and assigned the pilots who were to conduct these clandestine flights. It was 28 who collected the funds received in foreign drug sales and paid the employees' salaries. When new operators stepped forward offering to open new cocaine trade routes, 28 evaluated the worthiness of their proposals.

In addition, by managing the books, 28 was able to direct a portion of operating revenue to maintain the self-defense groups. The per-kilo price of Rodriguez Gacha's shipments was raised and lowered to reflect the additional cost of supporting the death squads. 28's method of operation went like this: If, for example, he was planning to send ten planes with a capacity for transporting seven tons of cocaine (700 kilos in each plane) at a cost of $70 million on the international market ($10,000 a kilo), he would charge $70,000 more. He would then deliver the extra amount to the national chief of the paramilitary squads, who would distribute the money among regional commanders of the defense squads.

By this time Rodriguez Gacha lived a life of wealth and privilege. His love of soccer had led him to buy a number of national soccer teams. By the mid-1980s, drug money owned the most important soccer teams in the country and players of international status. And in his many jungle-shrouded hideouts, alongside a cocaine laboratory or a coca plantation, there was sure to be a soccer field. Viafara often watched Rodriguez Gacha practicing his skill with volunteers, who always got a tip from the boss when the match was over.

Viafara said that Rodriguez Gacha was relatively Spartan in his personal life—he got up early, drank little, never touched drugs, and avoided foul language. But he dressed elegantly, with the proper attire for every occasion. In the jungle, he wore Bermuda shorts and short-sleeve shirts like those available at a Safari outfitters' store. At formal field lunches he was regaled in cotton suits.

Rodriguez Gacha had various code names, such as "the doctor" and "Don Andrés," but eventually he would become known as "the Mexican," in recognition of his affinity for things Mexican and his ability to capitalize on the lucrative trade route that uses Mexico as a transfer point on the way to the United States. His many ranches and contact points were named after cities and states in Mexico. One time he even pushed to change Pacho's name legally to Chihuahua.

The details of Rodriguez Gacha's private life are sketchy. Although the identity of his wife is not known, it is known that he had a daughter and a two sons. His teen-aged son Fredy quit school to join the drug enterprise full time, often working with the paramilitary squads.

Little by little, Viafara, who was now called "the veterinarian" by his comrades in the militias, was getting to know Rodriguez Gacha's inner circle. Most were retired military men who maintained links to the army that helped Rodriguez Gacha's enterprises. Rodriguez Gacha boasted of having prime contacts among there military men. "The government gives them medals," he boasted. "I give them money."

Rodriguez Gacha's activities thrived on more than just contacts with retired military officers, however. Viafara was there when active members of the military came to visit the drug boss. One Christmas the Medellín chiefs held a Christmas party at a ranch near the army's Barbula Battalion. Among the mirth and good cheer were the requisite payoffs. Each military officer got a bonus for another year's work well done. One officer kept Rodriguez

Gacha abreast of the government's antinarcotics operations, quickly delivering secret briefings to him.

In Magdalena Medio, Rodriguez Gacha had direct radio contact with the local police headquarters and the military command center at the army's Barbula Battalion. And whenever Pablo Escobar came to the area—he had a ranch in nearby Doradal— the local police backed off, giving him free access. Although air traffic in Puerto Boyacá was supposedly under military restrictions, these restrictions did not extend to private planes and drug flights managed by the two drug bosses.

Rodriguez Gacha made occasional efforts at self-promotion. Once he sought an interview with a friend of mine, Hernando Corral, who was an investigative reporter for the television news program "Noticiero de Las Siete." Corral was a seemingly meek, scraggly person whose moustache overwhelmed his gaunt face. But his friends knew that his mild manner went only so far; he was quite flirtatious and could salsa long into the night. He was also a former guerrilla; in his younger days, he had been a member of the National Liberation Army.

Corral met with Rodriguez Gacha on August 7, 1988, at the Mexican's ranch along the Magdalena river. The idea, Rodriguez Gacha said, was just to have an initial chat—no interview. "You people have not realized that this is an anti-Communist struggle," he told Corral, defending his work with the paramilitary squads. "I am doing this in order to defend democracy in Colombia."

Few people found out about this meeting while Rodriguez Gacha was alive; it was the only known meeting any journalist had with him. Corral did speak with Rodriguez Gacha again but by telephone, about a week after the assassination of presidential hopeful Luis Carlos Galán. In a sometimes rambling monologue, Rodriguez Gacha refused to talk about the assassination, though he complained bitterly about the government's crackdown following the killing. He also clearly realized that security forces were closing in on him.

In their conversation he warned repeatedly that he would never surrender to be tried in a judicial system that he didn't trust and that he considered Communist-controlled. "How can we let them try us in court if the judges are Communists?" he asked.

The violent tactics he and his colleagues in Medellín employed were a matter of self-defense, he said. "What would you do if they told you they were going to kill you? What would you do if they were hassling your children, your family? What would you do? . . . If they are going to try to kill you, you have to defend yourself."

He told Corral that he considered himself a "patriot" who has "fought for the people of Colombia. . . . I have dedicated myself to investing in this country; I love this country. Nobody believes this, but I am a patriot.

"They have taken everything. We have nothing left to lose here," he said. "But they haven't taken the money and the coca business." He joked about the United States' inability to halt the cocaine trade, saying "if we don't keep sending cocaine, the gringos will get mad at us." He said that he and his associates had large sums of money deposited in U.S. banks. (The United States and European countries have since frozen millions of dollars in bank accounts believed to be controlled by Rodriguez Gacha's organization.)

Although he refused to discuss Galán's assassination, at one point he said, with an air of disgust, that while some politicians are worth dealing with, Galán "always tried to screw us." Other politicians, he stated, always came to the drug bosses at election time asking for money. "You give it them, and then they forget all about you."

Rodriguez Gacha declared that the drug wealth reinvested in Colombia, often estimated at $5 billion, had kept the nation afloat financially and politically while surrounding countries floundered. Seventy percent of the nation's wealth, he noted, came directly or indirectly from the drug business.

"We are defending the people; we are fighting for the people. Had it not been for the drug traffickers, we would have had a civil war five years ago," Rodriguez Gacha said. "They aren't going to catch me easily; they'll catch me fighting, because this is a struggle to the end."

Speaking in simple language, often repeating the theme of his persecution and humble origins, Rodriguez Gacha explained that as a child, he wanted to work in farming. "I went to a vocational school to study agronomy. Economic conditions did not permit [me to finish]." However, he said he had provided a good education to his three children. "Let me tell you something. I am a man of the people; I am a humble man. With all this money, if I was from one of the five rich Colombian families, you wouldn't think twice about me. But as the person who is a campesino, a poor boy who has nothing . . . that means this is bad money."

He had chilling and passionless words about his relations with the news media. More than thirty journalists had been killed by drug traffickers in the past four years. "War is war," Rodriguez Gacha said. "If they don't bother with us, we won't bother with them. It's the intense types that are going to have problems."

The drug boss lashed out at General Maza Márquez, his principal foil in an Elliott Ness–style crusade against him and Pablo Escobar. "I have a tape intercept that proves that Maza accepted $10 million from the [rival] Cali drug cartel," Rodriguez Gacha said. The general, who had heard and confirmed the authenticity of the conversation with the drug boss, denied the charge, saying it was part of a defamation campaign against him. Asked repeatedly how the violence and bloodshed in Colombia could end, Rodriguez Gacha kept bringing up the proposal for negotiations. "This could all end if the government would negotiate. If they would think a bit they would send a messenger to talk to us," he said. "And if they are going to kill us one day, let them get it over with."

AN INFORMANT AND HIS SECRETS

Viafara's sudden appearance was not the first time that *El Espectador* had received this kind of visit. Although Viafara was by far the highest-level and most knowledgeable person to approach us, many people came to the newspaper claiming to have exclusive, ground-breaking information.

As early as 1987, *El Espectador* and *Semana,* as well as several television news outlets, were publishing stories based on sources who spoke of an alliance between the private militias and the cocaine bosses; these reports flew in the face of an opposite claim that the drug bosses were in league with the leftist guerrillas. That was the line propagated by the Colombian military and spurred on by the U.S. ambassador to Colombia, Lewis A. Tambs. On television, in weekly magazines, and in newspapers, there were occasional reports of a supposed split between Rodriguez Gacha and FARC, which had been protecting his coca fields and laboratories. The stories were systematically denied by both the army and the militia groups themselves, who insisted on referring to themselves as self-defense patrols.

At *El Espectador* I had written several reports about what was going on in Magdalena Medio. Toward the end of 1988, several peasants from Magdalena Medio, terrorized by the violence, came to our offices to testify to the atrocities that were taking place in the region. We published a chilling account of their charges.

In an interview with one of them, we told a dramatic tale of a man whose brother had been killed by the death squads. When the surviving brother decided to place the case before a judge, the militias responded by kidnapping his mother. Since then, the man could not go back to Puerto Boyacá. "When I realized that justice had no meaning, even though we could prove who had killed my brother—it was a sicario who was a member of the Puerto Boyacá death squads—I decided to come to see you to get the story out," the man said. "They are killing the peasants where I live. If you want to go there, we should hang a sign around our necks with our names on it. That way the militia will be able to check us out when we come to a roadblock, to see if we're on the list of suspected 'sympathizers with the guerrillas.' But we probably should put something else on the sign, something like 'I'm not a Communist.'"

I went to Magdalena Medio. The peasants showed me the roadblocks and the militias manning them; the tacit support of the army was obvious. Our report hit the streets of Bogotá but didn't make it far in Puerto Boyacá. The militias retaliated by blocking the distribution of *El Espectador,* seizing deliveries of the newspaper at the local distributor in Magdalena Medio. Not all newspapers received the same treatment, however. *El Tiempo,* whose correspondent in Magdalena Medio was Pablo Guarin, a founding member of the rightist militias, published a paid advertisement in July 1988 in which the squads answered the charges in an open letter addressed to me.

The self-defense groups not only rejected any connection with the cocaine bosses—they continue to reject the link to this day—but took credit for improving the lot of the people living in Magdalena Medio.

"We invite the journalist Duzán to see with her own eyes the schools and the new streets that have been paved in Puerto Boyacá, and to see further that they are certainly not used any longer by international communism."

The letter was signed by the mayor of Puerto Boyacá, Luis Alfredo Rubio Rojas. A year later, a judge would issue an arrest warrant against Rubio Rojas, implicating him in one of the ongoing series of massacres of peasants. Although Rubio Rojas was arrested, he was set free in 1989 in a raid staged by his comrades. Today, he is a fugitive from justice.

By 1989 the militias had managed to obtain a certain political currency in the nation, especially in the zones where they had beaten back the guerrilla groups. In 1988 the guerrillas had been forced to retreat, not in battles with the regular army but with these drug-financed militias. The "pacification" campaign conducted in Magdalena Medio had also been conducted in other parts of the country, leading the militia squads to declare they were winning the war on subversion. The steady stream of assassinations of members of the Patriotic Union succeeded in sinking the leftist political experiment. This was evident in popular mayoral elections in 1988, when the Patriotic Union saw an ebbing of its support, more like a full-fledged sea change, while the Liberal party began to retake positions it lost to its leftist rivals in 1986.

Landowners were able to return to their lands, and the areas that had suffered a strong economic depression were receiving an influx of drug money that brought a certain newfound prosperity. The drug bosses and their militias were so self-assured and so entrenched that by 1989 they were able to field their own political party, which they called MORENA (the color brown in Spanish and, in this case, an acronym for the Movimiento Revolucionario Nacional—National Revolutionary Movement). Their goals were to obtain legal status to field presidential candidates in the next election and to obtain equal treatment with the leftist guerrillas. "We are a rightist guerrilla movement. While the leftist guerrillas seek to overthrow the established order, we fight to preserve the national institutions," declared a spokesman for the group in an interview. MORENA was, to be sure, a right-wing movement, but a majority of its members were in the Liberal party whose regional leaders had become major landowners with a vested interest in the ideals of the cattlemen's association.

The army said nothing. In numerous interviews, no battalion commanders I spoke with ever admitted knowing about the right-wing drug armies. Every time a massacre occurred or a leftist leader was assassinated, the army contended that the violence was the work of the Communists.

Although the army commanders denied any connection with the militias and the drug lords, there was growing sentiment that such a link existed. Despite the fact that the drug bosses were operating in the same region as the militias and everyone knew where the militias were located, there never was a confirmed report of fighting between the militias and the army. The scant investigations that had been conducted following peasant massacres, which were carried out in spite of tremendous pressure on and death threats to judges who were hearing the cases, acknowledged that not only were some members of the army and police involved in massacres, but that the whole death apparatus came from Magdalena Medio.

Members of the Colombian government, or at least the key aides of President Virgilio Barco, were plainly aware of the alliance between the drug bosses and the militias, but their open acknowledgment of it was gradual, even though evidence was available as early as 1985. After the death of Jaime Pardo Leal in October 1987, certain voices in the government began to incorporate the subject of the militia groups into the public debate—especially after Hernando Corral produced a television report with footage of army-supplied militiamen fighting FARC. One of the people who began to speak up about the militias was Cesar Gaviria, Barco's minister of the interior. In a heated speech in Congress, Gaviria declared the existence of 122 paramilitary organizations.

It was only after the assassination of twelve judges in early 1989 that the government established a new branch of the national police, the Elite Corps. The Elite Corps was to be a specially trained counterinsurgency unit whose objective would be to dismantle the drug militias. Yet none of these activities had much of an effect on the national consciousness. It was Viafara who made the difference.

Fernando Cano decided we needed to break the story fast. There were ways to publish important details of Viafara's report without destroying the security of the ongoing police operations. Once the government had shepherded Viafara out of the country to the United States, we went ahead. On April 6, 1989, about six weeks after the meeting with Viafara, we published a story under the simple headline VIA AN INFORMANT. The article disclosed that foreign mercenaries were training the drug bosses and their subordinates in the use of explosives, armed warfare, and terror. It also stated that the drug militias had an entire arsenal at their disposal—M-16s, AK-47s, Galil 762s, MP-5s, and grenades—supplied directly by the corrupt Barbula Battalion, under the command of Colonel Luis Bohorquez.

There were photographs, too, showing Bohorquez along with some of the mercenaries, Henry Pérez, and many others. One such photograph was published in our second report.

The reaction was immediate. Bohorquez went before the television cameras minutes before the defense ministry was to announce he had been relieved of his duties. Choking away tears, he announced his retirement. "I love this uniform. And I regret to say that I will not permit it to be stained or stepped upon. . . . I am a soldier to the depths of my being. I am radically opposed to subversion. . . . And if that brings my dismissal . . . so be it." Despite the emotion, his words had a menacing quality, as if he were threatening that his downfall would not go unavenged.

Attempts to deny that mercenaries were training a drug army tried to repudiate Viafara's testimony. They accused him of being a small-time dope dealer and said he had stolen medicine from the militias and decided to desert for fear of being killed. But the government proved Viafara's information correct, and by the end of April, *Semana* magazine published details of a secret report by DAS, confirming the presence of mercenaries and naming each of them.

The secret report revealed for the first time the name of Yair Klein, a retired Israeli colonel who was the chief Israeli protagonist in the affair. Klein was a white-haired, fifty-four-year-old former Israeli tank commander with a robust, military bearing. Aside from being a colonel in the Israeli army reserve, Klein was president of Spearhead Ltd., an Israeli firm that provided military know-how and equipment to foreign clients; according to Viafara, Klein's Israeli associates told him that Spearhead also trained the U.S.–backed Nicaraguan contras in Honduras and the Christian Phalangists in Lebanon.

Viafara first met Klein in Puerto Boyacá in 1987. Viafara's detailed description of the visits by Klein and other Israelis included the hotels where they stayed, the dates they were there, and the names of each person involved. Klein moved about Magdalena Medio in the company of active members of the military. He and his men, including Mike Tzedaka, Spearhead's chief instructor, and Arik Afek, an Israeli citizen murdered mysteriously in 1990 in the United States, were presented as trainers who were to conduct personal security courses. Klein did not speak Spanish and communicated with his hosts by means of his translator, Teddy Melnyk.

It was not only the political situation that made the security business increasingly lucrative in Colombia. The Colombian armed forces and several Israeli armaments companies already enjoyed well-established relationships. Under Colombian law, the armed forces had budgetary independence; they were able to buy weapons as they saw fit without oversight from Congress or the executive branch. (Under the government of Cesar Gaviria, which took office in 1990, there is now civilian oversight of the defense department.)

From 1986 to 1989, General Rafael Samudio Molina, the Colombian minister of defense, bought sixteen Kfir fighter planes from Israel and greatly increased arms purchases. When I asked an Israeli embassy official what he thought Colombia needed with Kfir jets, he said, "That's their problem. Our job is to sell." Before Samudio was appointed, the United States had been the largest defense supplier to Colombia. Afterward, the armed forces and Israel had signed accords for training security organizations in Colombia, especially the escort contingent that protected high-ranking members of the Barco government.

The bodyguard assigned to me was proud to say that he was Israeli-trained. "You see a difference in the training between the gringos and the Israelis," he told me. "When you're under attack, the Americans teach you to try to avoid hurting innocent bystanders. For the Israelis the objective is the only thing that matters. They teach you to be ready to shoot at anything that moves."

According to the DAS document, Klein's instructions came through two Israelis already on the scene—Maerot Shoshani and Eitan Koren—who enjoyed excellent relations with General Samudio. Shoshani was the representative of the Klal group, an Israeli company that was selling arms to the Colombian government. Klein and Shoshani had met some time back, when Klein was president of Israeli Military Industry, IMI, the official armaments manufacturer for the state of Israel.

Klein proposed training sessions for the Colombian security police, DAS, as well as for the antinarcotics police, the air force, and the army. He also met with representatives of UNIBAN, a banana-growers cooperative that was being threatened by leftist guerrillas. But Klein came up empty-handed.

His luck was soon to change. In October 1987 Shoshani introduced Klein to the leaders of the Colombian Cattlemen's Association of Magdalena Medio. They had work for him.

A meeting was arranged with Pérez, by now functioning as Rodriguez Gacha's military chief. Luis Alberto Meneses, a cashiered army captain, was also there, as were other directors of the cattlemen's association. Meneses's job in the drug organization was to pay the necessary bribes to keep military and police officials in line. Klein would consistently deny knowing about any connection between Pérez and Meneses and the drug rings, insisting that the cattleman's association represented "defenseless peasants who sought to free themselves from the guerrilla yoke."

Also at the meeting were two Colombian army generals who the Israelis said never identified themselves. The generals told Klein that they supported the work of the cattlemen's association in their fight against the guerrillas.

In November 1987 a second meeting was held in Puerto Boyacá, attended by Klein and Arik Afek to negotiate a price tag for the training courses that were to be offered. Pérez and Meneses once again represented the cattlemen's association at that meeting. Klein sought $300,000 to conduct the courses, but eventually settled for $76,000.

In the six months in which the Israelis trained the militias in Magdalena Medio, the country began to experience previously unknown levels of violence: massacres of unarmed civilians and peasants shot at point-blank range, all killed by the militia squads that Klein and his associates were training. (In all, about eighty massacres of about fifteen hundred people took place in Colombia from January 1988 to January 1989.)

The first such recorded massacre was on Honduras and La Negra, two ranches in Urabá, in northwestern Colombia, in March 1988. A commando squadron from the militias rounded up forty peasant squatters who were living on ranch land owned by the drug bosses and murdered them.

The second massacre took place on April 11, 1988, at the fishing village of Punta Coquitos in the northern province of Urabá. The third massacre occurred in La Mejor Esquina, in Córdoba, in northern Colombia where seventy well-armed masked men entered the village during a *fandango*—a folksy fiesta. The commando leader took out a list and called out the names of peasants who were promptly taken aside and executed for allegedly being guerrilla collaborators.

The massacres were conducted with similar methods and identical weapons. In all the cases, DAS said, there was evidence that linked the crimes to military intelligence officers.

But the most important detail gleaned from investigations

and interrogations of those captured was that all the attackers were trained in Puerto Boyacá by foreign mercenaries. The DAS report concluded that "to judge the assault techniques used during the massacres at Urabá and Córdoba—the discipline, the use of insignias and uniforms, patrol techniques, the type of arms, and method of using them, the communications equipment and the personal security and identification measures—one can say that this new method of violence appears to be connected in some way to foreign training."

In early 1989, even after *El Espectador* had published the first exposé based on Viafara's testimony, the drug bosses were confident that Viafara's testimony would not have an impact. Pérez and Rodriguez Gacha again sought out Klein, asking him to conduct yet another training session. The fourth Israeli training course began on March 24, 1989, with fifteen students from Pacho, Medellín, and Puerto Boyacá. The coordinator of the drug militias was Oscar Echandía Sanchez, a retired army colonel, who linked up with the cocaine bosses and their militias after having served as military mayor of Puerto Boyacá. Only four of twenty-two students were given passing grades at the end of the three-week session. Those who did not pass were allowed to go home; many returned to their gangs. The course was financed by Pablo Escobar, Rodriguez Gacha, Pérez, and Ramiro Guzman, known as "Don Ramiro."

Since Viafara had deserted some time earlier, the tracks of the arms shipments might not have been uncovered. Indeed, there might have been no one to prove Klein had returned for the fourth training course. But Klein did not know that there was another deserter from the militia ranks. This time it was a more important figure, better situated in the criminal enterprise than Viafara: Oscar Echandía Sanchez himself.

Like Viafara, Echandía Sanchez had decided to come in from the cold and become an informant for the government. He had entered the militias because he thought it necessary to stop the guerrillas, but what he was living through had nothing to do with the idealistic preachings of anti-Communism and protection of homeland. He soon decided that the time was right for him to help the police. As course coordinator, he had access to a video training tape prepared by Klein. He absconded with a copy and brought it to the Bogotá offices of the national television network.

In June 1989 the video was broadcast throughout the country.

The reaction was swift. The presence of the trainers was greeted with shock and disbelief. DAS later used the tape to develop key parts of its investigation. For example, it discovered that one of the students Klein was training, with the code name Vladimir, was the same man who had been identified by survivors of several different peasant massacres as a leader of the commando-executioners. Vladimir was also identified by the survivor of the massacre of the judges on January 18, 1989.

Klein, who produced the tape as a business-promotion device, never considered that it might ever be broadcast. The tape showed that the students were at the command of the drug militias and that they were responsible for the majority of the massacres that were committed in 1988. It proved that the victims were not guerrillas. The killers had brutally murdered innocent peasants and twelve federal magistrates.

Klein and Arik Afek also appeared in the video, and their presence brought a swift indictment and arrest warrants against them. The warrant against Klein is still outstanding; he escaped arrest in Colombia, went to Antigua for a time, and then returned to Israel. Klein's student Vladimir was captured on August 1, 1989, in Medellín by the metropolitan police chief, Colonel Waldemar Franklin Quintero, who was the victim of a brutal assassination on August 16; Vladimir is still in prison.

Arik Afek, who also escaped arrest at that time, was found murdered in the trunk of his car at Miami International Airport on January 24, 1990. His killers have never been found. Afek's final visit to Colombia was in August 1989. In a clandestine interview with an Israeli reporter during that trip, Afek said that he was being followed.

"By whom?" the Israeli reporter asked.

"I think it's Mossad," Afek replied.

Echandía Sanchez's testimony confirmed Viafara's deposition but accomplished much more. It revealed the existence of an international conspiracy that linked Israelis to a web of monetary transactions through banks in the United States, Panama, and Israel; to corrupt government officials on the Caribbean island of Antigua; and to retired Colombian army officers linked with the drug cartels. All were working on a project much more ambitious than the government investigators had realized, one that sounded like it was right out of a James Bond novel: the creation of a survival school on Antigua, in which Klein would be a partner with the Antiguan government.

More than just a training center for the drug militias, who Klein still considered defenseless peasants, this would be a center for "freedom fighters" from around the world. The training site would also be the focal point for illegal Israeli arms. Klein would obtain the weapons from Israel and supply them to participants in the training courses on Antigua. When the "graduates" returned home, they would take their new weapons with them. Klein asked Echandía Sanchez to be an instructor at the Antigua school.

Klein was facing a number of problems in Magdalena Medio. There were shortages of technical materials, arms, and explosives and no ammunition. In addition, news reports—especially in *El Espectador*—and pronouncements by General Maza Márquez confirming Viafara's deposition on the presence of foreign mercenaries had made Magdalena Medio a site that was hardly ideal for Klein's operations.

On the other hand, Antigua had great advantages. The Israelis had excellent relations with the Caribbean nation via their local contact, Maurice Sarfati, an Israeli who had been doing business on the island since 1983. Sarfati was close to John Vere Bird, Jr., son of the island's longtime prime minister, member of Parliament, and a power broker in the Antiguan cabinet. He also had contact with Clyde Walker, the commander of the Antiguan police. The idea of a training center was also broached in Miami on October 5, 1988, at a meeting attended by Klein, Sarfati, and Walker.

Just when everything seemed to be going well for Klein, the Antiguan government, motivated by Colombian press reports and by investigations of Klein's illegal activities in Colombia, suddenly decided to reject the proposal on April 10, 1989.

On March 28, 1989, the Danish flagship *Else Thuesen* set sail from the Israeli port of Haifa with a cargo of arms legally consigned by IMI, the Israeli state armaments company, bound for Chile, Ecuador, Colombia, and Antigua. On April 22, the ship docked at St. Johns, Antigua, as planned, after an apparently uneventful Atlantic voyage. One container, containing 400 Galil rifles, 100 Uzis, and $323,205 in ammunition, which was destined for the Antiguan defense forces, was unloaded.

Two days after the *Else Thuesen* docked at St. Johns, another ship, the Panamanian flagship *Seapoint,* arrived. The *Seapoint* attracted no particular attention either, even though it was on a U.S. tracking list of vessels that could be carrying drugs. The rest of the cargo from the *Else Thuesen* was unloaded and hoisted aboard the *Seapoint,* and both ships set sail once more.

The entire operation was revealed about six months later, after the death of Rodriguez Gacha on December 15, 1989, when 232 Galils from this same shipment were found by Colombian police in hidden stashes on property belonging to the Mexican. The Colombian government asked the Israeli government for an explanation. The answer was a bombshell: The serial numbers of the weapons seized on Rodriguez Gacha's land corresponded to the weapons that left Haifa en route to Antigua.

A U.S. Senate investigation showed that Klein's company, Spearhead, issued close to $400,000 in payments for the arms to IMI, controlled by the Israeli government. Klein denied any connection to the case and rejected reports that the arms were paid for by Rodriguez Gacha's paramilitary forces, which he had trained. Klein said that the arms transaction had been between Maurice Sarfati and the government of Antigua.

Two of my colleagues, Ignacio Gomez of *El Espectador* and Peter Eisner of *Newsday,* then reported the real dimensions of the story. Eisner had decided to return to the field as *Newsday*'s Latin America correspondent after a four-year stint as foreign editor for the New York newspaper. With all the violence in Colombia in 1989, Peter, like many other reporters, came to the country in the midst of bombs exploding by remote control in the streets of poor and wealthy neighborhoods alike.

As the guns were being discovered, Ignacio Gomez, another able investigative reporter, faithfully recorded the serial number of each one in his pocket computer. He did the same thing with each serial number of the weapons found with the suspects in the assassination of Luis Carlos Galán, the Liberal party's presidential candidate. In June 1990, on one of his frequent trips to Colombia, Peter showed up at Ignacio's door with a present—a secret document Peter had obtained that was the packing list of the arms sent from Israel to Antigua.

Ignacio pulled out his own list, and the two excitedly began comparing notes. They read each serial number from their respective lists until something jumped to their attention: One of the guns on Peter's list of weapons sent to Antigua was also on Ignacio's list of weapons held by Rodriguez Gacha. And that weapon was later traced to the house of the suspects in the murder of Luis Carlos Galán.

Israel said that its only information about Klein's illegal activities came via news stories and reports from the Israeli embassy in Bogotá in April 1989. However, Israeli officials did know that Klein had been working illegally in Colombia for three years; the Israeli embassy acted only after Klein's illegal activities were made public.

Klein returned to live in Tel Aviv, where he was found guilty by an Israeli court of having provided military training and know-how in Colombia and Antigua without permission. He was sentenced on January 3, 1991, to a suspended one-year jail term with three years' probation. He also was fined $40,000, and his company was fined $35,000. He appealed the conviction.

Maurice Sarfati, who served as an intermediary in Antigua for the arms shipments, was living scot-free in Paris. It was Sarfati who falsified end-user certificates presented by Israel as proof that the weapons sale to Antigua was legal.

An official DAS investigation said that the arms trafficking via Antigua "was carried out with the knowledge of Israeli government officials," noting that the entire shipment had the approval of IMI as it left Haifa. Israel rejected any suggestion of official involvement; faced with an official Colombian protest, it blamed the government of Antigua. Antigua in turn conducted its own investigation, finding itself innocent of all responsibility in the case. John Vere Bird, Jr., however, was stripped of his cabinet post as minister of public works.

Following its investigation, the Israeli government declared that Spearhead employees had no connection with the Colombian drug cartels. Testimony by Viafara and Oscar Echandía Sanchez revealed not only that the cattlemen's association was financed by Rodriguez Gacha, but that Klein and his colleagues met face to face with the Mexican and with his son Fredy, who was one of the students shown in the training video made by the Israeli mercenaries.

The *Seapoint,* the ship that carried the arms from Antigua to Panama, was seized by Mexican authorities in August 1989 with a cargo of two and a half tons of cocaine.

Echandía Sanchez continued to provide information to DAS until May 1990, when the Antigua arms affair came to light and it became obvious that he was a principal informant for the government. Since then he has lived underground with DAS protection. Meneses, who served as an intermediary between the cattlemen's association and Klein, was arrested in 1990 but later released. It is believed that he returned to Magdalena Medio to work with the drug militias.

Backed by Viafara's revelations about the drug militias, DAS and the Colombian Elite Corps mounted a special mission in Magdalena Medio, code-named Operation Springtime. The mission began on April 4, 1989, when Klein's course on explosives had been going on for twelve days in Puerto Boyacá.

Once again, as on so many other occasions, news of the operation had already filtered through to the drug dealers. Despite all the secrecy, all the precautions, the government was finding it impossible to hide anything from the cartel. Just before the police commandos came in, the drug militias pulled up stakes along with the two Israeli instructors, Mike Tzedaka and a man identified only as Amancia, and moved to a more secure location. The drug sweep failed to find the kingpins, or even middle-level drug dealers, but it did come up with a record seizure of pure cocaine: fourteen metric tons.

Everywhere the police followed the tale mapped out by Viafara, they found things set up exactly as he had described them. For the first time, they seized the installations of the cattlemen's association while in search of a computerized file that Viafara said would tell the intimate details of the Medellín cartel's operations. However, when they got there, the files had been conveniently erased. The agents contented themselves with important material about Rodriguez Gacha and his finances.

When General Maza Márquez visited our newsroom to tell us the results of Operation Springtime, I had the same thought as when Jaime Pardo Leal exposed the assassinations of his Patriotic Union allies at the hands of the drug Mafia.

"They're going to kill this man."

Maza Márquez was of medium height, a robust man who was tough and impenetrable, yet jovial and warm. He had a piercing gaze; he focused intently on the person he was talking to, always pausing in silence to measure his reply. If an answer was to be tough, it came with a curt, coplike answer from pursed lips. And if it was to be pleasing, a smile erupted, and his brilliant white teeth illuminated the atmosphere around him. He was intense and engrossing, not an easy man to figure out.

The general's accent marked him as coming from the north. He was born in Ciénaga, a coastal city that was the scene of one of the most tragic events in Colombian history: the massacre in 1929 of four thousand striking banana workers by the Colombian army that was under the command of a Colombian army general acting on behalf of the United Fruit Company.

As a young man Maza Márquez always knew he would get into police work. He wanted to be a detective. Maza Márquez went to school in Barranquilla, a populous city on the Caribbean coast. Barranquilla was a principal cultural center, and Maza Márquez soaked up the atmosphere. He was always an avid reader and loved Cuban rhythms—*guaguango* and *son*. He was adept at entering different social and cultural circles, equally at home among the politicians and intellectuals of the Colombian coast. His friends ranged from army officers to Gabriel Gárcia Márquez, who was also born in the Caribbean North and is a distant relative. He had, perhaps, some of the traits of the ancient indigenous peoples of the Caribbean region, the Arhuac Indians, who were known for their aptitude in war and in politics.

Maza Márquez first became known in the 1970s as chief of investigations for the national police. He received credit for negotiating the release of kidnap victims when they had been seized by common criminals and guerrillas. I first met him when my uncle, Antonio Saenz, was kidnapped for ransom by a group of bandits in October 1979. In that instance, my uncle was able to escape his captors. What impressed me was that Maza Márquez, then holding the rank of colonel, was always personally on the scene and in charge. Unlike the average officer, who has few dealings with the public, Maza Márquez was an instant hit in the media. Reporters always had excellent relations with him, and he was well publicized and highly regarded. There was criticism of his tough tactics in extracting information from suspects, but such charges always were muted by his ability to seize the headlines. Rich and poor were all freed by Maza Márquez whose crime-fighting prowess was already winning him the nickname of the Colombian Kojak in some journalistic circles.

Like all law enforcement officers, his years of service were marked by the fight against the leftist guerrillas. He started out as a member of a military whose fast-track officers were educated in U.S. army schools, training that enhanced their anti-Communist stance. However, in recent years, because of the growth of the drug-trafficking problem there was a division of labor. The police, which Maza Márquez joined after a stint in the regular army, concentrated on combating drug crimes; the army focused on leftist subversion. In 1981 the national police created a special antinarcotics unit, which had achieved results in fighting the drug rings. But the cost was shattering; an investigation revealed that the 1986 assassination of Colonel Jaime Ramirez, chief of the antinarcotics squad, was an inside job. Only after Ramirez was gunned down did the scope of corruption within the police become known.

As a result, the Barco government in 1989 created yet another new police organism, the Elite Corps, intended to be a strike force whose goal was to destroy drug terrorism and the militias controlled by the drug bosses. The members of this new organization were well trained, well paid, and chosen for their spotless records; their names were kept secret to protect their identities. They were rotated in and out of the corps from other divisions in an attempt to maintain operational security. Maza Márquez, as the nation's chief of police investigations, provided the raw material for the Elite Corps's operations. Following the peasant massacres of 1988, he was again operating with a high profile. The Barco government, faced with heavy international criticism for human rights abuses, had convened a meeting of Colombia's National Security Council to deal with the massacres. The goal was to promote and infuse energy into investigations so that major crimes could be solved and stopped. Maza Márquez was the central figure in this redoubled effort.

Most government officials generally saw journalists as potential agents of an international Communist plot to discredit them and help the guerrillas. Only the reporters who fawned and paid deference to them were able to coax real information out of them. The officials professed to keep an informal list of guerrilla sympathizers, and if there was such a list, I was on it. There was not a great deal of logic to my being branded a guerrilla sympathizer; I had nothing against the military as an institution, nor had I ever been a Communist or a member of any guerrilla group.

But if I was suspect in their eyes, the feeling was mutual. The leadership of the army was not willing to accept criticism; any dissension must be Communist-inspired. If, for example, a battalion sought out guerrilla sympathizers, there were likely to be innocent, unprovoked deaths. When reporters wrote about these abuses of human rights, they landed in the same category as the victims: guilty by suspicion.

But Maza Márquez went a long way toward restoring my faith in the armed forces. When he was named chief of DAS and promoted to general, he quickly sought out journalists who traditionally were critical of the government and its security forces. He approached us with all the charm and wit at his disposal, ready to disarm potential critics in lively, open debate. Above all, we had a mutual interest in discovering the roots of the violence, the culprits of the massacres. As we both investigated the militias, the cattlemen's association, and the drug bosses, we were in close contact. Quickly, we recognized that we were targets of the same enemy.

"I admire people like you because I am a professional trained to face death and deal with that," he would often say. "But you are not trained; you are willing to face death all the same."

His opinions and views on drug dealing diverged from the conventional wisdom. He rejected the U.S.-promoted thesis that there was an alliance between the guerrillas and the drug dealers, with some hidden link to Cuba certain to be found. Rather, Maza Márquez believed the threat came from the private armies funded with drug money and supported by the rightist landowners and drug dealers in Magdalena Medio. In taking this view, he was attacked by longtime associates in the military, more than one of whom began to call him a Communist. In 1989, flyers were seen circulating in Magdalena Medio discrediting Maza Márquez and his work, charging that he was fronting for the guerrillas. This charge was as absurd in the Colombian context as saying that J. Edgar Hoover belonged to the Weathermen.

Rodriguez Gacha, seeing his operations fouled up by Maza Márquez's diligence, said in the interview before he was gunned down in September 1989 that Maza Márquez was being paid off by the rival Cali cartel. Others mouthed the same charge. Still others said that Maza Márquez's brother worked as the chief accountant for the Cali cartel. Maza Márquez angrily denied such charges and demanded that his accusers present evidence. None was ever forthcoming. Some U.S. officials subscribed to those charges and made other claims as well. The U.S. State Department prepared a dossier on him, in which it reported allegations that a woman in DAS custody had been tortured under Maza Márquez's command. Maza Márquez proved that the woman never existed and that it had all be a ruse. Nevertheless, he took pains to be cordial with U.S. officials, saying he wanted to maintain good relations, although he felt that they were no substitute for Colombian police work in combating the drug bosses. "We Colombians know more about fighting the drug war than the gringos," he said. "They don't know the jungle, they don't know the mountains, and they get frightened every time something happens. They shutter their windows and go home. What is it we have to learn from them?"

It certainly seemed that Maza Márquez needed little training from anyone. He had uncanny instincts and remarkable luck—having escaped at least six assassination attempts. "This kind of incredible luck comes from on high, from the divine source, a holy source of which I am a devotee.... I start feeling like one of the Untouchables."

The first attack on his life was staged by M-19, which put fifteen hundred pounds of dynamite in a car on his route to work. But because there was a traffic jam that day, Maza Márquez took another route, and the bomb, which had a remote-control device, was not detonated. Next, the National Liberation Army sent him a book bomb, which had a cover saying it was on the life of Lenin. But someone noticed it had glue all over it and got suspicious. Two agents took it outside and while trying to detonate it were severely injured.

The third attack would have gotten him, but he was saved by a lucky change to a more heavily armored car.

On May 27, 1989, in the evening, I was at Colonel Luis Eder España Peña's house, invited to a birthday party for him. Also there was General Octavio Vargas Silva, chief of the Elite Corps, who in due course told me quietly that one of our units had arrested a retired army captain named Huanumen and an active member of the national police, José Joaquin Rivera. And this captain was carrying papers that pointed toward an impending attack against me. I told him that I was certainly interested in seeing the material. We agreed to meet on the following morning at the home of the assistant police director, General Arturo Casadiego. But first I went to the Military Club, to the steam baths, as I usually do. While I was there a retired police colonel came up to me and told me matter-of-factly: 'Listen General, be very careful because I've heard several officers right here in the bath plotting against you.' I was amazed. I finished the steam bath, got dressed, went home to pick up my wife, and drove to General Casadiego's house as planned. Also there were General Gomez Padilla, the police director, and General Fajardo Vanegas. They showed me a portion of the papers where it was easy to see—and I can say from experience—that they were dealing with an intelligence analysis prepared for a man named Señor de las Flores. I knew that was a pseudonym for Pablo Escobar—Medellín, his base, is always referred to as the city of flowers [*flores* in Spanish]. The papers said, 'As far as Maza Márquez is concerned, we have him nailed and are just awaiting your instructions—at the very least we are going to really shake him up.' On reading the papers, I said, 'This is clearly a plot to kill me.'

So we started talking about what to do. And I said the best thing to do was to cut them off. On Tuesday, the thirtieth, two days later, I told them I could issue a release letting them know that we were on to the plan.

Well, I can say that the news of the plot was immobilizing. I stayed about one hour more with the other men, then said good night and went home with my wife. From home, I called my intelligence chief and told him to meet me at the office Monday morning, even though it was a holiday. I told him I had something to talk to him about.

When we got to the office, I asked him to get in touch with this Captain Huanumen to try to win him over and get us details about what they had in mind. At the same time I got a call from the presidential chief of staff, German Montoya, asking to come talk to me. He said it had to do with a family matter. He stopped by with two of his daughters-in-law. In a very troubled tone of voice, he told me that his son Gustavo had just been kidnapped. After a while, I left the office and went down to the car pool. I had an old Mercedes at that time. It was armored, but not in good working condition. In fact, it broke down that afternoon at the front gate. So I switched cars.

The following day I got up quite early. It was strange that when I went downstairs, they brought neither my Mercedes nor the car I had switched to, but a third car, an armored vehicle that had been used by President Betancur. It was fully armored and was quite heavy, so much so that they didn't use it anymore. Nevertheless, that was the car I rode to work in that morning. When we crossed Fifty-seventh Street on Seventh Avenue, I felt a sudden sharp thud and then the sensation of being dragged under the waves in the ocean, and I saw that a large number of projectiles were hitting the windows.

I shouted to the driver that we were being attacked, but it was a matter of seconds, and the car was already stuck and on the sidewalk. Seconds more passed, and I thought they were coming to kill me. But suddenly it all stopped. I got out of the car, and the sight was infernal. I was shocked to see that the bodies all over the outside of the car were my bodyguards, all smeared in blood. People crying, mutilated, half a body torn apart, lying there. Two of my bodyguards were severely wounded. One of them had his eye torn out; the other I could see was wounded and growing weak but standing by nevertheless. I hauled them both up and took them on my back to the military hospital. Many people criticized me afterward for what I did. But that's easy to say after the fact. At such a time of suffering, seeing these two boys so badly hurt, and I was well . . . I felt fine . . . I just had to do something, and I did it.

When we got to the hospital there was much confusion. Others who had been wounded in the attack were also arriving. I was there perhaps for half an hour until I was picked up by my men and taken back to the office. I started to realize that all this had been one huge conspiracy. . . . I sat down and wrote what I knew about the event. I consider it a faithful reflection of what Colombia has been going through.

He wrote his statement and then went out in front of the television cameras to read it himself; he stood there with a stern, hard gaze, and in his clipped, erudite language began to speak:

"I ask myself, Mr. Attorney General, if Colombians can believe that the drug cartels and the 'self-defense' groups supported by them want to achieve some sort of equilibrium for the stability of our democracy? Is it not in fact their intention to use all of their wealth to pay graft and foster corruption among government officials, in an attempt to control . . . political and economic power in this country? Let us take a look at what is happening. . . . Mr. Attorney General, investigate and you will find the answer that the nation needs to hear. Send your most honorable men. . . ."

The assassination attempt, he said, "has one positive result and that is that for the first time we no longer have to guess. . . ."

Maza Márquez was not only bringing the subject of the drug militias out in the open, he was hinting at evidence that military intelligence knew about the assassination attempt before it took place. Never before had any military officer acknowledged that corrupt military officials had joined with the drug dealers and corrupt landowners in a right-wing plot to seize control of the nation.

Relations between Maza Márquez and the military began to deteriorate immediately. Here was an attack on a high-ranking official, yet the army did not respond. They did not seize suspects; they did not set up the usual roadblocks in an attempt to stop the flight of the attackers. They made no statement to express their concern or to deplore the attack on Maza Márquez. They did nothing. The minister of defense, in fact, issued a statement denying Maza Márquez's charge of military involvement in the drug militias and in the assassination attempt.

Captain Huanumen was arrested, however, and was found guilty, along with two police officers. And Maza Márquez accelerated his campaign to hunt down corrupt police officers. Every police commander in northern Colombia was fired, and the chief of police, General Delgado Mallarino, was quietly retired.

But the effort to clean up corruption in the military quickly stalled. Only at the end of President Barco's term of office was something done. Barco dismissed five generals for their failure to pursue the war on the drug traffickers.

They did look at some corruption charges, but they did nothing to investigate how the assassination attempt was organized. It was quite unpleasant. One cartoonist drew a picture of me as a common gossip. The truth is that after the attack, I felt very bad. I had never felt so totally alone in my professional life. I saw everybody making excuses, and I, just having been the target of an attack that had left a number of people dead, where I saw firsthand the degree of danger that I was facing, saw that the organs of state had been penetrated by the Medellín cartel itself; I saw myself face to face with the Mexican; I felt like a David standing alone in front of Goliath.

But I came to the conclusion that I had to keep fighting. Very possibly, I told myself, I would never get out of it alive. Why should I have believed that I would be an exception? No one who had taken on the Mexican and Pablo Escobar had lived to tell the tale. They were murdered. Since Lara Bonilla they had started to pick off their enemies one by one . . . and looking at these recent events, all this elaborate infrastructure they had, I saw that they could even kill me in the bathroom. I began to mistrust everyone. Nevertheless, I decided to forge ahead. What was the motive? I saw that President Barco was quite strong in his resolve.

So I went back to work. A few days after the attack on me, in June 1989, the governor of Antioquia province was assassinated. The violence gripping the country following the attack on me was terrorism directed at the government itself. Our investigations concluded that the killing was carried out with the same modus operandi as in the attack against me—with a remote-control bomb device—evidence once again that these assassins had learned new techniques in carrying out terrorism.

On December 10, 1989, a bomb containing more than two tons of dynamite exploded at 7:30 A.M. in front of Maza Márquez's headquarters. The explosion was so massive that it was heard from one end of Bogotá to the other.

I had just entered my office. Usually at that time of the morning, I go out again to sit with some of the staff to have a cup of coffee and read the papers. For some reason, I didn't do it that morning. I went right into the office, which was the only place in the building designed to withstand a bomb blast. And for some reason, I had an important phone call to make, so I got up and closed the door, something I also seldom do. As I was dialing, I felt a massive blast that threw me to the floor. I got up as best I could and opened the door. The first thing I saw was my secretary lying on the floor, right where I usually had my cup of coffee. A wall had fallen on top of her, and she died instantly. I was anguished and could feel a pain in my back. I began to run anxiously about the building to see what was left. I felt infinite pain; I had never seen anything like this. The building was destroyed, and as I went along all I could see were lifeless bodies and the wounded. The majority were women, members of the administrative staff. The sorrow began to give way to deep anger.

That day I swore to myself that I would get them. I hated them, and I have been unable to overcome that hatred. Talk about drug trafficking, and my hair stands on end. It was Escobar and the Mexican who were responsible for that attack. We have a tape intercept on which Pinina, the chief of Escobar's assassins, is insulting another person for not having put enough power into the bomb. Eighty people died in that attack; more than 120 people were wounded.

In March 1990, a truck with more than one thousand pounds of dynamite was found near Maza Márquez's apartment in fashionable northern Bogotá. It was deactivated moments before it was set to go off. "That's the luck I'm talking about," he told me later, in one of the many meetings we had in the midst of all the bombings and attacks and threats. "I tell you, it all has to do with the Holy Spirit—Divine luck."

Throughout 1988 and 1989, Israeli, British, and Spanish mercenaries trained death squads in terrorist techniques never before seen in Colombia. With their help, the private militias of the drug dealers learned how to make incendiary devices, the latest technology in bomb production, the use of plastic explosives and TNT. They became familiar with the use of remote-control triggers and how to place altimeter-activated detonators to blow up airplanes. They learned how to make explosives from everyday materials, from potassium chloride and light bulbs and white sugar, from trigger devices bought in Israel, and from matches. They learned to make gunpowder and Molotov cocktails and to set up defensive perimeters with explosives. Some of the training dealt with evading the detection of explosives in airport X-ray machines and how to conceal electric circuits.

In 1989 and 1990, 25,000 Colombians died in the escalating violence that attacked every segment of society.

In mid-1988, Interpol and the British Embassy had advised DAS of the presence of British mercenaries contracted by the Cali cartel in the capital of Valle state. The full story broke on August 16 when the *Sunday Times* of London published a detailed report on the activities of the mercenaries. The British, like the Israelis, were schooled in special forces operations. They made two trips to Colombia. Their first trip was in August 1988 and contracted by Medellín. But their second mission in June 1989 was vastly different: They were hired to kill some of the men who paid for their first trip. At the top of their list was Pablo Escobar.

The British adventure in Colombia began when two Colombian army intelligence officers contacted Peter Tompkins, a well-known mercenary who had been working in Angola. They offered him work in Colombia to conduct courses for "paramilitary groups who were fighting leftist guerrillas with the aim of attacking the FARC headquarters at Uribe." Each mercenary was to receive $5,000 a month. One of the Colombians, a colonel, said that military intelligence was working with Rodriguez Gacha toward that end. According to Tompkins, Rodriguez Gacha wanted to stop all guerrilla activities because the guerrillas were competing with him for control of cocaine exports. Rodriguez Gacha was to pay all expenses, and military intelligence would take care of their entry into Colombia, providing them with arms on arrival and avoiding problems with immigration at the airport. Unlike the general training assignment of the Israelis, the British would have specific tasks: to seize and destroy Casa Verde, the headquarters of FARC; to kill FARC's leaders; to block all access to the mountain hideout, and to stop the supply routes to the zone.

But the British were not able to carry out that plan. The arms never arrived, and they had a hard time adapting to jungle conditions. Worst of all, the antidrug raids that were becoming more frequent at the time forced the militias to keep breaking camp and to relocate to safer territory. The British settled for providing a training course and left Colombia toward the end of August 1988. They returned, however, in May 1989, but this time they were contracted by the rival Cali cartel with a single, hazardous assignment: to kill Pablo Escobar and Rodriguez Gacha.

Relations between Cali and Medellín had been deteriorating since March 1988 when Cali operatives set off a bomb at a Medellín building controlled by Pablo Escobar. Medellín held Cali responsible for that attack and charged the Cali cartel members with providing information that led to the capture and short imprisonment of Jorge Luis Ochoa in 1987. Many drug investigators attributed the rift to a fight for market control in the United States, especially over the high-price New York and Washington markets, where Cali holds a monopoly in cocaine sales. But that was not the only reason. The Cali drug bosses were much more involved in legitimate business interests. It was one thing to fight among themselves, but attacking government and civilian targets was something else. They rejected the violent actions taken by Medellín, using words that could have come right out of a movie: "It's bad for business."

A friend from Cali gave me a telling example of the difference between the two cartels. A man he knew had participated in a

drug shipment and had the bad luck to be captured by the antinarcotics police. In jail, this man decided to threaten the judge
who indicted him. When Gilberto Rodriguez Orejuela, the head of
the Cali cartel, found out about that threat, he sent a message
through an intermediary: "We don't kill judges or ministers. We
buy them."

In the many tape intercepts obtained by the government, the
infighting was evident. Escobar and Rodriguez Gacha often tried
to seek a broad underworld consensus for their destabilization
strategy but to no avail. Unlike the Medellín drug organization
that launched a frontal assault on politics—with Escobar reaching
Congress as an alternate delegate and Carlos Lehder creating his
own party—Cali preferred behind-the-scenes, back-channel dealing. What it needed it could obtain through business contacts, not
through bombings and political campaigns. Rodriguez Orejuela
never bothered to seek elective office or to form a political party.
When blood spilled at the hands of the Cali cartel, it was a result
of internecine battles for primacy in the business. Never did the
violence reach out to the citizenry, never did it alienate the political establishment. The Cali cartel was not interested in buying up
large tracts of land, joining with rightist forces to fight the guerrillas, or winning popular support among the peasantry by creating social welfare programs in the slums. Rather, it set about
making money and doing so in the legitimate business world.
While Escobar and Rodriguez Gacha were shunned by the Medellín power brokers, their Cali counterparts owned banks, security
agencies, and sugar refineries, and were shareholders in the local
racetrack—the major traditional enterprises in the region where
they lived. Rodriguez Orejuela took pains to develop and maintain
good relations with the nation's power brokers and counted among
his friends key politicians and industrialists.

Moreover, Rodriguez Orejuela had worked hard to earn his
nickname, The Chess Master. He had obtained the drug-trafficking indictment filed against him in the United States and offered
himself up for trial in Colombia. He subsequently was acquitted of
those charges and so lived in Colombia as a perfectly legal member of society.

He once called the newsroom at *El Espectador* to remind us
cordially of his status in the world. The occasion for his call was
the publication of a story describing a police raid on his daughter's house. Nothing had been found in the raid, and the young

woman was not charged with a crime. "By the way, this violence is really terrible," he said. "You and I are both victims of Pablo Escobar. The violence he is causing is terrible, and I understand what you're going through because I'm in the same situation."

The Cali drug bosses had reason to be put off by the high profile adopted by the Medellín cocaine dealers; not only was it bad for business, it was diametrically opposed to their attempts to blend into a smooth-functioning economic system.

Cali had been spared the violence that characterized other major Colombian cities. The calm was shattered, however, with the onset of the war between the cartels. Bombs shattered radio stations, drugstores, and other buildings owned by Rodriguez Orejuela and his associates. As if in retribution, important members of Medellín's assassin squads were being gunned down in the street. Every intelligence agency in the country had been alerted to the presence of the British mercenaries in Cali—their rude attraction to local night life and women made them easy to spot. Despite their high profile, the British decided to carry out their attack on Escobar and Rodriguez Gacha. On June 4 they launched a commando raid on a ranch owned by Escobar near Medellín— they had received information that he would be there. They flew from Cali in two helicopters, painted with the markings of the national police. One of the helicopters was actually piloted by a police captain, Gustavo Gonzales Sandoval; overladen and flying through bad weather, it crashed several miles short of the target, killing the pilot. Peasants crowded to the site to find four battered men, who spoke no Spanish. Rather than accept the peasants' help, the men tried to flee on foot. They were rescued by their mates from the other helicopter. These mates had gotten lost and had landed three hours by land from the site of the accident. They paid a guide 100,000 pesos—about $2,000, an enormous sum for such a thing in Colombia—to hike through the mountains with them to the crash site. Then they radioed back to the other helicopter, gathered up the wounded and all the arms that were on board, and fled.

ZERO HOUR

All the members of President Barco's cabinet entered the great rectangular meeting room in the Nariño palace at precisely 11:30 on the morning of August 18, 1989, and took their places around the large Guayacan-laminated conference table reserved for the Council of Ministers. They looked toward the empty seat at the center of the table, reserved, according to protocol, for President Barco. Barco arrived promptly and launched into an announcement in his customary distant yet straightforward manner:

"I want to inform you that a series of quite strong measures are being studied in response to the critical situation we face in the country today. And I want to sound out your opinions. I would, therefore, ask that none of you leave the palace this afternoon because I'm preparing a speech for television this evening and would like you to read it first."

He then directed one of his aides to start reading the decrees. There was a nervous silence in the pale green room; the ministers could hear the sound of each breath they took. The Colombian leaders, whose portraits hung on the walls, were silent witnesses to this important occasion. This was to be one of the longest and most difficult meetings in recent Colombian history. Behind the president there was a portrait of Santander, known as the Man of Laws and as the conspirator who plotted unsuccessfully to take the life of Simón Bolívar, the Great Liberator.

Bolívar's portrait did not hang here but had a place of honor elsewhere in the palace. Facing Santander were paintings of four of the fathers of Colombian independence: Camilo Torres, José Joaquin Camacho, Francisco José de Caldas, and Antonio Villavicencio. On the wall to the right there was a striking painting by Alejandro Obregón, the well-known Colombian artist. Entitled *The Eagle of Violence,* it depicts the destruction of the state under siege, synthesizing in an eloquent way the brutality that had traumatized the nation.

Already suspecting that something extraordinary was taking place, the ministers realized quickly as the decrees were read to them that the measures Barco was proposing were without precedent. They amounted to a veritable declaration of war on drug terrorism.

One measure authorized the seizure and detention of anyone who was suspected of dealing drugs or having committed acts of terrorism and the imprisonment of such persons incommunicado for up to seven days. Another measure authorized the seizure of the property of drug suspects, even before they were found guilty of a crime. Anyone whose name fraudulently appeared as the owner of any of these properties to hide the true owners would be punished with a fine and up to ten years in prison.

Barco wanted to pull the rug out from under the drug dealers: to give more latitude to the security forces to pressure suspects and to obtain information without having to seek a court order to do so. The idea was to force them out of the safety of their hidden sanctuaries and draw them into the open. Barco's staff had scrutinized the decrees carefully, finding them legally airtight.

But one decree had a specific intent all its own: The government would once again allow the extradition of drug dealers to the United States. The drug dealers had fought the resumption of extradition tooth and nail because it meant they could be tried and probably receive long prison sentences in the United States.

At least one person at the meeting had known about the decrees before the meeting began. It was the young lawyer who was the newly appointed minister of justice, Monica de Greiff. Monica was eighth in the rapid succession of justice ministers in fourteen months, a turnover worthy of the *Guinness Book of World Records.* She was the first woman justice minister in Colombian history. "They named me because they were running out of justice ministers," said number seven, Guillermo Plazas

Alcid, with a note of sarcasm. He lasted only four months in the job.

De Greiff had been summoned prior to the general meeting by aides and given a copy of the decrees for review. She scarcely had time to read them when the president came into the antechamber, greeting her in his cold, stoic manner. From behind his thick eyeglasses, he turned his gaze on de Greiff and asked, "Do you think the Supreme Court can rule the extradition decree unconstitutional in the manner it is presented here?"

"No," she said. "The decree in judicial terms is irrefutable."

The president said nothing. He moved on to another subject, saying that he had called a full cabinet meeting at 11:30 A.M. to present the decrees. Then he turned and walked out of the room.

It was a classic game of poker, with only his closest personal advisers in on his strategy. Extradition was the ace up Barco's sleeve to be drawn at just the right moment. Only three of the cabinet ministers—Orlando Vazquez Velasquez, minister of the interior; General Oscar Botero, minister of defense; and de Greiff—had known about the decrees ahead of time, and they were informed only hours before.

To avoid any chance that the Supreme Court might overturn his executive ruling, as it had done before, Barco based the new decree on what seemed to be an irrefutable principle: the right of the president to issue laws under a national state of siege—and no one would deny that the nation had been living under a state of siege for most of the previous forty years.

The decree specifically suspended the article in the regular Colombian penal code that requires the application of an international treaty with corresponding countries for extradition to take place. That suspension allowed extradition to be authorized by executive order, bypassing the Supreme Court.

It was immediately evident to everyone in the cabinet that if the president's intention was to revive extradition, the drug cartel would take the decree to be a direct declaration of war. And it was equally clear that this would be a war without quarter.

No one spoke about it, but deep down, all the cabinet officers knew that this session could cost them their lives. There was a feeling in the country at the time that Colombia was overwhelmed by terrorism and that the government had lost its ability to cope with the drug trafficker–inspired violence. At the newspapers, we were writing about a new act of terrorism almost daily. In a way, what was happening in the cabinet meeting that day was a reflection of what was felt on the street. We Colombians knew that we had to take some momentous step—and that such a measure could have dangerous repercussions for all of us. That step had to be the resumption of extradition to the United States.

Since July 1988, when Barco had decided to freeze the extradition process, until this day in August, drug-directed terrorism against the government had been gradually increasing. Since May, when General Maza Márquez had miraculously averted an assassination attempt, the violence had moved into the cities. In Bogotá, the battle waged by Rodriguez Gacha to control the emerald trade had taken to the streets. More than a dozen people had been killed in July alone. And in a demonstration of the crudeness with which Rodriguez Gacha ran his private system of justice, among those attacked was the mayor of the town of Chia, located near Bogotá, who was ambushed just minutes after he publicly denounced Rodriguez Gacha; luckily, he survived the attack.

I was deeply affected by one attack because I knew the victims well. It took place at El Dorado Airport in Bogotá on March 3, 1989, a Friday, at 6 P.M., one of the busiest times of the week. A sicario assassin had gotten through security with a machine gun and emptied his magazine, firing at the leader of the Patriotic Union, José Antequera, a friend who had often come to my house for dinner and parties. He died on the spot. Such was the ferocity of the attack that three of the seven bullets that hit Antequera went through his body and wounded Ernesto Samper, a well-known, high-ranking official of the Liberal party, and another close friend of mine, who had the bad luck to have stopped to talk to Antequera. Samper was seriously injured but survived. In the midst of the melee, the sicario was gunned down by Samper's bodyguard. Samper's wife rescued her husband, putting him on a luggage cart and leading him away. Protecting him with her own body, she took him to the hospital.

These attacks were devastating. We were completely helpless. People were being killed not only by contract, but simply because they were on the street at the wrong time. I couldn't tell which was worse. To this day, Samper, who ran for president in the 1990 Liberal party primaries (and is a leading contender in 1994 presidential polling), still has four bullets lodged in his body. People joke that he carries the "heaviest artillery" of any presidential candidate.

In Medellín the escalating drug terrorism began to target high-ranking government officials, as in July 1989 when the governor of Antioquia state was murdered on his way to the office. A bomb was detonated by remote control in his car; the force of the explosion was so strong that his body was almost disintegrated. This assassination caused particular outrage and disgust in Medellín, where the jovial, democratic-minded governor was universally respected and loved. Most outrageous of all was the way he died, torn to shreds, not even leaving a body to inter.

During the months of July and August, there were three assassinations per week; judges were being picked off like ducks in a row. I was friends with many of these judges, or a friend of their friends, and we all felt the nightmare they were living through. All the judges had been involved in investigating the murders ordered by the cartel and the paramilitary squads. In most cases, when they got word they were targeted to be killed, they quickly issued arrest warrants against the drug bosses and then fled the country.

But the judges who did not flee were killed. On Wednesday, August 16, 1989, a brazen assassination took place that would drive the judicial system over the brink. That afternoon Bogotá Municipal Magistrate Carlos Valencia was assassinated after he indicted Rodriguez Gacha and Escobar for the murder of Guillermo Cano. The week before he was assassinated, Valencia had called Justice Minister de Greiff to ask for protection because of the constant threats he was receiving. De Greiff gave the order to protect Valencia with bodyguards and to provide an armored car. But on the day Valencia was gunned down as he left his office, the armored car still had not arrived.

When Minister de Greiff arrived at the funeral services for Magistrate Valencia, she was forcibly prevented from entering. "Nobody wants you here," one of Valencia's relatives whispered to her.

With Valencia's death, forty members of the judiciary had been murdered in three years. Valencia's killing provoked a new wave of indignation among his colleagues and associates. As a form of protest, judges who had drug cases before them submitted their resignations, charging that they could not operate under conditions in which their lives were constantly in danger.

The organization that represented lawyers, judges, and their associates, the National Association of Jurists, besieged and disgusted by so many threats to its members, came out in favor of a massive resignation of Criminal Court judges to protest the lack of security.

On August 18, the day that President Barco called the cabinet meeting to announce his war measures, ministers had been awakened at 6 A.M. with the news of yet another killing: the murder of Colonel Waldemar Franklin Quintero, commander of the Medellín metropolitan police. Franklin Quintero had been at the forefront of the fight against the drug dealers and their armies and therefore took his place on the drug bosses' hit list of the nation's political leadership. The courts were on strike and the government, unable to stop the terrorism, was being held accountable for the violence.

From the moment at which the cabinet meeting began until 8 P.M. that night, Barco, preparing for his televised address, neither spoke nor offered any opinion about what was taking place. Always impenetrable and unmoved, he dedicated himself to listening as each of his ministers talked about the decrees.

The debate surrounding extradition grew, and tempers were on the rise. Tense, desperate, strained to the limits, the ministers were in the middle of a battle without knowing exactly who was fighting whom. Such was the menacing vise of the drug traffickers that the ministers even began to mistrust one another. They all measured what they said, fearing that someone present might have sold out to the drug bosses.

"We all know what this decision means. The question is, knowing that, are we prepared to submit the country to what comes next?" asked Julio Londoño, the foreign minister, talking about whether to accept the consequences of approving extradition. He put his finger right on the uncertainties they all felt—and for which there was no convincing answer. For an instant, even President Barco, solid though he appeared throughout the day, seemed hesitant.

The possibility that Barco might have doubts brought an immediate reaction from the ministers and aides who supported the measures. Some of them, including the minister of defense, went to the chambers where the president was waiting and again debated the subject behind closed doors. Such was the weight of this historic moment, however, that none of the ministers, not even those who had apprehensions about the desirability of extradition, considered the possibility of resigning.

Everyone knew that with Barco one could not vacillate. Either you would convince the president with your arguments or you would go along with him and sign the decrees.

At 5:30, when the president called once more for the Council of Ministers to read his speech, most of the decrees had been signed by everyone in the cabinet. The debate about the timing of the extradition treaty was closed, and the president was prepared to accept only one proposal made at the session, which was offered by Education Minister Manuel Becerra.

"I believe that it is not possible to leave Monica de Greiff all by herself," he said. "If she is the one designated to sign the arrest warrants against the Mafia chiefs, it does not necessarily have to be her burden as well to sign the extraditions. It might be a good idea to have the extradition orders signed by the National Council on Narcotics."

De Greiff felt relieved. The cabinet and the president approved that motion. Under the new formula, the ministers of justice, defense, agriculture, communication, health, and education would jointly sign authorizations for extradition.

The proposal—or at least its source—surprised many of those in the chambers, since Becerra had previously served as president of the America soccer club in Cali owned by Miguel Rodriguez Orejuela, the brother of Gilberto Rodriguez Orejuela, the presumed chief of the Cali cartel. At the beginning of the Barco government, *El Espectador* had begun an investigation of Becerra. After he found out about it, he showed up at the newspaper one morning loaded with documents to prove that he no longer had any connection to the Cali soccer team and that even though Miguel Rodriguez Orejuela was the brother of the presumed chief of the Cali cartel, he was not facing any criminal charges and was a well-known public figure in the Cali sports world, which was indeed the case. A few months after Becerra's visit, Miguel Rodriguez Orejuela went underground—an indictment in which he was named had been issued in the United States. Nevertheless, the Becerra episode had been closed, and his explanation apparently had satisfied the president, who first named him governor of El Valle State, and later minister of education.

Despite Barco's trust of Becerra, that day many ministers and aides, without saying so, looked upon him with certain reservations, especially when he warned that the extradition decree could lead to the unification of the Medellín and Cali cartels. "Extradition will put them under the same umbrella," he said.

Yet if there had been any doubt concerning his commitment to the government's measures, his proposal had buried it.

Ana Mena, the minister of mining, voiced another more general concern: "I would like assurances that the people extradited will be the chiefs and not the small fries."

The ministers had repeatedly asked Defense Minister Botero and General Maza Márquez about their ability to place their forces on a virtual war footing against the drug bosses. The president, always imperturbable and impassive, looked toward his military chiefs, and responded, "The armed forces have the capacity to deal with this." Maza Márquez, who often attended these meetings as a de facto member of the cabinet, said that he was prepared to act strongly: "We are informed of the whereabouts of the bosses and we have the means to capture them. I think we can catch Pablo Escobar."

The preoccupation about the armed forces' ability and commitment was quite valid. The national police and DAS were the lead agencies in the war on drugs, and they were facing up to the task. But during the first two years of the Barco administration, the army had been reluctant to enter the fray, arguing that the drug problem was eminently a police matter and that the army's involvement would only weaken its operations against guerrilla groups. Botero's predecessor as defense minister, General Guerrero Paz, had told the president on one occasion: "Listen, Mr. President, we are committed to support your policy of negotiating peace with M-19, but please do not ask us to get involved in drug interdiction."

That statement was really a smokescreen for the hidden reality that army intelligence had been seriously compromised by the drug-trafficking organizations and that many brigade-level generals were being investigated for their relations with the drug militias. These new measures, established as wartime edicts, would codify the army's entry into the drug battle to face the same people with whom some members of the military were cooperating behind the scenes.

"Upon their entry into the battle, the first thing they'll have to show is that they themselves are not corrupt," a high-ranking aide to Barco told me. "If they don't respond and get the job done, they're out."

Barco read the assembled ministers the speech that he was going to deliver on television. It was already evening, and after the intense talks, the ministers listened silently, their faces showing weariness and strain.

At around 8:30, moments before he was schedule to speak, the phone rang in the adjoining reception room, and General Maza Márquez was called out of the meeting. When he returned, one could immediately see that something had happened. Barco stopped reading as the general took the floor. "I have the sad duty to inform you, Mr. President, that there has just been a terrorist attack on Senator Luis Carlos Galán."

For the first time, Barco's distressed, preoccupied look melted, and he seemed genuinely, personally struck by this shattering report. He withdrew to consult with Maza Márquez, and within ten minutes returned to the cabinet room and sat down. His face had once again taken on that look of remoteness and self-control. He then added a new first paragraph to the speech he was about to deliver.

"I address you tonight to explain new measures adopted under stage-of-siege provisions, at a time in which, with justification, the nation finds itself indignant and distressed by the grave acts of violence which have taken place in recent days. Deplorably, Luis Carlos Galán, Liberal party presidential candidate, has been the target of yet another terrorist attack. Senator Galán has been taken to a hospital. We pray to God—for him and for the country—that he recovers from this difficult moment."

Then he continued with the rest of his speech.

"The criminal organizations and the drug dealers have unleashed a wave of murder and death. They have attacked representatives and leaders of every sector of the country and all its institutions. Judges, political leaders, soldiers, citizens, and public officials have been victims of this barbarity. The violence affects us all. It is not an offensive against the government or against the system of justice. It is a war on the nation. And for that reason, the nation must give its answer."

Surrounded by his entire cabinet, the president read his speech live from the presidential palace, something that he had never done before. "Today more than ever we need to show that this is a joint decision. Now there is more reason than ever for us to be united," he told the ministers before the speech.

As the president went on the air to read his announcement, Luis Carlos Galán was still alive. The very possibility that he might die drove Colombians over the brink—the announcement of the war measures and of the resumption of extradition was greeted with immediate and unanimous approval.

"This is certainly a difficult moment," he said in closing his speech. "But there have been other such occasions, and Colombia has endured. We must not lose sight of our goal because that is what these violent men want to happen. To fall into despair is to play the game of the terrorists. We will carry on, decisively and firmly, rather than give in to arguments against a common enemy. We must win this battle. I am certain that we shall succeed."

Less than an hour after the broadcast, Barco got the news that Senator Galán was dead.

News of the attack on Galán reached me while I was at a diplomatic cocktail party, in the midst of a conversation with my colleague Enrique Santos Calderón and Philip McLean, who was the chargé d'affaires at the U.S. embassy. All day rumors had been brewing that Barco was about to make a major policy address. The possibility that there would be a resumption of extradition spread through the press corps. We, like the rest of the nation, could sense that tough measures were about to be enacted.

McLean had asked us what we had heard about Barco's impending speech, and we had argued the merits of resuming extradition. There were those who believed that McLean in his position as chargé d'affaires was even more important than the ambassador himself. On receiving the news about Galán, McLean furrowed his brow and, with a gesture, motioned to his numerous bodyguards to prepare to leave immediately.

As McLean left, he swept along with him the majority of government officials, academics, journalists, and presidential aides who were at the gathering. Ordinarily Galán himself would have been there, but he was on the campaign trail and had declined the invitation. He was on the hustings—a front-runner. That night, instead of sipping cocktails with diplomats, he was on a campaign swing through Soacha, a few miles from Bogotá, as the Liberal party candidate for president.

Some friends came back to my house around 8 P.M. to monitor

what was going on. The radio reports were confusing, so I telephoned Rafael Pardo, one of President Barco's aides. However, Pardo, in his customary clipped, serious tone, told me only what we were hearing on the radio: "He is apparently wounded, but we don't know what condition he is in. They're taking him to the hospital right now."

When it was apparent that the president's office had no additional information for us, all we could do was sit in front of the television and await further news. A cameraman who had been covering the campaign swing to Soacha was able to capture the sad and dramatic footage of the attack. The power of the image, with all its devastating force, showed us in slow motion how Galán, one of the most protected men in the country, moved fatefully into the trap that had been prepared for him. The jostling crowd in Soacha's town square raised him on their shoulders: His face jubilant, his arms raised as if celebrating a battle victory, he was filled with vigor and energy. As he was hoisted to the stage, six assassins who were camouflaged in the crowd spread out to take their appointed positions. One of them, apparently located at the foot of the podium, fired three shots at Galán. One of the bullets perforated his aorta, producing internal hemorrhaging to such a degree that this wound alone almost certainly killed him. These shots were followed by volleys of gunfire. One of Galán's bodyguards threw himself to the ground to protect the already dying man with his own body. Swiftly Galán was taken to his armored limousine, which then raced to the nearest hospital. A Liberal party colleague, who helped carry Galán to the car, later said that his friend had still been conscious. "Don't let me die," Galán said, a distant gaze already descending upon his countenance.

The president sent Eduardo Diaz, the minister of health, to Kennedy Hospital, where Galán lay wounded. Diaz was taken to the operating room, but as he donned hospital garb so that he could go in, an officer walked up to him and said, "Don't bother putting it on, Minister . . . he's dead."

Eduardo felt as if the world were collapsing on top of him. He went out immediately to call the president and inform him about what had happened, but he found that the few telephones available were occupied by radio reporters who already had begun to broadcast the news. He finally found a public phone and made the call.

"He's dead, Mr. President. Dr. Luis Carlos Galán is dead."

"Come back right away," was all Barco said to him.

Eduardo went outside in the company of three other ministers who had arrived at the hospital after him. The crowds were surrounding the bulletproof cars of the ministers, blocking their way. For an instant Eduardo thought he would be dragged out and lynched. The radio was broadcasting the news, and people were weeping, disconsolate but angry. Eduardo finally found his car— the only one that was not armored—and got in with the other ministers, while one of the other ministerial cars was taken over by a group of supporters of the dead senator. Inside their car, the four ministers had an uncomfortable feeling of impotence, anger, sadness, and fear.

President Barco called back his ministers for an extraordinary cabinet meeting. In the hall of the Council of Ministers one could sense the uncertainty that follows such a harsh blow. "Sadly, I must inform you that Senator Luis Carlos Galán has died," Barco said. At his side was Gabriel Rosas, a member of Galán's New Liberal faction who had served as minister of development and had accompanied Galán throughout his political career. Rosas could not hold back his tears.

He had also gone to Kennedy Hospital and had seen his friend and political ally dead. "They have killed Galán, Dr. Rosas. Please take up his cause," one follower of Galán had implored him as he left the hospital.

With the same pain and powerlessness that showed in his face when he met the Galán follower at the hospital, Rosas looked to Barco and said pleadingly, "Mr. President, what can we do? Help us! Help us!"

"I want to express condolences to you, Gabriel, on behalf of the New Liberals . . . this loss is deeply saddening for the country," Barco replied.

Amid choking tears Rosas tried to answer, but the words came haltingly. "I am happy to have been one of the supporters of the measures that you have just announced. The death of my friend Luis Carlos confirms for me more than ever that the path we have taken is the appropriate one."

The president turned to the minister of defense, Oscar Botero. "We have to move to the offensive. This is going to be quite a prolonged war. I am today establishing the Center for Joint Operations, an organization that will coordinate the three armed forces and which will function in all cases when we are engaged in war."

"Yes sir, commander," Botero replied, calling Barco by his title as commander in chief of the armed forces. "We will begin immediately to search for the drug dealers and to occupy their properties."

At that moment there was unanimity about the correctness of the wartime measures Barco adopted. The doubts of the few who might have vacillated were galvanized with the majority upon word of Galán's murder. All that could have been done had, in fact, been done. All that could have happened in a single day had, in fact, happened. Nevertheless, the situation of the country was such that, it was clear, more tragedies would follow. And with whatever came next even the harshest measures would seem to fall short.

The president adjourned the cabinet session that evening with a final note: "Go home and get some rest because tomorrow is likely to be a very busy day," as if this one had not been long enough.

One of nine children of a middle-class family and a descendant of the *comunero* (revolutionary), Galán, one of the first *criollos* to challenge authorities during the Spanish colonial period, Luis Carlos Galán was a unique figure in Colombian politics, dominated as it was by the offspring of families who were high in the hierarchies of power. A well-spoken, likable person, he had in a deft thirty-year career become one of the transcendent figures in national politics.

Carlos Galán was still quite young when he came to the newspaper *El Tiempo* where he wrote his first stories as a cub reporter. At the paper he connected easily with a select group of reporters who not only became his inseparable friends, but also served as coconspirators in a romantic liaison he was developing. After work the group would usually go out together to chat, debating the political scene and the future. Gloria Pachón, a bright, self-assured young woman, had unwittingly left Luis Carlos hopelessly smitten, and he successfully courted her in the company of the entire press corps. They eventually married.

I was introduced to Galán when I was fourteen, at a dinner organized by the principal of my high school. The principal was an unabashed admirer of Carlos Galán and had adopted at our school Galán's plan for joint governance by students and administrators, a policy that Luis Carlos had pushed for in the public university system to democratize internal debate. The idea was a novel one, but it did not last long.

What began as power sharing quickly turned into anarchy, so the students' power was quickly reined in. Luis Carlos never found out that the same problem was the case at my school, which was privately run. Imbued with these new democratic airs and full of ourselves, we rebelled against the principal one day after she fired a teacher on grounds we thought were unjust. Under the umbrella of cogovernance we called a general strike. What followed closely paralleled the experience in the university system. Filled with indignation, the principal quickly lost her love for Galán's democratic experiment and expelled fifteen girls from the school. Not surprisingly, that was the last that was heard from our idealistic principal about joint control at our school.

It was a minor issue, of course, but it seemed, in miniature, to reflect what was going on in the country. Neither at my school nor in the country at large were we prepared for so much democracy all at once. Galán was the first to recognize that problem. "I'm not interested in becoming president just for the sake of getting there," he said to me more than once. "What I have tried to do, above all, is to cultivate a process of political education so the nation and its citizens understand the value of democratic institutions and learn to use them to their own benefit."

By 1978 Galán had become convinced that there had to be fundamental changes in the political structure, that the two traditional political parties had become wrapped in self-absorbed bureaucracies and converted into mere centers of political patronage. He decided, therefore, to found a dissident wing within the Liberal party and called it New Liberalism.

His proposition from the outset was to seek changes in passé political habits, to infuse a new social consciousness in political life. It was an effort to modernize the Colombian state for the benefit of all Colombians rather than a handful. Galán was, above all, a liberal who knew how to analyze the values and aspirations of the long-suffering Colombian urban middle class.

"Galán, more than a politician, was an idealist, a fundamentalist, a man of principles," said President Cesar Gaviria, who was his closest aide during the campaign and who was elected president in 1990. His political line found strong sympathies among college students and among those of their parents with liberal sentiments. These parents were solidly middle class, conservative in their habits, who paid their taxes religiously and saved every cent for their children's education. One could compare them to middle-class Americans who clip coupons for the supermarket and pay their taxes regularly and have their own homes, although they never finish paying them off.

Something was still lacking, however. As one leader of a grass-roots barrio put it, "Galán still has to get down deeper, to get even closer to the real people." The truth is that in some of the barrios, like those of Medellín, the "real people" were being trained as some of the sicario assassins who would eventually kill the young political leader. For them, talk about democracy had not the slightest connection to reality. "All that stuff belongs to goody-goodies who have a mother and a father in the first place," one of these sicario gang members told me.

Luis Carlos waged his first presidential campaign in 1982. He lost, although political analysts considered the large number of votes he received to be a broad triumph and a sign of things to come. But the victories were still hard to come by. Galán, who had always done well in public opinion polls, never matched expectations on election day.

After he lost the parliamentary election in 1984, it was time for reflection and analysis. Many of his assumptions were revised, not so much in conceptual terms as in terms of organization. Luis Carlos decided it was time to start traveling, to move around the country once more.

In 1986, after Barco was elected president, Galán took the most important step in his political career. After ten years of being a dissident, he decided to dismantle the barriers his faction had created within the party and join the mainstream once more.

Although many of his colleagues resented his decision and saw it as a form of surrender, Luis Carlos used his acumen as a political leader not only to coax most of his fellow dissidents along with him, but also to set things up so he would be welcomed back into the fold. In large part his reentry was made possible by the great political affinity that existed between Galán and Barco. Both were virulent critics of a political echelon that had abandoned itself to bureaucracy; both had tangled with the power structure because of that stand. Barco saw in Galán a powerful ally for his policies and a stalwart defender of his administration. They were united not only by their beliefs and by their roots in the same part of the country, Santander, but by their same preoccupations. One of the main ones was the threat of drug trafficking. By the end, their personal contact had been on the rise.

Barco, who rarely used the telephone, not even to speak with his own ministers, spoke almost daily with Luis Carlos.

At the time of his death, Luis Carlos was clearly at his zenith. He had successfully bridged the fundamental gap between dissidence and political reality: He had done what had to be done. Now back inside the party, he had begun an aggressive new campaign. Three days before his death, opinion polls had given him a clear preference among Colombians to be the next president. Nothing appeared to stand in his way.

Gloria was already in bed when she was informed of the attack on Luis Carlos by her secretary, Lucila. She hung up the phone and got dressed quickly while she called to the children to get ready to leave for the hospital. The whole time she had been telling herself that nothing bad had happened to Luis Carlos. They got to the Social Security Hospital at around 9 P.M. She remembered being besieged by people asking for Luis Carlos's blood type, which she told them was A negative, a relatively uncommon type. Rumors were still circulating that he had been wounded in one arm and that he was not seriously hurt. She kept telling herself that these stories were true. And she was conscious of not wanting to scare the children.

Finally someone came up to her and said that Luis Carlos wasn't even at this hospital, that he had been taken to Kennedy Hospital, which was closer to where the attack had taken place. She left immediately. When she arrived, there were many people milling about waiting to find out about their political leader. Gloria and the children were taken to a room where the bodyguards had also been taken. She was told that one of the bodyguards, who had used his body to shield Luis Carlo, was dead, as was the Soacha city councilman, who was killed instantly in the volley of gunfire. But no one said anything about Luis Carlos. Finally, a doctor came up to her and led her to an adjoining room. She motioned for the children to follow. And then, through a half-open door, she could just make out Luis Carlos lying on a bed. The doctor grasped her arm and led her to one corner of the room.

"I'm sorry to have to tell you that your husband has died."

Only at that moment did Gloria realize that Luis Carlos had been dead all along and that no one had dared to break the news to her. She looked at the children and felt profound grief enveloping her. Luis Carlos would never be able to fulfill the promise he always made to them when they complained he was spending too little time with them. She recalled the words he repeated when he needed to find a way to talk himself out of their complaints: "There will be time, there will be time, for us to enjoy ourselves like a normal family."

One year after the death of Luis Carlos, I interviewed Gloria in her apartment in Paris, where she had been sent by the government to serve as Colombian ambassador to UNESCO. Tears came to her eyes when she recalled that night. What she had felt, she said, was so terrible that she was still unable to express it. "It is as if I myself had been killed. From that point on, I started living something else, a life that had been given to me on loan, as if I were no longer myself. As if they had taken my life away from me."

On the day he died, Luis Carlos left home as he always did—quickly, without eating breakfast or having time to chat with the boys as he sometimes was able to do. As always, Gloria recalled, he was in a good mood. Gloria noticed nothing strange. Or perhaps it was that she had decided to not worry anymore about security. Gloria had spoken with Luis Carlos three times during that day. One of those times it was to remind him that he had to discipline Juan Manuel, their oldest son, who apparently had left the house the night before without permission.

For several weeks, ever since Luis Carlos had received indications that something might happen to his children, he had ordered them to stay home after they returned from school. But Juan Manuel, in the full bloom of his sixteen years, disobeyed his father's orders and went to visit his girlfriend.

The other thing that Gloria had told him was that he should avoid climbing up on trucks and should not let people raise him on their shoulders—an act that seemed especially dangerous to Gloria.

Gloria never remembered seeing Luis Carlos nervous about security questions. Nevertheless, she now thinks that he avoided talking about all the threats he received so he would not worry her excessively. But she remembered that after the murder of Guillermo Cano in December 1986, he said something that left a deep imprint on her. "I am condemned," he told her.

Around the time of Cano's death, Luis Carlos decided to leave the country for a while. He had said that what was going on in Colombia was absurd and that he would have to stay away. DAS was constantly discovering ambushes planned against him.

Whenever particularly solid information was available, they warned him to take special precautions. At the time, I lived down the street from the Galáns, and I could always tell when something was going on because the security provisions around their apartment would be increased. Every morning I could hear the caravan of security vehicles and armored cars leaving the garage next door. I remember one day counting twenty-five bodyguards.

Threats that went beyond the routine, that spoke directly of attempts on Galán's life, began to surface in August 1989. Oddly enough, no one gave them much credibility. Luis Carlos had heard them all and decided to go ahead with the campaign swing. It was only after the attempt on his life in Medellín on August 6 that Gloria saw him really worried for the first time. He was in Medellín participating in a forum at the University of Antioquia when the chief of police pulled him aside.

"We have just broken up a plot to kill you. Don't be alarmed now because we have everything under control," he told the presidential candidate.

One block from the university, the police had discovered an abandoned vehicle equipped with a grenade, two rockets ready for firing, two revolvers, and a radio communications system. The car was found at a spot where the motorcade carrying Galán and Minister of the Interior Orlando Vazquez Velasquez were to pass by. An anonymous phone call to the police enabled them to find the assailants who had planned the attack in the barrio of Manrique, one of the slum districts that surround Medellín. Many of the sicario assassins contracted by the drug Mafia live in Manrique and the other outlying slums. Like all makeshift squatter areas, Manrique was built on the side of a mountain. The streets were not really streets but steep labyrinths that hid the sicarios when authorities or rival gangs tried to move in on them. The police found these men, however, and managed to surround them. Three suspects were captured after a gun battle in which one policeman was killed. The group confessed to having planned to launch one rocket against Galán's car and one against that of his lead bodyguards, using the grenade to finish them off, if necessary, or to cover their flight. Knowing that Galán had planned to come to Medellín, they had concocted the scheme weeks in advance. The men were working with a $400,000 war chest to carry out the attack.

Luis Carlos returned from Medellín anxious and upset. What

perhaps troubled him most was that even though the news media had published every detail of the assassination plot in Medellín, many people dismissed the entire affair. Others thought that the frustrated plot had been directed not against Luis Carlos Galán but against the minister of the interior.

Gloria simply had no idea what was going through Luis Carlos's mind. If he had really been anguished and distressed, he would have suspended campaigning. But he chose not to do so. Few knew that Luis Carlos leaned toward the metaphysical and had a particular interest in the influence of the stars. He had his horoscope read in early August, as I knew because we went to the same astrologist, Mauricio Puerta. Among other things, Puerta had followed the astrological movements during the peace talks between the government and the M-19 guerrillas. Frequently, on his own initiative, he informed government negotiators about his astrological readings. According to Puerta, Luis Carlos, a Libra with Libra in the ascent, was facing a violent convergence on the days in question. Mars, the god of war, was passing through the Twelfth House, where hidden enemies reside. That, in laymen's terms, meant that his life was in danger. Perhaps recalling his fateful astrological chart, Galán had put on his bulletproof vest that night, en route to Soacha, thinking that the precaution could avert his destiny with death.

The day after his death, Galán's body was borne to the Plaza of Bolívar in the center of Bogotá, which was packed with thousands of Galán's supporters. When Barco and his ministers arrived, they were reviled with contemptuous jeers. "Justice, justice!" came the shouts from the throngs of people crying for the fallen candidate. "Assassin! Assassin!" they called out as the scornful shouts rose in pitch. One felt both the affinity people had for Galán and the atmosphere of hostility his death provoked toward the government. The people felt orphaned and were deeply outraged at the drug Mafia. I joined the huge line of Colombians who were marching to pay their final respects to Galán in the Congress of the Republic. As I stood there, I recalled how Colombia was filled with contradictions. In this same spot, five years earlier, Pablo Escobar, as an elected alternate representative, had gone head to head with Galán's uncompromising New Liberalism. I felt afraid because for the first time there seemed no way to halt the onslaught of a narco-controlled state. I was not sure we were strong enough to fight back.

The assassination of Luis Carlos Galán was felt in Colombia much the same way that the killing of Benigno Aquino was felt in the Philippines, or the murder of Pedro Joaquin Chamorro was felt in Nicaragua. It was a blow that made Colombians react in unison as never before, that filled them with an indignation that surprised the drug dealers themselves. Galán's murder convinced Colombians to go along with the only weapon that the drug Mafia feared: extradition to the United States. One week later, the Supreme Court would declare that Barco's extradition measures were constitutional in what was considered the ultimate endorsement of his policy. "With Luis Carlos's death, we lost not only our present, but our future," declared former President Misael Pastrana.

Fear had been replaced by furor.

In Washington, Barco's decision was received with jubilation. At the White House, President Bush immediately declared his unlimited support for "the war on drugs declared by the people of Colombia and their president."

One week after the death of Galán, the declaration of a war on drugs by Colombia and the United States was the top item in the news around the world. From one moment to the next, Colombia saw itself invaded as never before by news media from around the world. Many of the reporters who came already knew Colombia and thus were not surprised to see people walking down the streets, cars driving around the city, and people dancing salsa in discotheques. But since Colombia had always been in obscurity with little news interest, the large majority of the reporters sent to the country had not the slightest idea of what they would face. A crew from one American television network showed up at the newspaper wearing bulletproof vests. Others, assuming that Pablo Escobar walked freely about on the street, called to ask for his telephone number, as if an interview could be set up as easily with Escobar as with a Hollywood movie star.

In late August 1989, I came across a story in the French newspaper *Liberation*. It was prominently displayed on the front page with a headline that must have surprised Escobar himself: WORLD EXCLUSIVE: AN INTERVIEW WITH THE CHIEF DRUG BOSS, PABLO ESCOBAR.

The report was wrong from beginning to end. The exalted world exclusive with Pablo Escobar was in reality an interview that my friend and fellow reporter Hernando Corral had conducted with another drug boss, Gonzalo Rodriguez Gacha, the Mexican. The French correspondent had gotten the names mixed up.

In short order, this invasion by the news media managed to alter Colombia's image. Colombia's problems were not well understood; nobody knew who was who in the cartels; it was not clear whether the country was governed by Pablo Escobar or Barco. The only thing anyone knew was that Bush and Barco had declared a war on drugs in a country called Colombia.

This declaration of war, which the world celebrated optimistically by way of their television screens, came across differently in Colombia. A few days after the measures were approved, the entire Barco cabinet began receiving the first telephone death threats at their homes. "No matter how many bodyguards you have, we are going to kill you. We know the position of the Council of Ministers on extradition, and we have infiltrated palace security," said a letter signed by the Extraditables. If there was any lingering doubt as to whether their lives were in danger, that ended with the swiftness of the threats. "The day we signed the first extradition order I was completely certain that they would kill me," one of the cabinet ministers told me. That minister had suffered heart spasms because of the all the pressure he was under. The concern about death that the ministers felt was even more evident on the streets and in places of business. The war of nerves intensified even more when a communiqué from the Extraditables was sent to the news media, declaring total war on the oligarchy and on all Colombians who supported extradition.

While the nations of the world sent their messages of solidarity to President Barco on his decision to fight drugs, the government announced in the news media a reward of $200,000 for anyone who could provide information on the whereabouts of Pablo Escobar and Gonzalo Rodriguez Gacha. Throughout Colombia, one could smell death and perceive the inequality of the battle before us. I was waiting for the next act of violence.

THE BOMBING, FINALLY

A shattering sound like thunder woke me up early on Saturday, September 3, 1989. The echo and the vibrations against the mountains made me realize that a high-powered bomb had exploded somewhere. I was immediately stricken with the horrible premonition that the newspaper had been attacked. I automatically reached for the telephone and called *El Espectador,* hoping that my feeling was wrong.

"Margarita," I said nervously, "what's happening?" My hand shook as I cradled the receiver.

"María Jimena, it's a bomb! It's a bomb! I don't know what's happening!" the receptionist shouted, her voice choking. In the background I could hear the sound of glass falling. My premonition had been correct.

"Is anyone dead?" I asked.

"I don't know anything! The only thing I can say is that the whole building is wrecked!"

I looked at the clock. It was almost 7 A.M. I hung up and then called Juan Pablo Ferro, the news editor at the paper. My call woke him up.

"Juan Pablo, they blew up the paper!"

"Huh, what? Is anybody dead?" he stammered, still groggy.

I told him what I knew—almost nothing. We agreed that I would pick him up and go quickly to the office.

Within minutes we were weaving through the morning traffic toward the industrial outskirts of town, saying little, hoping this was only a nightmare, broken and dispirited by radio reports of the carnage and destruction.

When we got within a few yards of the office, we were stopped. The army had set up a roadblock, securing the area where the only people who wanted to get in were the employees of the paper it had not protected before.

"You can't go in; it's closed off," a soldier said, adopting an authoritative tone. "Only the owners can go in."

That was just fine, said Marisol Cano, one of the younger members of the family who has published the newspaper for a century. Diminutive but tough, she held her identification card in the air to let him know who she was.

The soldier paid no attention.

"It's incredible," she screamed, tears of rage welling in her eyes. "For a week we were asking for protection without anybody listening and now, after the fact, without any reason at all, after it's all over and done with, they won't let us go in."

Her tone was so explosive that the soldier seemed to shrink back. He made no protest as we crossed police lines.

Then it all became real. As we moved toward the building, we saw that everything was wrecked. Across the street, a cement plant was little more than a smoldering skeleton. The facade of the customs house on the corner was ripped away.

And then we stopped at the littered hulk of our newspaper, cement and bricks all around, a nightmarish vision of what was once a modern, well-kept enclave. I remember how the production chief came stumbling out of the place, wided-eyed, to warn us.

"Prepare yourselves," he said. "When they called me, they said that there was just some broken glass. But my office is gone; there's nothing left."

I got my bearings by noticing the pieces of a bust of Don Luis Gabriel Cano, who founded the newspaper in 1889. This was what was left of the front entrance. I climbed a staircase filled with debris and blood. As I walked through the building, through the groans and dust, the way darkened, I found that the ceiling was gone and all was in ruins, with the wounded still lying on the blood-splattered floors.

The roof had been blown off, and the main press machinery

was covered with shards of glass and pieces of the ceiling. There was a penetrating cold throughout.

One worker, severely wounded by a piece of glass that had pierced his forehead, sat on the floor; a messenger who had been trapped in a closet was found close to death. The scene looked like a bombed battlefield.

Outside the building, I wandered toward the site of the blast—the ruins of what had been a gas station—following a trail past security guards and groups of foreign reporters. A bomb that had been concealed in a truck with about 275 pounds of dynamite had dug a deep crater. There was a safety device on the gasoline storage tanks at the gas station, scant inches below the ground. Had the tanks blown up, half the industrial district of Bogotá would have gone with it.

It was Carlos Junca, the news editor on duty that night, who first noticed the truck and called the police. "We'd like you to check it out," he told a local precinct officer after seeing the truck pull up in front of our lightly guarded building.

The police called back—at least they did that much. And fast, too. "No problem, nothing at all," whoever it was at the police station told him. "They have an electrical problem and got stuck. We'll give them a push. Nothing to worry about."

Junca wasn't satisfied with this explanation because he had noticed that the headlights on the truck were still on. He didn't need to be much of a detective to realize that something was wrong. But he still had to put out the final edition, so he put his suspicions on hold.

The streets were quiet, and there was a mountain chill in the air when Carlos left the office late that night in his old Renault sedan. As usual, the city was deserted at that time of night, and only the imposing mountains that encircle it were witness to the tension that was all around. Carlos had agreed to meet some friends at a salsa bar. He wanted to hit the dance floor and drink rum, hoping he could dissolve the strain of recent days. Since Luis Carlos Galán's death two weeks earlier, Bogotá was like a city laid siege by an enemy one could not see, but who lurked undetected, plotting his nighttime attacks. People locked themselves inside their houses to hear the bombs going off from the safety of their homes.

When Junca rounded the corner on Sixty-eighth Street after

leaving the building, he saw the truck once more. But after rerunning his conversation with the police over in his mind, he again brushed off his suspicions and headed toward the Café Libros.

The morning was clear. At about the time Carlos was dragging himself home downtown, when the sun begins to cast its morning shadows and the mist weaves in and out of the three lines of mountains that slice the Bogotá plain, the industrial district around the newspaper was waking up. It was Saturday, but people were beginning to stir, buses were picking up passengers, and the streets were getting more crowded.

The watchman at the newspaper office spent the night as he always did, relaxing and listening to the radio. At first light, he saw four husky men get out of the truck, go across the street to have coffee at one of the many breakfast stands along the avenue, and then return to the truck.

The men then pushed the truck to the front gate of the newspaper. The idea, they told the watchman, was to work on the engine in the parking lot, so they wouldn't block traffic.

"No way, you can't come in," he told them.

So the men pushed the truck next door to the gas station, parking it less than fifty feet from the side of our building.

Nearby, people were lining up on the sidewalk to catch one of the many buses that traversed the avenue. The buses were stuffed to overflowing with people hanging out of the doors for dear life. These were some of the first victims of the bomb blast.

As I stood in front of the crater, I realized that it could have been worse. If the bomb had exploded half an hour later, the kindergarten for employees' families would have been open. Its little classrooms in back of the newspaper had been ripped apart; miraculously, the only thing that was still intact back there was the altar to the Virgin. I felt some sense of relief then, because I knew at least for this moment, nothing more could happen to us. The previous week had been infernal. Since the president had issued his wartime measures, the bombardment had begun in Medellín and was slowly extending to all the cities of the country. And we had received a communiqué from the drug bosses declaring "total war" on the oligarchy and on all those who opposed them.

The day that our newspaper was destroyed, bombs exploded at the offices of both the Conservative and New Liberal parties in Medellín, killing one person. In addition, three bombs blew up the branches of the Cafetero, State, and Commerce banks in Medellín.

Three *fincas* (country estates)—belonging to August Lopez, the president of Bavaria, the nation's largest brewery; Edgar Gutierrez Castro, an ex-interior minister; and Ignacio Velez Escobar, president of the Conservative party in Antioquia—were set on fire. Two explosive devices, each with forty pounds of explosives, were found and deactivated at the Medellín bureaus of the nation's two principal radio networks, Caracol and RCN. There were terrorist attacks against popular restaurants in Medellín, Bello, and Itagüí as well. According to DAS, the Extraditables planned to kidnap ten notable public and private figures in Antioquia state that week, with the aim of trading them for prisoners held for extradition, and to attack the Rionegro airport. Threats on commerce in Medellín were also on the increase.

In Bogotá, "the war," as people were calling it, was less visible. Nevertheless, the attacks had been aimed primarily at the financial sector. There also had been an attack on the Institute for Nuclear Studies.

So with all these attacks, we had actually considered the possibility of a bombing at the newspaper. Information had come to the newsroom that the plan was to bomb *El Espectador* in broad daylight, when twelve hundred employees would be working. As I recall, although we figured that the drug dealers were planning something, we resisted the notion that an attack of such dimension would take place. The feeling of anticipation was so strong, in fact, that all week I had been unable to write my column. Juan Pablo Ferro, the news editor, felt the same way. Luis Gabriel Cano, who had stepped in to fill the role of patriarch upon his brother's murder, was the voice of reason and composure throughout this period. Nevertheless, fearing the worst, he had called the local military commander that week to ask that the inadequate security measures at the newspaper be reinforced. His calls were not heeded. Meanwhile, he had tried in vain to renew the building's insurance. No insurer was prepared to issue a policy.

I had met with General Maza Márquez the previous Wednesday to discuss the anticipated extradition of the first Colombian to the United States since President Barco had imposed the new measures. A strong reprisal by the drug dealers was sure to follow.

"Tell the Canos to go home early and that they shouldn't be going out," the general had said. "We're preparing at this very moment to extradite someone on a DEA plane."

I asked him specifically about the possibility of an attack on the newspaper. "Look, María Jimena," he said. "I see this as a fight between the drug dealers and the government."

That morning, the cold reality was evident. Maza Márquez had been wrong.

As I looked around, other reporters and employees began to arrive. We were told that amazingly no one had been killed, although seventy-eight people had been injured, some seriously. Armed with brooms, we began to sweep away the debris as if brooms could eliminate the destruction around us. We attacked the mess with a restless energy after our days of stupor. As we swept, foreign reporters arrived, asking questions and taking photographs. In the pressroom, the workers meticulously began pulling shards of glass out of the machinery to see what could be salvaged.

Suddenly I saw Fernando Cano walk in. His arrival was unexpected, to say the least, because he and his older brother, Juan Guillermo, had been forced to leave the country clandestinely. For the past year they had been facing a barrage of death threats while we published a series of stories about paramilitary death squads and their links with the drug dealers. These stories led in turn to revelations about the Israeli trainers who were arming and providing assistance to the drug militias.

Following the death of Guillermo Cano and the initial reaction of solidarity among journalists, there had been a retreat. Only *El Espectador* and *Semana* were producing significant investigative pieces about the drug Mafia. The death threats became frequent. There were calls to the Canos' private phone numbers at home, even though both brothers were changing telephone numbers frequently.

"If you keep on writing those stories, we'll kill one of your daughters," one caller told Fernando when he answered his home phone one day. Juan Guillermo was also threatened and fled the country first, thinking that things might calm down after his departure. But the threats to Fernando got worse and worse, and he was forced to leave as well. The absence of both brothers disrupted the newspaper, and Juan Pablo Ferro and I were faced with the difficult task of trying to keep things together. We couldn't bear another loss.

The Cano brothers took up exile in Spain. But reports of the bombings and of the general situation back in Colombia looked so bad that after one year, Fernando couldn't stand being away any longer. What we didn't know was that Fernando had gotten back the night before, planning to surprise us on Saturday morning. The surprise we had waiting for him was far greater. As Fernando entered the wrecked newsroom, I looked at his young, hunched-over frame. It was as if I could picture a gallery of all the people that the newspaper had lost in this unequal battle we had waged against the drug traffickers: his father, Guillermo Cano, murdered; six reporters killed; and the newspaper's attorney, Hector Giraldo, who worked on the assassination of Guillermo, also murdered, two months before the newspaper had been bombed.

How our lives had changed!

I could imagine that Fernando had the same thoughts. His sense of humor and his unaffected manner were gone. Beaten down, his face had lost that refreshing openness that I had seen since we had been together in school.

We did not speak; he did not even offer one of those bad jokes he would make to remind us of his mastery of gallows humor. There was only a strong, warm embrace; the tears said it all.

The Cano family was under constant threat of death, forced to travel to and from work with an armed escort and to have their children escorted to school by bodyguards. All the while, there were the telephone death threats, warning that the children would be killed, that they themselves would be the next to fall under fire.

But the Cano brothers seemed to take all the threats as a burden they had borne and would always have to bear. Since the newspaper's founding in Medellín a century earlier, they had paid for their independence—their grandfather imprisoned, their newspaper fire-bombed, their father assassinated. Neither Fernando nor Juan Guillermo would stop because of the threats, which had become part and parcel of publishing *El Espectador*.

At my side was Camilo Cano, Fernando and Juan Guillermo's younger brother, warmly embracing his mother, Ana Maria. Camilo, twenty-two at the time of his father's death, was studying international relations at the university, but had decided, despite his mother's misgivings, to take up journalism. Ana Maria was a native of the Spanish province of Cataluña. Her family had emigrated to Colombia to flee the Franco dictatorship. If anyone knew violence and exile, it was she. But how could she have imagined the destiny that would befall her in Colombia? Yet there she was, a widow, weeping on the shoulder of her son Camilo, knowing that he too might be killed one day. Her gaze was fixed on some distant point; she was the image of steadfastness and resolve.

That was when the indignation descended upon us. It was a strange sort of energy that sought to salvage everything possible from the ruins. There had been no phone calls to anyone—not one word—yet workers, reporters, and the managers had all come to the office. It was as if this wrecked building had become a refuge from our fears.

There amid the ruins we realized that the drug dealers feared us and what we stood for. Although the building was destroyed, the drug dealers could not stop what we were doing. Our anger gave birth to a commitment to keep fighting, to keep writing about these men, to keep publishing what frightened them so much.

We found our determination in the voice of our wizened senior editor, José Salgar, who called out, *"Seguimos adelante"* ("We will carry on"). It was a simple phrase, yet it became the theme of the day.

Reporters and other workers began arriving, and we found strength to put out a newspaper in which we journalists were the news. We put together a makeshift newsroom. The pressmen came along and said that they could run the machines if we would supply the words. It was a modest edition, the newspaper that *El Espectador* published on Sunday. But it came from the heart, from the gut. At the top, there was a banner headline, taking the theme that old Salgar had called out amidst the debris, "Seguimos adelante."

For the first time in a week both my colleagues and I found we were able to write, as if we had awakened from an infernal slumber. And as we wrote, we saw that we had all changed drastically. Journalism was no longer a civil right but an act fraught with danger. At 4 P.M. the newspaper was evacuated. For security reasons, a security cordon, patrolled to its last-minute detail by army patrols, surrounded the wreckage. This was the last sight I saw as I left the office that afternoon. For better or for worse, we learned to write from the trenches.

"The day that *El Espectador* decided to publish after being the victim of such a bomb attack was a day and decision that would change the concept of what journalism in Colombia is all about," said Gabriel García Márquez in a conversation with me some time later.

Two weeks later the newspaper's bureau manager and circulation director in Medellín were murdered as they went home for lunch. The bureau received a message at that time: "We don't want this newspaper on the street in Medellín." Then a bust of Guillermo Cano that had been placed in his memory in a Medellín square was blown up by the Extraditables. For about a month, despite the threats, some people were still willing to accept the risk of selling *El Espectador,* but they needed military escorts to do so. Such was the state of freedom of expression: a newspaper that had to be sold from behind military lines. The situation became untenable. The newspaper decided to suspend circulation in Medellín and close its offices there. In August 1990, a year later, the newspaper returned to the streets.

But even then *El Espectador* had become an underground newspaper. There had been so many threats against the reporters and salespeople at the Medellín office that *El Espectador's* official presence had assumed a radically different profile. Reporters worked anonymously from their homes. No one went to the bureau office.

Newspaper vendors continued to receive warnings from the drug traffickers: Sell *El Espectador* at your own peril. Some newsstands continued to sell the newspaper, which often came into town from the airport under armed guard. They would hide copies under the counter, offering to sell them to regular customers or those who seemed safely removed from the drug wars.

And *El Espectador* was nowhere to be seen in the suburb of Envigado, the birthplace of Pablo Escobar, where he was later imprisoned until his escape in 1992.

Four months of all-out war against the drug dealers were beginning to take their toll. Bogotá seemed like a bombed-out city. Although the economic losses were incalculable, the purported "war on the oligarchy" declared by the Extraditables had affected people from the middle and lower classes the most; they had been the principal victims of the bombings and terrorist attacks. In the barrios south of Bogotá there was anger: "One of the bombs that blew up in Quirigua destroyed my house, and now, another bomb has blown up my stand. I don't know why innocent people have to pay so high a price for a war we have nothing to do with," one man told a television reporter.

In the affluent suburbs, especially around Eighty-second Street, a Bohemian district that was the equivalent of New York's SoHo, the salsa clubs and restaurants were empty. In this area, usually a hangout for teenagers who attended the best private schools, one could find clutches of Colombian and foreign reporters circling the streets in search of news. The cantinas were not empty, although fewer people went out on the streets. The atmosphere was charged in anticipation of the sudden danger lurking everywhere. Army units patrolled the streets; the people who ventured out to dine or drink with friends did so daringly, with the feeling that anything might happen, that at any second a bomb or the sound of gunfire might pierce the silent chill.

A friend of mine who worked at a clothing store told me a rumor she had heard. "They say that Pablo Escobar and the Mexican are planning an attack on Eighty-second Street to retaliate for so many sicarios having been killed in Bogotá and Medellín. They say they want the rich people to know what it's like to have one of their children killed."

But the stronger rumor, coming in several different versions, was that a luxury car had run over a man in the Calera district and had left him there to die. The dead person, so the rumor went, was Rodriguez Gacha's son, and the Mexican had decided to take his revenge by setting off a bomb in a discotheque on Eighty-second Street so he could kill some rich kids. There was no indication that this was really so but such was the atmosphere; at private schools, bomb scares were regularly emptying out classrooms all over town. Some parents reported that their children had come home crying, saying they had been told the Mexican was killing little children in shopping centers and plucking their eyes out.

The mass paranoia even struck the newspaper; we took every type of emergency call conceivable, and it naturally took an emotional toll on us as well.

"Hello, I'm calling because I heard that the Mexican has poisoned the Bogotá water supply. Is it true?" asked one caller.

"Well, I'm not sure whether he was the one who did it, but the Bogotá water supply has been poisoned for a long time now," Juan Pablo Ferro answered with a kind of gallows humor. Actually, he was telling the truth. Bogotá's water comes from the Bogotá river, which for some time has been undrinkable because of the sewage and chemical waste that turned it into a cesspool.

But it was not all paranoia and wild imagination. The police found and took away a dynamite pack that had been hidden near the door of a school attended by Barco's grandchildren. Thanks to an anonymous phone call to a security guard, a bomb was also found before it could blow up the offices of *El Tiempo*. And three weeks after the attack at *El Espectador,* a terrorist bomb destroyed the Santander regional newspaper *Vanguardia Liberal*; a telephone caller said the Extraditables took credit for the attack.

Everyone went to sleep with the fear of being awakened by the sound of a bomb going off. The explosions bounced off the mountains, and their impact made the windows in my apartment, located at the foot of the mountains, vibrate. But the sound was like a short, echoless thud.

Once again we were receiving death threats on the telephone. Many of my friends, like Enrique Santos Calderón, had to leave the country for a while. The same source who had contacted me to propose a conversation with the Ochoas in 1986, after the assassination of Guillermo Cano, had sent word to Enrique that "Escobar wants to knock you off. He doesn't like the way you're writing." Immediately, Enrique decided to leave the country surreptitiously, and he stayed away for about a month. Something similar had happened to Felipe Lopez, the director of the magazine *Semana,* a weekly whose reporting of charges about political alliances with the drug bosses had served to uncover the hitherto unknown dimensions of the cocaine business. Felipe was a Colombian dauphin—crown prince, that is, the son of ex-president Alfonso Lopez Michelsen. As such he was a member of one of the preeminent families of the Liberal party.

Trim and well dressed, Felipe was so tall that we joked about how could he know anyone tall enough to notice that he was going bald. Felipe, who had a degree in business administration from Harvard, had learned about American journalism close up. He was pragmatic and sharp in his analysis of events; under his tutelage *Semana* had become the image of skillful, profound journalism. He was meticulous in his work; he did all the backup checking on the reliability of sources and their stories; he was the publisher, but he had his hand in the investigations being carried out. His insistence on doing drug stories had made *Semana* the center for the best information about what was going on. The magazine published profiles on the drug dealers, both the well-known figures and those who were unheard of, and exclusive stories about the links among the drug bosses, the army, and the politicians. And it reported contacts between the drug dealers and the government. It even went to the extent of producing a rap sheet on Pablo Escobar that exposed all the assassinations for which the Colombian judiciary held Escobar responsible. In the past five years, 70 percent of the front covers of *Semana* were related to drug dealing. No Colombian publication had ever devoted so much space to the subject, not even *El Espectador*.

Felipe maintained that his insistence on publishing drug stories was just good business, that he worked the way he did just to sell magazines. But the fact was that *Semana* was a prime example of how good journalism could be financially successful without killing the journalists.

Semana's formula for reporting on the drug trade was to tell the entire story without taking a position on extradition. "We never took sides; we only registered what was taking place," Felipe explained. The magazine presented the drug dealers as criminals but showed the weakness of the Colombian justice system in failing to produce sufficient proof to convict them. It would send its correspondents to write stories about drug murders in Medellín, something that *El Espectador* and other publications rarely did because of security concerns. But it always referred to Escobar in dispassionate, at times almost novelesque, terms, portraying him as an modern-day version of Robin Hood. Escobar liked the manner in which *Semana* dealt with his personality.

This policy on reporting gave *Semana* a security trump card to uncover the drug business that *El Espectador* never had. Nevertheless, *Semana*'s formula was not foolproof, and its reporters also began to receive threats. One of the drug bosses had gone as far as to say, "In reality, our enemy is not *El Espectador*. It is *Semana* magazine." The magazine's investigations editor had to flee the country when rumors spread that Escobar had issued an execution order against him. And Felipe left the country for a while after a source passed along the information that he was to be a kidnapping target.

Many journalists changed phone numbers frequently to cut back on the amount of threatening calls. I did not think that changing phone numbers was a good idea, primarily on journalistic grounds, because it seemed to keep away friends more than enemies. Once when I switched numbers, the phone didn't ring for several days. When it finally rang, I answered quickly, only to hear a voice tell me: "Watch out, because we don't like what you're writing."

The following day one of my neighbors stopped by. "María Jimena, my bodyguards say that all week they have been noticing guys driving up in cars and motorcycles asking if 'that reporter' lives here," he told me nervously. "I think you're being followed; why don't you get away for a while?"

That night I felt an eerie sensation of fear such as I had never felt, a feeling that surrounded me with a deep sense of being alone, with fear in the pit of my stomach. I was frightened for what might happen to my mother and to Sylvia. I called them and asked them not to go outside and to keep their guard up. I remembered that about a week earlier, a friend who had some contact with the Medellín cartel had called to tell me that my name had come up in a conversation with Pablo Escobar. Escobar had mentioned that he saw me on a talk show on CNN and was impressed that I had criticized the Bush administration's drug policies. Escobar "thinks you have an interesting point of view," the informant told me. "He wants to talk to General Maza Márquez. And he thinks that since you know the general, you can let Maza Márquez know."

I thought about it and decided not to get involved as a conduit for this sort of message. "Listen, you know what else Escobar says?" the contact asked. "He says that if people don't start listening to him, this country is going to see a lot more violence than there's been already."

I slept in the hallway that night instead of my bedroom, recalling the manual on security precautions we had been given by Colombian intelligence agents. The instructions said that sleeping in the hall or in a room without windows is a good safety measure since glass and debris from a bomb explosion are less likely to penetrate. The following day I moved quietly to the home of one of my cousins. Within a week I was back at work, but left the apartment only to go back and forth to the office every day, always at a different time and always taking a new route, accompanied by bodyguards in both directions. I stayed away from parties and get-togethers.

One of the few times I went out was when Juan Guillermo Cano, my day editor, told me that we had been invited by DAS to take a course on security and the use of handguns.

I thought it was a joke. Us, doing target practice? Everyone was serious. The following Saturday, several members of the Cano family, José Salgar, and I went to the DAS training school to be instructed on how to fire a revolver, among other things. It wasn't the first time I had held a weapon. When I was in the mountains with M-19, Jaime Bateman had given me an Uzi for my "protection," saying that an army attack was imminent and they wouldn't be asking who were the reporters and who were the guerrillas. The attack never occurred. But I started to notice that the guerrillas felt a kind of libidinous attraction to their weapons, fondling them as they would a lover, almost in ecstasy at the touch.

My father used to carry an old Smith and Wesson revolver wherever he went, although I never saw him use it. He had it ever since the time of La Violencia, when he had been chosen as a councilman in a Liberal party town that was under siege by armed Conservative groups. Once, robbers actually used that gun against me. One night, about six months before the bomb attack at my house, I heard the sudden noise of people breaking in and thought that the right-wing militias were coming to kill me. I could hardly believe the sense of relief I felt when I saw the thieves surround me. They held the Smith and Wesson at me and rubbed it up and down my body as they tied me up.

"This is a robbery," they shouted, but my reaction must have been a big surprise. I was happy.

"A robbery? Take whatever you want."

So much for my father's gun.

Neither Fernando, Juan Guillermo, nor Salgar had ever loaded a pistol or even seen a Berretta before. Nevertheless, the sense of panic all around was so great that they were ready to learn. Here they were, dutifully taking weapons training, surrounded by their bodyguards. Something was wrong. It was absurd to think that we would be using guns to protect ourselves. The very idea gave me a chill—the same fear I had felt when I was given the Uzi in the guerrilla camp; then, I accepted the gun, though my principles told me not to because I was afraid of dying in a gun battle. The instructor of the course, an army colonel dressed in black, gave us a security briefing, which, above all, showed how confused the authorities were in dealing with the drug traffickers.

"The terrorist-Communist enemy always takes advantage of the best weapon of all, the element of surprise," he kept repeating insistently. Afterward, he showed a U.S. videotape about security precautions, which presented several ways to evade an attack by "Communist terrorists." A simple U-turn, we were told, can save your life if you see the road ahead blocked; you could also turn off the highway in another direction. I wasn't convinced which was more dangerous, the supposed attack or the U-turn, especially since the cars in Colombia are manual-shift cars with small engines that can't maneuver too easily—not the fancy American models shown on the tape. None of the examples given on the tape dealt with the most virulent type of attack we were likely to face—sicarios riding motorcycles. And the term *drug trafficker* never came up in the conversation. The insistence that we needed to learn to defend ourselves from Communist terrorism was so great that I whispered to Fernando Cano, "I guess the colonel hasn't heard about perestroika."

"Maybe it's not so much a course in personal security as a course in national security," Fernando joked.

Forced to travel about with bodyguards and to change houses and telephone numbers frequently, I decided to push up a trip I had planned to the United States, where I had been invited to attend a journalism conference. I got to El Dorado airport on the outskirts of Bogotá early on the morning of December 10 for a flight to New York. Shortly after I arrived, I was casually looking out the window in the international wing when I saw something so sudden, so beyond horror, that the image of it will never go away. A jet that had just taken off blew up in midair. I saw pieces of flaming metal fall out of the sky.

It was an Avianca domestic flight, a shuttle between Bogotá and Cali. Many of the family members of those on board were still at the airport, and their screams of horror and cries of grief reverberated throughout the building. None of the 120 people on the plane, most of them young executives going to Cali on business, survived.

RODRIGUEZ GACHA

On December 15, 1989, four months after the assassination of Galán and during a wave of terrorism never before seen in Colombia—during which more than fifteen hundred Colombians had been murdered—the news was broadcast around the world that José Gonzalo Rodriguez Gacha, the Mexican, and his son Fredy, had been killed in a battle with Colombian police. That morning I was being interviewed at the office by the BBC, which was preparing a documentary about *El Espectador*. Upon hearing the news, I catapulted out of the interview and went running into the newsroom. Everyone was crowding around radios.

Our first reaction was fear—then uncertainty about the reprisals that this killing might unleash. And what I saw in the newsroom was reflected to a large extent throughout the country as the news got around. "I know that what I'm about to say is not very Christian, but I'm happy that Gacha is dead," said one editor. "Finally someone's been killed on their side, not a judge, a minister, or a reporter," said another.

I was remembering the words the Mexican used in his interview with Hernando Corral: "If they get me, I'll go down fighting," he had said in his distinctive, rough-hewn way. Although Rodriguez Gacha had turned Colombia into a bloody battlefield and his death produced a great feeling of relief, there was still something disquieting about his death: Right up to the final battle, everything had followed the course he had set; he had decided to become an outlaw, and he died on his own terms.

The jolting news was followed by a police news conference at which officials began to offer a closely managed account of what had taken place. According to the version provided by DAS and the national police, the "successful operation had culminated in the killing of the Mexican," thus dismantling a terrorist plot to destabilize the country further. Rodriguez Gacha, Fredy, and six men assigned to protect them had been ferreted out, thanks to a police dragnet—the Mexican had been found on a ranch in Tolú, his headquarters on the Caribbean coast. According to General Maza Márquez, "the Mexican was there celebrating his last terror attack on DAS headquarters, in which seventy Colombians were killed." In the ensuing siege, the drug traffickers had returned fire with high-powered weapons. Fredy was the first to die in the cross fire—a bullet from above had hit him in the head. Three of the bodyguards were also killed. According to Maza Márquez, Rodriguez Gacha had left Fredy behind as bait, while he tried to effect a desperate escape. He and two bodyguards raced off in a truck, but crashed in a nearby banana plantation under heavy fire. Rodriguez Gacha then got out of the truck, seized a weapon, and began firing. He was killed in the ensuing exchange of gunfire with the police.

Swiftly, however, contradictions began to surround the various versions of how Rodriguez Gacha was hunted down and killed. First DAS had said there was one police helicopter. When Colombian reporters got to the scene the night of the firefight, frightened farmers consistently spoke of two helicopters.

The official versions themselves were also contradictory. While Maza Márquez had said that Gacha was in Tolú to celebrate a terrorist victory, he would later change his story: Rodriguez Gacha had been tracked down in Cartagena, far to the north, where he was working on details of an important cocaine deal to the United States. According to this version, the Mexican had been ordering large quantities of food from his favorite restaurant in Cartagena. Word that he was in town had been passed to a DAS agent. The Elite Corps and DAS began tracking him, all the time knowing that he had infiltrated the security forces and had informants everywhere.

Maza Márquez therefore devised a diversionary tactic, sending two units to Barranquilla, farther east, to make it look as though the police were off target and searching for a cocaine shipment somewhere else. Rodriguez Gacha bought the story when an informant told him about the Barranquilla operation, but not for long. The truth came out later that night, Maza Márquez said in a subsequent interview. "At that moment he decided to flee; he took refuge near the Pegasus port in Cartagena and quickly fled on a cigarette boat with his son Fredy and the bodyguards."

Once Rodriguez Gacha managed to escape, at around 11 P.M., the police lost his trail. It looked like the operation would fail. For eight hours that night, Maza Márquez said, he had no more contact with police units in Cartagena. It was only at 11 A.M. the next morning when he was advised that Rodriguez Gacha had been killed in Tolú. "We took down Gacha," he was told.

Later the general said that a single police official, Colonel Vélez (not his real name), commanding a police helicopter and a launch, had decided not to give up the chase. On his own and out of contact with headquarters, he and his men set out before dawn and tracked Rodriguez Gacha all the way down the Caribbean coast to Tolú, near where he was supposed to have his headquarters at Puerto Escondido. Suddenly, and by chance, they found a speedboat whose occupants admitted that they had transported Rodriguez Gacha, Fredy, and the bodyguards.

Rodriguez Gacha was chief of the paramilitary groups in Colombia and had an army of assassins at his disposal throughout the country. He was capable of unleashing terrorist acts on a scale that had never been seen in Colombia. Yet police said that he had been hunted down and killed by a police major with a handful of men operating one helicopter and a police boat. Militarily it was a victory of epic, almost miraculous, proportions.

Although miracles do happen in Colombia, in this case celestial forces were not the only ones accompanying the Elite Corps on its mission. Immediately after Rodriguez Gacha was killed, there were strong indications that U.S. special operations teams had played a role.

At about the same time that Maza Márquez was informed of Rodriguez Gacha's death, a lone figure was stripping off his green jungle fatigues at a safe house somewhere in Bogotá. He wore the insignia of no nation and no identification of any kind. I will call him Dave Barretta, not his real name, but it doesn't matter—no one knows his real name. His personnel records and his active service file were expunged of most of his deeds in service to the United States. He was the elite of the elite U.S. Special Forces, a veteran of the Vietnam War, as well as of operations in Central America. He was a West Point graduate, forty-two years old, and he was moving slowly. The excitement was there, but the bones were aching, and perhaps, he confessed, it was just as well that this was the end of the road. He had just come back from Tolú and when word came back that Rodriguez Gacha was dead, Dave would be out of a job. Barretta's mission had been to seize Rodriguez Gacha and bring him back to the United States to face drug charges—not to kill him. He had accompanied the Colombian Elite Corps, some of whom he had trained, in the chase after Rodriguez Gacha. When they caught Rodriguez Gacha at Tolú, the helicopters had come under ground fire. Barretta gave the order to fire, and the Colombian Elite Corps shot all drug dealers dead.

The problem was that he was supposed to bring the man back alive. Given the presidential ban on foreign assassinations, Dave was sure he was through. The first indications up the chain of command made it seem like he was right. However, things quickly began to turn in Dave's favor.

Public reaction to Rodriguez Gacha's death was overwhelmingly positive. President Bush quickly sent a letter to President Barco, congratulating him on his steadfastness in fighting the drug traffickers. The following day Colombians saw the grim evidence firsthand. Television pictures showed a body easily identified as Rodriguez Gacha lying on the ground with the bodies of Fredy and his aides, their bodies intact and sewn up as if they had undergone a quick autopsy.

The image of the Colombian police dragnet and a great victory for the national psyche saved Dave's job. He went back to the United States, was praised for the operation, and continued on the job, sometimes working as an army operative and sometimes working for the Central Intelligence Agency or other clandestine organizations in the U.S. government.

Dave told more than one person about his mission. "He was proud of what he had done, although he hadn't planned on killing Rodriguez Gacha," said one veteran investigator, who was at the American embassy when Barretta came back from Tolú. "What else could he do when he came under fire? They had to shoot back."

After Dave's acknowledgment we at *El Espectador* confirmed the U.S. role in Rodriguez Gacha's death with other sources.

Three other sources in the Pentagon and the U.S. Congress confirmed that at least three members of the U.S. military participated in the operational area. A senate aide who saw a top-secret report on the operation told us that a handful of special operations troops participated along with a large contingent of Colombians, but that the role of the United States had been preeminent. A U.S. intelligence source went as far as to say that the Colombian police presence had been a facade. "Officially we say that the Colombians did it. But the truth is that it was us."

The mission had been designed with what is known in the trade as full deniability: U.S. officials would be able to deny knowing anything about the mission. Dave later joked with a friend: "If you try to say that I was there on the operation, I can prove that on that day I was sleeping with your sister."

He said that the personnel for this operation were specially chosen, that they operated under deep cover, sometimes as members of the active military and sometimes temporarily transferring back to civilian life.

Congressional intelligence committees were actually notified of the joint mission to capture Rodriguez Gacha via a top-secret presidential finding, in which the mission was characterized as an operation in the national interest, according to the congressional sources. Four American operatives of Hispanic origin were designated to operate the electronic gear packed into two helicopters that were receiving tracking information from a satellite that could detect the drug dealer from above. At least one of the helicopters belonged to the U.S. Southern Command. The Colombians handled the firepower.

"Troops in Colombia? No. That's the entire answer," President Bush told *Newsday*, which prepared an extensive report on the killing of Rodriguez Gacha. When I asked General Maza Márquez the same question, he laughed and, with a cynicism that was uncharacteristic of him, repeated verbatim his version of events with Major Vélez and one helicopter.

"North American troops? We're the ones who know the turf. They have nothing to teach us. On the contrary, we could teach them a thing or two."

By the way, he said, the DEA had promised a reward to the seventeen members of the Elite Corps who participated in the operation. But we haven't seen the money. . . . We gave them a reward ourselves of a million and a half pesos [about $3,000].

It was not only Maza Márquez who was receiving idle promises from the United States, which was pledging a lot more than it was delivering. After the attack on DAS headquarters, FBI agents went to inspect the wreckage, promising help with reconstruction. "The building was completely remodeled with Colombian money, and we never heard anything from the FBI," Maza Márquez told me.

"You want to know the only thing that DAS has received from the $65 million the United States promised Colombia in military aid?" Maza Márquez went on: ". . . a bus and a few signal machines to intercept radio messages."

When the United States promised bulletproof vests for judges, it sent impossibly heavy flak jackets instead. When it promised aircraft, it sent planes for the army guerrilla effort and little help for the police drug operations. And often, when U.S. agents showed up on Colombian special operations, things went badly awry. Consider what happened when the U.S. Marshals Service sent a secret contingent of agents in 1989. Its presence might never had been known had it not been for an incident that caused an uproar in the Colombian government. Marshals who were apparently trained in capturing criminals overseas and bringing them back to the United States were supposed to target one of the drug bosses and bring him back for trial. The cartel had other ideas. When the U.S. operatives returned home, they brought no criminals but something better instead—a "great find"—a video-tape on which the wife of a supposed member of Rodriguez Gacha's gang charged that General Maza Márquez was getting payoff money from the Mexican.

The Americans knew nothing about Colombian intrigue, nor did they know who Maza Márquez was or that the whole story was nothing more than a con job by the cartel to foil the general in his almost personal war with Rodriguez Gacha. The U.S. Marshals Service took the word of the woman on the videotape as the truth and dispatched a report to the State Department. When President Barco traveled to New York for the U.N. General Assembly session that fall, he was solemnly advised of the "charges" being levied against Maza Márquez.

The general was furious, criticizing the Americans derisively. "While the Mexican says that I'm being paid by the Cali cartel, the U.S. Marshals say that I'm paid by him. . . . Those guys are really nuts," he said. The chargé d'affaires at the U.S. embassy,

Philip McLean, finally went to DAS headquarters to apologize directly to the general, saying the entire matter was based on a misunderstanding.

The Rodriguez Gacha operation fit in perfectly with the United States' approach to the drug wars. As early as August 1986, President Reagan had sent the 193d Infantry Battalion, stationed in Panama, to Bolivia, along with six Black Hawk helicopters. The mission of the operation, known as Operation Blast Furnace, was to locate and destroy coca-paste laboratories and illicit coca plantations in the Beni region. Three months earlier, Reagan had issued Executive Directive 221, declaring that drug trafficking was a threat to national security. The measure was interpreted as allowing the expansion of the U.S. military role in the drug war.

In 1988, a presidential election year in the United States, narcotics was emerging as an issue with which the American public was most concerned. A poll conducted by the *New York Times* and CBS showed that 48 percent of those interviewed thought it was the most serious foreign policy concern the United States was facing. In answer to another question, 63 percent of those interviewed said that the war on drugs was more important than the war on communism. At that time, the U.S. Congress approved the 1988 drug bill, which included $15 million in aid to the Colombian armed forces, but only $5 million for the protection of judges.

In 1989, after President Bush took office and Luis Carlos Galán was assassinated, Richard Thornburgh, the U.S. attorney general, said on the NBC program "Meet the Press," that the United States should consider sending troops to Colombia if that country requested such help. It was well known that Colombia had not made and would not make such a request. On September 3, Bush's chief of staff, John Sununu, said much the same thing on the CBS program "Face the Nation." On September 5, President Bush presented his antidrug plan, pledging $76.2 million in military aid for 1990, a 900 percent increase over all the military aid sent to Colombia in the previous decade. Within a week, the United States sent the first contingent of military personnel to Colombia—ten trainers assigned to provide training in the use of the helicopters being sent to Colombia. The Colombian armed forces protested the arrival of the American trainers. On September 19, U.S. Secretary of Defense Richard Cheney declared that "detecting and countering the production and trafficking of illegal drugs is a high-priority national security mission" for the Pentagon. Finally, in November 1989, a U.S. Justice Department brief from the Office of Legal Counsel authorized the FBI and other federal enforcement agencies to seize drug traffickers and other fugitives without the consent of the host country.

In 1991 the United States signed an agreement with Peru to send military advisers to help fight the cocaine trade. It was also using a web of current and former CIA, Defense Intelligence Agency, and special forces operatives in its drug operations from Panama southward.

Five days after Rodriguez Gacha was killed, December 20, 1989, the United States invaded Panama, formalizing—as if there had been any doubt—the entry of the U.S. army into the war on drugs. By the end of December, when twenty thousand American troops still had failed to track Noriega down, there were strong indications in Colombia that the United States had decided to send a flotilla to patrol Colombian coastal waters, and on January 4, the aircraft carrier *John F. Kennedy* and the frigate *Virginia* set sail for Colombian international waters from their base in Norfolk, Virginia. It was a short step from a naval patrol to a naval blockade.

The Colombian government was indignant. The invasion of Panama, which shares a border with Colombia and which was Colombian territory until the dubious United States–brokered independence of 1903, had been roundly rejected in Bogotá.

"We reject all use of force," said Julio Londoño, the foreign minister, at the outset of the invasion. The position of the Barco government was not only to reject the United States' action, but to preclude any possibility that something similar could one day happen to Colombia. Of course, the situations were vastly different and there was no imaginable scenario of an invasion of Colombia, but rumors and anti-Americanism swirled about in places like Medellín and Envigado, the home of Pablo Escobar.

At the newspaper we began to receive odd phone calls. "What's the latest on the invasion," asked a woman calling from Envigado, which, she thought, would be the first to feel the wrath of U.S. war planes. In Itagüí, many people began to build barricades and to hoard food. There was talk of signing up to fight the Americans when they came.

"Wasn't there a mayor in New York who said that Medellín ought to be bombed?" a resident of Itagüí reminded me, referring to an ill-chosen remark by former New York mayor Edward I. Koch about how to halt the spread of cocaine in his city.

Gabriel Silva, the president's foreign policy adviser, found out about the flotilla on January 5, in a story published in the *Washington Post*. Alarmed, he immediately called Londoño, who also had not been informed of the naval movements. Silva considered the action a serious move by the Americans; together with German Montoya, the presidential chief of staff, Londoño telephoned Barco, who was out of Bogotá at the time.

"We have to send the toughest protest possible to the United States," Barco told them, incensed. Within minutes Philip McLean was summoned to Nariño palace and was apprised of the Colombian protest:

"The Colombian government considers this to be an act of unilateral aggression which endangers the fight against drug trafficking. We have not given, nor shall we give authorization for the placement of American ships in Colombian international waters. If this is done, it will be considered a hostile act which places in jeopardy the cooperative fight against drug trafficking," Montoya told McLean. (McLean said privately in conversations with reporters that he also had not been informed of the naval action. He said he had angrily objected to the action in a swift call to the State Department.)

The following day the Colombian foreign minister released a communiqué denouncing the blockade, saying that "Colombia has never participated nor would it participate in any joint operation with the United States." The unilateral decision of the United States to blockade Colombian waters came from the flush of success in Panama. The Pentagon had decided to increase its presence in the region. Toward that end, the U.S. Southern Command had obtained the approval of the Colombian Naval Command in the Atlantic, even though that command had neither the authority nor the autonomy to approve such an operation.

"This tendency of United States diplomacy to seek approval of special operations via second and third parties or with substitutes is their method of avoiding having to confront the authorities they should be talking to; this is the way the Americans are scoring goals without our knowing what they're up to," said a former aide to Barco. "Maybe that's what happened in the operation that finished off Gacha . . . and we never even knew about it."

Nevertheless, this time, apparently, someone in Washington

leaked the story. By the time the flotilla got to Puerto Rico, it was recalled. The White House said that the entire operation had been a misunderstanding and that the Bush administration had never thought of imposing a blockade on Colombia. President Bush also telephoned President Barco, again saying that it all had been a mistake. "Many thanks, Mr. President, I expected nothing less of you," said Barco in a clipped, but cordial, response.

On February 15, 1990, Cartagena was gearing up to be the site of a drug summit with Barco, Bush, President Alan García of Peru, and President Jaime Paz Zamora of Bolivia. Several days earlier, an NBC report revealed that the Colombian drug bosses had bought SAM-7 hand-held missiles with the intent of attacking Bush upon his arrival. The news provoked alarm in the United States. In addition, there was a report from DAS that agents had captured Benjamin Aponte, a Medellín trafficker, with ten surface-to-air missiles; they were not SS-7s, as was charged, but home-made missiles. DAS did not release the information, attempting to avoid alarm. The type of missile wasn't significant—just the fact that missiles were being sought on the international market in Colombia, right before the arrival of four presidents in Cartagena, seemed, at the time, a threat of major proportions by the drug dealers.

The information came out a week after the summit meeting. The White House press corps protested as Washington prepared to house them in an airport hangar in Barranquilla, miles up the Caribbean coast from Cartagena. Several U.S. news reports spoke about impending Colombian terrorist plans to attack American judges working on drug cases. Bush—the representative of the world's largest drug-consuming nation—deigned to spend three hours in Cartagena. The American news media painted his appearance as an act of courage, but it was little more than a photo opportunity.

Whatever the press releases said about economic issues, the only war being fought was military. The United States pushed as hard as it could to bring the armed forces into the drug fight. In Peru and Bolivia, the pressure tactics were successful; in Colombia, the United States faced a relatively stronger civilian government and, therefore, more opposition to its militarization effort.

One key pressure tactic in all three countries was so-called certification in the war on drugs. Economic aid was conditioned on the U.S. government's perception of whether a given country was

doing enough to combat drug trafficking. Under this highly sub-
jective, highly political process, Bolivia and Peru were "decertified" several times and faced a cutoff of needed economic support.
Meanwhile, countries that were considered more strategically
located, like Turkey, Pakistan, and Mexico, slid through without
being decertified, even though they were also infested with and
corrupted by drug trafficking.

The United States constantly found ways to tie economic
agreements to its policies. It began pushing for the defoliation of
the coca crop in places where subsistence farmers had never been
given a viable alternative for survival. In Peru, as a result, President Alberto Fujimori had to sign an economic agreement with
Washington that acknowledged that the eradication of coca plants
would be a requirement for any future economic aid.

But even when the governments acceded to the pressure,
additional economic help never came. Despite the smiles and
handshakes at the Cartagena meeting, Colombia's proposal under
the Andean Trade Pact for reduced tariffs on coffee, flowers, and
other key exports apparently languished in some back room of the
U.S. Congress.

The other pressure tactic used was military—the United
States forced its military advisers upon the countries. While civilian officials were denying the presence of American troops, the
Colombian military was virulently protesting the need for any
such presence in the first place. Upon hearing news reports in
late September that the United States planned to send military
advisers to Colombia, Defense Minister Botero's reaction was
swift and succinct. "We have no need for foreign troops," he told a
news conference.

In mid-August 1990 the concern about the presence of U.S.
troops caused more than bruised sensibilities. U.S. transport planes
had brought in radar equipment under a bilateral aid agreement
pledged by the United States. But when the planes arrived at their
Colombian military destinations, Colombian troops on hand
blocked the exit of the American servicemen on board. The Colombians said that the two sides almost came to blows.

The U.S. soldiers, whose arrival hadn't been anticipated, were
assigned to take care of the radar equipment. But there was no
mention of such personnel in the treaty agreement on the aid. The
argument about the radar equipment persisted for some time.
When the Bush administration began making preparations for

the Gulf War, the gear was sent back to the United States. Colombia was no longer on the radarscope. Months later, after the Gulf War, the radar equipment was sent back, one unit going to the south of Colombia on the Peruvian border and another to the Caribbean coast. According to Silva, foreign policy adviser for both President Barco and President Gaviria, the radar installations have reduced the number of illegal drug flights, but closing Colombia's borders just meant that new routes were developed in neighboring countries.

In June 1990, about six months after the death of Rodriguez Gacha, people began to notice hundred-dollar bills floating down the Pacho river, which cuts through Pacho and the Cundinamarca valley. The forty-year-old drug boss had been buried in Pacho, near his hometown, with all the honors of a man who had been the region's most important benefactor. The residents of Pacho sat in mourning for three days and three nights. "He was very good to us," one woman told a television reporter. "Every time we had a problem he helped out. He did more for us than any politician around here ever did. Who's going to help us now?"

So when the U.S. greenbacks started appearing in the river, many believed that the generous soul of the Mexican, in repose on high, had come to their salvation once more. "It comes from up there," said one such person, gesturing to the sky, grabbing a fistful of wet American bills.

It was a miracle. There was a constant pilgrimage of the faithful to the banks of the river, fishermen angling to haul in the bills. And, of course, there were endless rumors about where the money was really coming from.

The most popular story was that Rodriguez Gacha had buried millions of dollars before his death; when the river waters rose, they flooded the hiding place and brought the bills downstream. Some said the ghost of the Mexican was patrolling the river's shores and that he was seeding the money into the waters himself. Less spiritually minded souls merely thought that Rodriguez Gacha was not really dead and that he had decided to return clandestinely and dump money into the river as his way of continuing to take care of the afflicted residents of Pacho.

People from nearby villages started coming to Pacho to take advantage of this rare phenomenon. Eventually the government took note and imposed a curfew. Within three weeks, Pacho had been placed under military control, and the army patrolled the banks of the river.

The military solution was symptomatic of President Barco's new policies. He had issued his wartime measures on August 18, 1989, and Minister of Defense Botero had pledged the army's entry into the drug war. The armed forces, formerly reluctant to get involved, were now fully engaged. The police and the army both were out on raids, seizing contraband and occupying the property of known and suspected drug traffickers. The measure was intended to put the dealers on the run, to flush them out of their hideouts; it seemed to be working.

Pacho had been the Mexican's sanctuary, but he, too, had been shaken out and was now dead. After Rodriguez Gacha died, the authorities raided two ranches in the area around Pacho—named Fredy One and Fredy Two. In addition to the large cache of arms that Klein had sent from Israel via Antigua (it was proved later that one of these weapons had been used to kill Luis Carlos Galán), they also found about $65 million, hidden in a well-camou-flaged underground vault, and eventually rounded up a total of more than $200 million. Rodriguez Gacha had buried the money in scattered, strategically located properties as an emergency stash. The residents living along the river weren't concerned with the intricacies of the drug war or the military operations, however. They knew business was still booming. All they saw was that the army showed up as soon as the money started washing down-stream. "Here everybody always knew where the Mexican was liv-ing," a local resident angrily told me. "The army has come here to keep us away from the river, so they get the money instead of us." The anger at the outside military interference increased. The mayor demanded that the army immediately get out of town.

On July 23, 1990, two officers from the Colombian Armed Forces Military College ransacked one of the vaults owned by the Mexican and fled the country with the money, one day before they were to receive a special medal from President Barco. Their haul was estimated at anywhere between $9 and $36 million. No one was talking, and the men had vanished. A military court eventu-ally found them guilty of stealing the money and expelled them from the army.

Despite the military buildup, the biggest prey still eluded all efforts to stop him. General Maza Márquez was taking every opportunity to tell reporters that the capture of Pablo Escobar was imminent. But on at least four more occasions, Escobar escaped the traps set for him by the Elite Corps. The general continued to insist that the police knew Escobar's whereabouts, that they had him pinned down and surrounded, but no arrest was made. This bravura started to work against Maza Márquez. "It was what we called the underwear theory (Escobar always managed to get away at the last minute without having time to get dressed). Maza Márquez was talking about it all the time, but nothing ever happened," one high-ranking official told me.

Adalberto, the lawyer who had represented both Rodriguez Gacha and Escobar, gave me the most plausible explanation for Escobar's ability to slip away from police and military dragnets. "If the authorities know where Pablo Escobar is, why don't they ever catch him?" I asked. He answered with a cynical smile: "Listen, half the army and the police are protecting him. The other half are trying to kill him."

More often than not, it is those who are expected to wage a war who are most interested in avoiding one. The military did not see the war on drugs as its battle. An army enhances its prestige only when it has a clear-cut chance to win; this was a no-win situation.

"Colombia is carrying the weight on its shoulders of the sins that the world blames on us and us alone. We should recognize that the balance sheet for the entire drug problem is skewed: We have the bad image, while the profits for what is an illegal business go to other countries . . . the dominant factor is money and the essence of drug dealing is economic," said General Fernando Landazabal, the first interior minister in the Betancur government.

The Colombian army always had been primarily a counterinsurgency force that had been fighting subversion for more than thirty years and considered that mission its principal challenge. In that regard, it was like other Western armies, which saw the cold war as their war. Drugs did not fit in with this narrow vision of the struggle against communism.

"The army could be more successful in the antiguerrilla struggle if it were not engaged in counternarcotics activities, which means, most of the time, performing police work," said General Rafael Samudio Molina, Barco's first minister of defense. "We are protecting judges and public buildings. All of these are police matters that distract us from our operational activities and training."

The fear of corruption in the upper echelons of the military hierarchy and specific cases like the money stolen from Pacho always figured prominently in military arguments against continued activities in the drug war. Opening such a major initiative against an unknown enemy with so much power to corrupt was, in the view of many generals, a huge risk that could destroy morale throughout the armed forces. Above all, the experience of Operation Lightning Bolt, carried out in 1978 under the Turbay government, was still fresh in everyone's memory.

Operation Lightning Bolt was the army's first major initiative in the drug war, aimed at dismantling the marijuana trade that was gaining strength in the Guajira peninsula and all along the Atlantic coast. Although the army registered record quantities of marijuana seizures, the operation fell well below expectations. Not only did the marijuana Mafia extend its crops to other parts of the country, but the military found that it needed more and more men every time it went out on an operation. Military casualties were high, with a serious demoralizing effect among the troops, who agreed with the generals on the real enemy.

Operation Lightning Bolt ended after two years, and the police took over the responsibility for the war on drugs. This relationship did not change significantly in Betancur's administration. In 1982 the antinarcotics police command was formed, charged with conducting special operations and reinforcing the police strategy in fighting the drug dealers. Despite Barco's generosity in increasing the military budget during the first three years of his administration, all but a few generals refused to enter the fray.

Nevertheless, Barco was convinced that the problem demanded military participation. He converted the issue into a personal crusade. While he praised the military in public, behind the scenes he was discreetly cleaning up military corruption.

Newspaper stories linking members of the army to the drug militias' massacres of peasants were always strenuously denied by Minister of Defense Samudio Molina. In 1986 the Barco administration began a quiet campaign to clean up the police. In 1988, thirteen hundred members of the police had been removed, including most of the police commanders along the Atlantic coast. And Barco kept going. In 1990, at the end of his regime, he made a bold and surprising announcement—the military high command was being replaced. The purge reached such levels that Barco considered naming a civilian as vice minister of defense, something that had not been done for forty years.

Part of Barco's strategy was to place more trust in DAS, General Maza Márquez's organization, which was not originally intended to be the lead agency in the war on drugs. DAS had been formed in 1950 with the idea of creating a "civilian intelligence service," separate from military intelligence and in the direct service of the president. As time went on, public safety functions became militarized in Colombia, and all the recent DAS directors had been military officers, not civilians. General Maza Márquez, named DAS chief in 1979, became the key player. DAS became the intelligence "eyes of the president." It was no exaggeration to consider the general to be at the same level of importance as the minister of defense. The prominence of DAS produced tension between Maza Márquez and the army, which was displeased with its waning influence.

While Barco pressured the military, he also courted them. Like no president before him, he went religiously to all military ceremonies. Furthermore, he went out of his way to praise the armed forces for their valuable role in "fortifying democracy" at the very moment that they were facing criticism for their ties with the drug-financed private militias. Despite steadily increasing evidence of this and other forms of corruption, Barco never spoke out in public on the subject. Every time that "the prophets of calamity"—as he referred to the news media—reported that the armed forces were trampling on human rights, he rose to their defense. "Those who wrap themselves in the flag of human rights to defame the armed forces are committing a great injustice. . . . The armed forces of Colombia have defended human life and democracy, honor, and the well-being of all with unquestionable loyalty. If some of their number are involved in excesses and abuses . . . they are traitors to the institution they serve. These isolated cases will never serve to blemish the civic tradition of the armed forces. Such cases, whomever they may be, should be punished as examples by the very institution they betray."

Like a teacher who repeats a lesson endlessly to drum it into his students, Barco talked endlessly of the democratic tradition and the commitment of the armed forces to the rule of law; he accentuated their achievements in fighting guerrilla subversion and always ended by insisting on "the vigorous presence of our armed forces if we want to neutralize other violent forces."

Barco backed up his commitment by tripling the defense budget and allowing a considerable increase in the standing forces, from 62,000 to 100,000 troops. In 1988, after the death of Attorney General Carlos Mauro Hoyos, Barco called the U.S. ambassador, Thomas MacNamara, and asked for U.S. military aid. Even Washington was taken aback by the request. Although the Bush administration was a fervent supporter of the militarization of the drug war, the U.S. Congress had blacklisted Colombia as a country not worthy of receiving military aid. (As a result, Colombia turned to Israel and became a good client for burgeoning Israeli weapons sales.) Barco previously had tried to obtain loans in the United States for weapons purchases but failed, since American banks were included in the congressional ban on weapons sales. But Ambassador MacNamara and the Pentagon lobbied Congress to approve Barco's request, and by the end of 1988, Congress had rescinded its ban on military aid. The first military purchases following the lifting of the ban were two dozen combat helicopters. They were delivered just after the death of Galán and two days after Bush announced a new $65 million military aid package to Colombia for fiscal year 1990. But the helicopters were erroneously reported in the United States as being part of Bush's new commitment to military aid for the drug war and evidence of the speed with which the U.S. government was disposed to act. In reality, it was a prior purchase and had nothing to do with new military aid.

The first shipment under the new military aid consisted of a single UH-1H helicopter sent from the U.S. antidrug operations in Peru. It arrived with a flood of publicity, MacNamara and Colombian luminaries in attendance, surrounded by a crowd of reporters. One detail not mentioned that day was that the helicopter was a reject that had to be repaired before it could fly.

In October, part of the military aid shipment promised by Bush arrived—jeeps, automobiles, flak jackets, and four Hercules C-130 transport planes. For the army, ten more UH-1H helicopters were sent. Barco assigned his aide Rafael Pardo to ensure that the shipments from the United States met military and police requirements. Apologetically, American officials explained that the fiscal year was ending and that this was the only equipment available off the shelf.

The fact was that the military aid that arrived in 1989 was much more suited to the antiguerrilla operations than to the war on drugs. "There is no restriction on the use of this equipment," Ambassador MacNamara said in response to a question at a news conference for U.S. reporters.

Once again, Bogotá and Washington had something in common. Both governments were convinced of the need for military participation in the war on drugs. It was hard to tell which was more convinced than the other. Was it Barco, who was trying to draw in the military even though it was facing international criticism for its strong ties with the militia marauders who killed innocent civilians? Or was it Bush, who was happy to give military aid to an army that was going to use it to fight a Soviet- and Cuban-financed Communist subversion campaign, even though that enemy really didn't exist anymore?

There were raids and record seizures of cocaine and arms caches, and the army had a much larger budget than ever before. But the military was using much of the foreign military aid to fight guerrillas. "If there was any reality in the thesis of a narco-guerrilla conspiracy, the army was focusing more on fighting the latter: subversion," said Juan Tokatlian, a political analyst in Colombia.

It was not long after the war measures came into effect that complaints from the military surfaced once more. "Not only do they tell us that we have to seize landholdings, but they tell us that we have to safeguard them as well. We should have to surround every one of these ranches in a military cordon. There aren't enough troops for that. And anyway, it's quite possible that these same properties will end up being returned to their owners," complained one brigadier general who was engaged in the operation of property seizures. (The lands were eventually returned to the family members of the drug traffickers because the Supreme Court ruled that the seizures were unconstitutional.)

Meanwhile, the army had founded many of the paramilitary groups, and the financing and control of these "self-defense" militias was taken over by the likes of Rodriguez Gacha in Magdalena Medio and Fidel Castaño in Urabá. The connivance of the military with the paramilitary squads hampered the effectiveness of Barco's war measures. Theoretically, the army was involved in the war on drugs, but in practice a division of labor was maintained. Thus, the police and DAS remained on the front lines, while the army, with only a few exceptions, maintained a low profile.

LA COMUNA NORORIENTAL

On the hillsides of Medellín, the slum barrios sprout up in a disorganized array, haphazardly devouring the slopes. Life is in constant peril. With periodic torrential rains, pieces of the mountainside sometimes break loose, and mud-slide avalanches can drag an entire neighborhood into the valley below.

One of the barrios perched on the mountainside is known as La Comuna Nororiental—The Northeastern Collective. Streets in La Comuna wind up the steep incline and disintegrate into a mesh of rocky trails and indecipherable labyrinths—a bazaar for drugs, arms trafficking, and assassins. The majority of the fifteen-odd murders committed every day in Medellín take place there too.

In these proletarian barrios over half the population is unemployed. Most of those who work are day laborers or do odd jobs; mothers earn their daily bread as servants in the grand mansions of El Poblado, the section of Medellín where the wealthiest live. But in the slums, nearly half of all high-school students do not graduate (compared with 35 percent in the rest of the city), and 60 percent of the people who live there are squatters who have no legal title to the houses they have built. Whereas statistics show that there are twenty-seven square feet of recreation land per person in Medellín, the figure for La Comuna Nororiental is about one square foot per person.

In these barrios the power of hard cash, the money from drug trafficking, has subverted all the codes of social behavior. Here the name Pablo—it can only mean Pablo Escobar—is spoken with admiration for the sports centers he built and the social programs he promoted, things few traditional politicians have done. In this place where few families include a father; where worshipers venerate the mother, the Virgin, and guns; and where the people haphazardly migrated from the countryside to the city, the drug bosses found the raw material to commit their assassinations and other crimes.

This is the birthplace of the sicarios—"the children who kill." The sicarios were first used to settle accounts in the drug Mafia's vendettas, killing people who didn't meet payments or who failed to come through with a delivery. But when the drug traffickers increased their terrorist attacks on the state, the sicarios ended up killing judges, police, cabinet ministers, four presidential candidates, leftist leaders, unionists, and journalists. The sicarios started using violence to defend themselves with knives and switchblades against people who were more dangerous than they; now they are professional assassins, skilled in handling sophisticated arms. Many of them were trained by Israeli mercenaries from whom they learned to detonate car bombs and pressurized devices for airplanes.

There are slums in many cities; Medellín is not unique. Slums have grown and proliferated in concert with the disorganized development of Latin America's cities. They have various names, *favelas* in Rio de Janeiro and *pueblos jovenes* in Lima, but they are all the same. The slums of Medellín are not even the worst. On the contrary, for those with money and legal property titles, Medellín has one of the highest coverage rates for public services in Latin America and one of the highest rates of students obtaining a university education. The contrast between the landed and the slum dwellers is profound.

Furthermore, the problems of slums (or ghettos) and homelessness are also growing in the United States and other industrialized countries where the per capita income is much higher than in Colombia. No wonder. The same problems of drugs and violence are at the core of social inequality wherever there is poverty.

The sicarios of Medellín are the most recent product of the tremendous impact of drug trafficking in a society dominated by social inequality. They have "the opportunity to find in the violence and in the drug trafficking their dreams, to be protagonists in a society which has closed them out," said Alfonso Salazar, a writer based in Medellín.

From the time they are children, the sicarios use violence to show they have guts. The money and power they receive are a symbol of prestige. But few of them really make money. Just like the drug dealers who hang out on street corners in New York City, they'll never accumulate much wealth. They want to become legends, to be tough, to bring home money and presents for their girlfriends.

After the death of the Mexican—"that man gave us work"—and with the search for Escobar, car theft, murder, and kidnapping multiplied in Medellín. The Extraditables showed no sign of letting go and fortified themselves with sicario gangs. *Semana* estimated that about three thousand sicarios were operating in Medellín.

Many foreigners first heard of Medellín and its cartel in the early 1980s. Their image of the city was that of some sort of untamed jungle outpost from which fiendish drug cartels processed and exported their wares. The hyperpopular television show "Miami Vice" played no small role in spreading the frightening image of the Colombian drug dealers throughout the world; although the show's characters were accurate for that small group, the program did wide and reckless damage to the reputation of the whole country.

Medellín is, in fact, the second largest city in the country, and was the first industrial center of Colombia long before the arrival of the drug traffickers. Far from being some backwater campground, it is a city of five million people. The proposal by then mayor of New York Ed Koch to bomb Medellín was like suggesting that in the 1920s everyone in Chicago was a bootlegger and that U.S. authorities could enforce Prohibition (and get Al Capone) by dropping bombs on the city.

In the barrios where the sicarios lived, a new generation of young leaders started working to improve conditions and to fight the image: "In the United States, they believe that just because you live in Medellín, you have to be a drug dealer. And in Colombia, when you say you live in La Comuna Nororiental, everybody thinks you have to be a sicario," one such leader told me.

Since the early 1900s, Medellín has been the epicenter of Colombia's industrial growth. Facing land that was largely not productive, *paisas* (residents of Medellín) began to leave their home regions in search of better opportunities in other areas, in much the same way that rugged American pioneers settled the West. The paisas developed a reputation for being hard workers, willing to take the risk needed to settle new lands. The tremendous conquest of these Colombian pioneers brought quick rewards; Medellín became an important commercial and financial center that would determine the country's future industrial development.

In the early 1950s, as Colombia began to industrialize, poor farmers were lured to the city and they developed into a well-paid working class. But the labor force grew too rapidly, and there was not enough work for everyone. The first rings of urban poverty developed, contributing to the eventual creation of two separate cities divided by social inequality. The situation became more acute with La Violencia, which forced even more people to migrate from the countryside to the cities. Many people simply abandoned their small plots of land and went off to seek their fortunes in the great provincial capital: Medellín. Many children of these chronically unemployed saw in drug trafficking a way to survive since they too could not find work.

Drug trafficking was more than just "an emergency escape door from the lack of alternatives," as one person put it. The idiosyncrasies of the region also played their part. "Paisas don't know how to be poor," said Alvaro Uribe, one of Medellín's young politicians who throughout the years has embodied the paisa spirit by being courageous enough to confront an old political class that tied itself to the drug traffickers. His family history shows the complex relationship of Medellín and the drug Mafia. His father, who was assassinated by FARC, was a horse trader, which brought him into contact with Fabio Ochoa, the father of the drug-dealing Ochoa brothers. Alvaro Uribe knew the Ochoas, as did many people in Medellín. Yet he decided to wage an election campaign in which he opposed the generation of politicians that had ties with those drug dealers. Ever since, he has received numerous threats on his life. Nevertheless, he managed to win election in 1992 as senator from Antioquia State, forcing a long-time political boss, Bernardo Guerra Cerna, out of office.

"In Antioquia everybody feels they are the boss," Uribe once told me. "The economic onslaught that was sustained over so many years left an imprint on the paisa personality: They love money." Medellín grew without a structured, thought-out urban plan. While the riches that developed were not shared among the classes, Medellín did manage to transform itself into a modern city.

The drug traffickers even reached into the upper economic strata, taking advantage of a serious economic recession in the 1970s. "The business sector of Medellín, perhaps motivated by a need to escape the economic depression and spurred on by ambition, initially reacted in an interesting way as they faced the nascent drug phenomenon: They disregarded basic moral and ethical principles. They actively engaged in doing business with these emerging impresarios who brought with them seemingly limitless financial resources," wrote Colombian priest Julio Jaramillo Martinez in his book, *De la Barra a la Banda.*

Slowly, Medellín's business class was lured into drug trafficking by the sound of money. "There was no social consciousness of the fact that this illicit business could become criminal activity," said Uribe. Underground business dealings and contraband were certainly well known here, where the wealthy imported pianos and French crystal by mule train; even the church bells in the Rionegro valley were custom-made and brought in from Europe. Later the paisas progressed to the contraband of cigarettes and home appliances. In any case, when the drug traffickers set up business, the operations initially didn't raise many eyebrows. "There was no perverse intention of breaking the law; rather there was a spirit of doing what it takes to be a businessman," Uribe added.

Little by little, drug trafficking moved up the social ladder; members of the most important families were soon investing their money in cocaine shipments through the process known as *la apuntada.* These were consignment deals in which an investor could purchase shares in a drug shipment. The drug dealer provided the cocaine and served as the shipping agent. If the shipment was successful, everyone made money; if it was not, they were insured. The process also made it difficult to link the investors with the drug bosses who organized the deal in the first place.

Although the drug dealers at first cooperated with the wealthy families, they soon began to attack those with land and money; their rampage took on characteristics of a class struggle. Escobar, Rodriguez Gacha, and their lieutenants were all poor street toughs who worked their way into the business, buying respectability along the way. Escobar was considered a crude and violent man (which was why doors slammed shut on him). His rhetoric was populist, and he posed as a kind of Robin Hood who helped the poor and disenfranchised of the slums of Medellín who rarely received much help from the government.

The Extraditables took direct action and declared war on the oligarchy, blowing up banks and burning down the fincas of well-known families or persecuting and kidnapping the landowners until they were forced to sell.

Perhaps the family who best represents what happened to the upper-class paisas is the Ospinas. A family of presidents, they were descendants of President Mariano Ospina Pérez of the Conservative party, who was in power at the outset of La Violencia in 1947. Several of Ospina's grandchildren became important partners of the Medellín cartel, working closely with Pablo Escobar and the other drug bosses. But other members of the Ospina family fought the drug dealers. For example, when Alfonso Ospina refused to sell his lands, he was kidnapped and murdered.

In 1990, Medellín reached the height of chaos and violence. An average of fifteen people were being killed every day. There were more than 100,000 unemployed; at least 140,000 children had no access to education.

I first went to La Comuna Nororiental in 1983 on a reporting trip with Cardinal Alfonso López Trujillo, the archbishop of the diocese of Medellín. Following the decision by Justice Minister Rodrigo Lara Bonilla to tighten the screws on the drug business, the newspaper was receiving a huge amount of information. In letters and telephone calls, people were eager to tell us about Escobar's relations with certain members of the political class, as well as his links to several soccer teams. But I was most interested in the material we were receiving about Escobar's connections to Colombia's most sacrosanct institution: the Roman Catholic church.

After much investigation and after obtaining confirmation from several sources, I published a report about two priests in the Medellín archdiocese who had worked side by side with Pablo Escobar on Medellín Without Slums, the social welfare program Escobar organized in 1981. Only in 1983, when Pablo Escobar was expelled from Congress amid charges about drug trafficking, did López Trujillo decide to prohibit the priests' participation in the program. Even so, for three full years, the priests worked with

Escobar inaugurating sports arenas, housing, and other new projects in La Comuna Nororiental.

Although the participation of the two priests had been public knowledge—photographs of them were even published in Escobar's newspaper, *Liberal Movement,* that circulated in the area— the report caused indignation in the Medellín archdiocese. They were outraged at my suggestion that the archdiocese—and accordingly, Cardinal López Trujillo, a highly respected prelate in Vatican circles, a man rumored to be in line one day to be the first Latin American pope—should have known the truth about Pablo Escobar's sources of money before 1983.

"You know, María Jimena, I think that there is something behind all this, that there is some dangerous ideological motivation, quite possibly Communist in nature," the cardinal told me on a visit to the newspaper, during which he also warned that he would sue unless we published a retraction to our story. "If you persist in besmirching my name, I will stop you because I am going to launch a very vigorous campaign in Congress. And I will talk to government officials so that they know all about what you are doing to me," he threatened. But I published no retraction, and he filed no suit.

In 1983 the Medellín Without Slums campaign was treated with great respect. At the time the groups that later became known as sicarios were no more than local street gangs. Cardinal López Trujillo's major concern continued to be the spread of Liberation Theology, not drug violence. The clampdown on the M-19 guerrillas by the security forces combined with the meager presence of the political parties and the absence of government social services had, in effect, reduced La Comuna Nororiental to a renegade state within a state. Any "laws," such as they were, were imposed not by constitutional right but by private forms of justice. The only "legitimate" institution was the church, which was in no position to confront the problem. Distracted by the battle to eradicate Liberation Theology and tainted by the power of drug money, "the church could not carry out its evangelical mission," said the Reverend Francisco de Roux, a Jesuit academic who studied the phenomenon of violence in Colombia.

Priests and bishops received large donations from the drug dealers for their parishes and said nothing. The practice became known as *narco-limosnas* (narco-charity).

More than anything, the Colombian church was an economic

power whose skills of persuasion were felt in the grand spheres of power as if it were any other economic lobby. But outside the political back rooms, the church's lack of influence was remarkable. Although the church vehemently opposed the use of contraceptives—approving only natural methods—Colombia became the Latin American leader in family planning and the first Latin American country to reverse the population explosion. The country's family planning centers were considered pilot models for the rest of the continent. But the surge in the number of new religious sects, even evangelicals in Medellín, was a telling sign that the church was losing ground and influence.

Many of the drug dealers were devoted to the church. Carlos Lehder invited Monsigor Castrillon, the bishop of Pereira, to bless his Posada Alemana. Only when the drug dealers were forced into hiding did the church decide to end its silence. Monsignor López Trujillo stopped the church's work with Medellín Without Slums, and the Episcopal Conference issued a statement rejecting the narco-limosnas.

My sister, Sylvia, was always my best source on La Comuna Nororiental. The Colombian justice system had issued arrest warrants against the first band of sicarios, the Priscos, for the assassinations of Justice Minister Rodrigo Lara Bonilla, Guillermo Cano, and Magistrate Vaquero Borda, among others. As Sylvia had discovered, the Priscos were already a legend in La Comuna. On Children's Day, October 28—a celebration little known elsewhere in the world—they always held a party. Along with them came everyone else in the barrio, even the police. "For the best disguise, there was a tricycle for first prize; they handed out dollar bills as well. . . . People liked them, but also feared them. They were generous, but always for the purpose of exercising control," Father Tobón, a priest who was responsible for forty-four parishes in La Comuna Nororiental, told my sister in an interview.

"They say that one of them committed suicide, but the truth is that one of his brothers killed him," Father Tobón said. The Priscos held a big fiesta when the attorney general was killed, complete with roast pig for all. People contended that they had nothing to do with the assassination of Galán "because they were supposed to be Liberals themselves," Father Tobón added.

While I was immersed in investigating the first paramilitary militia groups financed by the drug traffickers (who found their raw material in these outcast neighborhoods), Sylvia, with a much more sociological bent, was reading everything she could about the psychology of gangs. She had gotten to know a couple of gangs in Bogotá and had managed to get into some areas where few other journalists had succeeded in penetrating. While I tried to find out when and how the foreign mercenaries were training the hit squads formed by the drug traffickers, she was finding out about how they dressed; what they talked about; which heavy-metal rock bands they liked; and how, to her surprise, they were fervent believers in God and the Virgin. Seeking funding for more research, she accepted an offer to work on a British documentary. It was this job that eventually led to her death.

Ever since we were young, Sylvia and I always fought over silly things. I was the strong-willed older sister, and Sylvia, the second of three children, continued to suffer as my "little sister." But we were finally putting such things behind us. Now, thinking that the whole world was stretched before us, we began to plan for the future. We thought about writing a book together or even starting our own documentary film-production company. She was far more irreverent and analytical than I and had become an implacable critic of my work. She could always slice through the Gordian knots that journalists like me get caught in. But every time I asked my sister to let me see what she had written on the gangs, she always turned me down. "I have to polish it up first," she would tell me.

Sylvia's ghost must have bellowed with laughter when, a short time after her death, her husband, Salomón, after hours of fiddling with her computer, finally managed to recover the rough materials that Sylvia had gathered in Medellín. He gave them to me as they were, "unpolished."

Among her notes, I found an interview that Sylvia had conducted with Alberto, the chief of one of the many bands of sicarios in La Comuna Nororiental of Medellín. What follows is, in effect, our last collaborative effort, published four years after her murder.

The Magníficos of Medellín

The video stores in La Comuna Nororiental are heavily stocked with episodes of "The A-Team." The sicarios rent them and watch them intently, over and over again. They point out and analyze the mistakes that are made and applaud the way Fass, Murdock, and Barakus, under the command of Hannibal Smith, all living underground because of a crime they didn't commit, always manage to evade capture. For Alberto, they are perfect heroes. His gang has often been in tough straits on the verge of being caught by the law or by their enemies. They got the name the Magníficos from two girls who hang out with the gang. "We're going find a name for you," they told the boys one day. "They came back and said they were going to call us the Magníficos and it stuck—from then on we were the Magníficos."

In Alberto's world, where the link between fiction and reality doesn't mean much, they forget that the violence of American movies is clean: bombs go off, but you don't see the dead people; guns are fired, but no one ever dies.

The Magníficos under Alberto began living off death by taking away the lives of other human beings.

He's always wearing expensive Reeboks. He loves to go trail-biking on expensive 500-cc motorcycles. Life is a succession of sudden instants, like a gunshot, a goal. All that matters is the present. Live for the day. Alberto has no time to reflect; he just listens to Hector Laboe, a popular Puerto Rican salsa singer. He loves tango; he cheers with every goal scored on Sunday by his favorite soccer team, Atlético Nacional. In his world, death is the only sure thing there is. He is completely centered on what he's doing, even when he's about to kill somebody. "In this work, it's me number one and me number two. After that, who the fuck cares?"

He is in good physical condition and plays soccer as much as he can. He doesn't take drugs; the only person he trusts is his mother, nobody else, especially not the members of his gang. "Your best friend is the one who ends up selling you out."

He's also a man of experience and has much success with women: A poll taken at San Javier School showed that many high school seniors would like nothing better than to have a boyfriend who is a sicario just like Alberto.

The toughness on his face and the words he uses reflect the despair of someone condemned, of those who "were born to be pushing up daisies," of those who could never start over again even if they wanted to. Alberto is cold-blooded. Everybody knows it. He's tough, and he's an old-timer. Alberto is nineteen years old.

If he lives to be twenty-five, he can feel like he accomplished something. It means that he's earned the right to a "career" as a professional assassin in one of the more famous gangs, like the Priscos, the Nachos, or the Tesos—these are the gangs who win

204 □ DEATH BEAT

the all-important contracts with the drug Mafia. And, if they are very lucky, they can get to be bodyguards of one of the big shots like Pinina, Pablo Escobar's military chief until March 1990, when he was killed in a police ambush in Medellín. He was already old by gang standards. He had made it to thirty.

Most of the sicarios kill each other off; the ones who don't, die like Pinina or get killed, set up and knocked off by the Mafia bosses themselves. "The Mafia is hard-core, you know," Alberto says. "Suppose that I got the contract from a mafioso to kill somebody. 'Yeah, know what? I need you to kill this guy,' he says to you; 'go and kill him.' But you know that down the road, the same dude that gives you the contract can turn around and do you. The thing is that you get sent to take out one of his enemies, get it? And the guy that was the enemy probably has some friends and the dude that hired you thinks that someday those friends will catch you and make you sing. Your life is always screwed . . . always fucked up."

But being in the Mafia for these boys is a way to climb up the ladder, to move up, "to be somebody." It is not only a way to come up with million-dollar contracts, but it's the best school for learning to be a professional in the art of killing. Many of the sicarios hired by the Mafia receive arms training in the techniques of using explosives, in new methods of kidnapping. They also use these skills on their own chores. When one of the bosses goes down and "there's no work," common crime increases in Medellín. After the surrender of the Ochoa family and Pablo Escobar, car theft and kidnapping tripled in the city and in Bogotá.

Alberto has profound respect for Catholic law. He goes to mass without fail, and every time he commits a murder he prays to the Virgin de Carmen. "If they kill me, she will receive me in purgatory." He goes to confession after every homicide to eliminate any lingering pangs of conscience. He wears a medallion blessed by Nuestra Señora de Perpetua Socorro—"she watches over me"— and Saint Judas. Like many other sicarios, Alberto places them on his ankles. In his wallet he has pieces of paper reading: "Halt, the sacred heart of Jesus is with you."

They say that when a sicario is buried, the rest of the gang races all around La Comuna Nororiental on their 500-cc motorcycles in tribute. There are no tears. They fire guns in the air. Sometimes they take the body out of the coffin and give their departed friend one more ride around town.

"Do you believe in God?"

"Yes. When I'm on my way out to pull something off, I always pray. I believe in God and the Virgin."

"Isn't it a contradiction?"

"I believe in God, man! I always pray for Him to protect me, all right? Nothing bad's gonna happen to me. But no way . . . sure, the law of God is Do Not Kill! But you always kill! If one guy doesn't do it, somebody else will."

Judging by the number of people who go to mass, the church finds its most ardent parishioners here. Families become more religious still when they have sons who are sicarios . . . nothing is left for them except to pray.

Priests like Father Tobón are treated with a certain respect for being the representatives of God on Earth. It is he who will forgive them, because he represents "the forgiveness of God." This divine status does not stop him from receiving threatening phone calls every now and then, though up to this point there has been no case in these parts of a priest being killed by sicarios.

The religious devotion of the sicarios is seasonal. They believe firmly in the sacrament of penitence but go to confession only during Holy Week; on those days, of course, the crime rate decreases considerably in La Comuna. So Father Tobón takes advantage of Holy Week to preach from the pulpit about reconciliation, to talk about the meaning of life and Christian values. In his sermons he emphasizes the value of human life and even came to the point of uttering the word *sicario*.

Their devotion to the Virgin is ambiguous. They pray to Her but feel guilty. They feel that they are damned when they get past ten murders yet still maintain the hope that the Virgin is so good in Her grace that She will pardon them. This fixation on finding forgiveness was evident when Pablo Escobar decided to choose a priest, the Reverend Rafael García Herreros, as the intermediary when he surrendered to Colombian authorities in June 1991. "Pablo deserves God's forgiveness. . . . In the eyes of God, all men are created equal," the priest said on the day that he arrived with Pablo Escobar at the Envigado prison.

Alberto is a professional driver and an auto mechanic, but he doesn't have a job. When he has to fill out an employment form, he lists his profession as "student making the rounds, looking for work."

"What does it mean to be a sicario?"

"For me, it's a guy who likes what he's doing. You know what I mean? He likes to do it. And he does it because he wants to and not because anyone makes him do it."

"A sicario is a professional killer, isn't he?"

"Not always. For me, a professional killer means that he has always been doing that and that he knows how to do things."

They talk about death and killing as if they were part of a normal job that you do like any other. "When you make a contract with someone to kill a certain person, that guy that you hired is a sicario. Or a beginner if you want to put it that way. Can you dig it?"

Sicarios also do robberies and other underworld business. But they feel like amateurs because they really know one thing, one way of killing. For them a professional assassin is someone who knows the business well, who studies it over and over again from different angles, so that he doesn't get caught. "The sicario is different. The sicario only kills. And he makes a living from taking other lives. It's not like thieves who spend thirty or forty months in jail for stealing a watch. I'd never do that. I mean, I'd never steal a watch."

None of them wants to be a doctor, teacher, or fireman. Their only other career aspiration: to be soccer players. They're obsessed with soccer but only root for Atlético Nacional because "many kids playing for them have come from here." So scoring a goal becomes part of their special vocabulary. "Hey," they say. "I scored a goal that time, I scored."

Sicarios weren't born this way. They became murderers because of "what was in the air," because of bad influence. "Before they brought me to Medellín, I was completely sane." Many began using violence to defend themselves from others who were more violent than they were. In the barrio where Alberto lived, his house was across from a *jibaradiero*—a place where they sell basuco. The barrio bad guys showed up there and started hassling them all the time. That was the first time he got into a fight. Alberto remembers it very well because he was only seven years old. "When the bad guys saw that we were really going to fight, that we weren't going to get pushed around or anything, they backed off. The gang came together from that bunch of guys." They would only fight over a dispute in the local soccer game. "But we only used our fists . . . we fought in self-defense." They switched quickly from knives to guns. Now Alberto is always armed. "Yeah, because I have lots of enemies. People from other areas, you understand what I mean?" He has a 9-mm pistol because it's easy to carry.

He got his first "job" because he was flat broke. "A biker showed up at my house. He had a 500-cc bike. So, I'm on the corner, get it? I don't know this guy, but I did know the guy riding with him on the back of the bike. So the guy driving gets off and says, "You know what . . . I have a job for you." So I say, what is it?

"Now, I have a *compa* [short for *compadre* or "pal"]. We were always together since we were little, him and me, messing around. I told them that I'd do it, whatever it is, but only if he comes with me."

They didn't tell him to bring a gun, but they did say to bring a knife. They took him to a bar. "There was a lady there, right? All fancy and everything. So it was to kill a woman, right? We were going to bump her off, right? So I killed her when she was getting off a bus on her way home. I stabbed her like three times."

Alberto got the pay that he asked for: two motorcycles, two guns, and 200,000 pesos ($500). "We did it on a Friday, and they paid us the day after."

"Were you afraid?"

"You know what I did? While we were waiting to kill her, we bought a pint of *aguardiente* [Colombian anisette-flavored sugarcane liquor], but we didn't drink the whole thing, like, because we couldn't get drunk. It was only enough, like, to calm me down."

He said that the first time he killed he did feel something: "I don't know, killing someone, like, who hasn't done anything to you, like, killing 'em in cold blood . . . but no way, you like didn't think about anything but the money, because I was like broke. The day after I did the thing, was like Valentine's Day—we have money and the bikes—everything."

When the sicarios kill for hire they do it without even knowing who it is they're killing. And the people paying them don't tell them if the person they're killing is a union leader, a journalist, a politician, or a mafioso. "Sometimes you go and take a look before it goes down," Alberto admits. "You watch the person. And if the person is real cool you say: I won't do it and I pass it off on another member of the gang. It's happened. Killing somebody that's too cool is no good."

"Would you handle a contract to kill a mafioso?"

"I'd think it over. You can kill him real quick. But the problems come later with your family."

"And when the Mafia hires you to hit union leaders and journalists?"

"That's a much bigger problem. That's really heavy killing."

"So you don't do that kind of job?"

"You take a chance if the deal looks easy. If it doesn't, you
don't try. If you say to yourself, I can make it through this one,
you do it. But you have to think it over pretty much."

"Do you ever have doubts about whether you should kill somebody or not?"

"No! As far as that goes, if there's money in it, that's cool.
That's all I need."

After the first time, death and the act of killing become part of
a routine. But frequently, in the solitude of his own room at night,
the sicario is attacked by remorse: "When you get into bed at
night, you think of the person; it gives you trouble to get to sleep
thinking about him. But he's already dead, so what are you going
to do?" he tells me. "You know that sometimes you want to bring
the person back somehow, but what's done is done. You have to
think before you act. Before I do something I think about it first.
Because after a hit, you get real exhausted, and the only thing
you know is you don't want to go back to jail."

Strangely enough, sicarios like Alberto don't use drugs, not
even when they're about to kill somebody. "I've always liked to
drink but not a lot. But no drugs. Marijuana's the only thing that
people do around here. The friend who tries to get you to smoke
basuco is not my friend. I've never been into that."

They know that if a sicario is getting stoned, he can't be doing
a good job. There are, of course, sicarios who smoke basuco, but
they are a small minority. "The big bosses don't want to be hiring
drug addicts who do bad work," I was told. Nevertheless, statistics
in Medellín showed that more and more sicarios were becoming
street dealers and that many of them were using as well.

Alberto's love of guns began when he started watching American
westerns on television. "You know what I mean? Cowboy movies."
The first gun he remembers was a friend's single-action shotgun.
The first gun that he owned was one that he stole from a neighbor. "I wanted a gun, so even though this guy was a neighbor and
all, I ripped it off. And I learned how to use it by myself."

On the slopes of the mountains you can hear the sicarios doing
target practice. They buy their guns on the black market, often

from the police themselves. And they go out to start shooting. They practice over and over again until they can just snap their wrists and fire. At the beginning Alberto was afraid to shoot because he couldn't stop his hand from moving. "The first time that you're gonna shoot—like a .38—the bullet doesn't get there. You don't hit the target because you haven't had the practice. When the powder discharges, it moves your hand, you know what I mean? And you always, like, tell a new guy, that he has to hold it with two hands." Today Alberto brags about his sure one-handed shot.

As chief of the Magníficos, Alberto laid down his own rules and recruited people "who got put out front." The money from all the hits gets divided up equally. The rules of the gang are clear and precise: "Anybody who is a snitch gets killed. He goes down."

The solidarity among members of a gang is as fragile as their lives. The sicarios trust no one but themselves. And they know that even their best friends can end up being the people who kill them: "In our gang, for example, the guys here now are all friends, sure," says Alberto. "But the day you least suspect it is the day they're laying down money to knock you off, any one of them . . . the truth is that none of them has gotten to the point of trying to fuck me over. But you have to think that it's always a possibility, that money sucks."

"What's the money for?"

"To eat. We don't live off the air, you dig? And to buy bullets and guns, you know what I mean? The more guns we have, the stronger we get. Oh yeah, like we also need bread to buy sneakers."

"Do you save any money?"

"You make money, you spend money. When the money comes in, you have to pay for shit. You need more bullets, your shoes wear out. So then you have to go out and buy bullets and you have to buy shoes. And if there's anything left . . . you go out for a shot of aguardiente."

"So you kill for the money?"

"Yeah, sure, like, no clue."

But the truth is the sicarios don't kill only for money. Killing also means status in the eyes of their friends. Alberto brags that he's a big shot, known, "famous." He's already proved "he's got what it takes," that he has guts. "When you get to be known, you're the one that's hired for the hits, you know what I mean?

People come looking for you," he says with a degree of arrogance. The sicarios use their power in the barrio in their own twisted way of looking for respect. Each gang has its own territory, its own barrio, its own block. On their turf, they are the law; the only justice applied is that which is imposed by them. The rules depend on the mood. "A guy that's really tough can get ticked off real easy . . . if you're a trained killer, like, you're gonna kill for no reason, when somebody makes you mad."

They kill for any reason at all. Because something bothered them, because they woke up that day in a bad mood, or because they just felt like killing somebody. Sometimes they could kill somebody because they didn't show up for an appointment. "We have a friend who plays by the rules. So if he lends you a gun and says to bring it back at 4:00 and at 4:00 you don't bring it back . . . at 4:30 he kills you. That's the way he is: do it right or die. It's by the rules."

The first time that Alberto shot somebody, it all happened in a flash, in a chance encounter. "I'm with a buddy one night. We're hanging around, doing nothing. We're on some steps and on this side of me there's this drunk, you know what I mean? We're going up the stairs. So I stop here, next to him, you know? Like no big deal, and I'm taking a leak, you know? And while I'm pissing, he pushes me, you know? He thinks we're gonna rob him or whatever, I don't know. So he pushes me again and I get pissed off, you understand? I pull out the gun and I shoot him twice. That was it."

Like many gangs, Alberto's A-Team started out doing small-scale "jobs" in the barrio. But they soon branched out. "You wanted to improve, to get better, to get out of the barrio and do work in El Poblado," says Alberto. El Poblado is the residential neighborhood where the big, wealthy families live and where more recently, drug dealers and successful sicarios have set themselves up.

"We wanted to get out on our own and pull off bigger deals. We wanted to get into those places where the big Mafia guys live, where they have everything—Betamax, televisions, cars, everything. We wanted all that stuff."

"What do you call crime?"

"Breaking the law."

"Have you committed any crimes?"

"Yeah, I was in jail for a while. See, laws were made to be broken, you know. But let me tell you something, lady, not everybody in that jail is a criminal. There are innocent people in there! I'm telling you, the law—doesn't work at all."

Even though he knows what it means to break the law, the sicario doesn't have any problem crossing over the line. The strong arm of the police is the only law they know about. They see how the police come into their houses on a bust, breaking things and mistreating innocent family members. After Barco's war measures were adopted following the death of Galán, the roundups and the raids increased in these barrios. "They went into a house without warning, busting up everything, asking about our boys," said one mother in the barrio known as Manrique. "Many times they took them away without leaving word of their whereabouts, saying that it was because they were sicarios."

It got to the point where many young people who went looking for work in Medellín would be turned away for the simple reason that they live in La Comuna. "How do they want to put an end to sicarios, if when somebody tries to get a job he has to say that he lives somewhere else?" asked one of the many youth leaders who have cropped up in La Comuna.

Police harassment is just one problem. In La Comuna, dealing with the law is shorthand for corruption: It has nothing to do with justice. "I like to work in Medellín more than any place else because here you can have cop friends on the inside," said Alberto. Corrupt cops work with the gangs. They sell them guns and ammunition, and they take advantage of the situation by shaking down a piece of the action for themselves.

"In this world where law has always been a synonym for abuse, persecution, and mistreatment, killing a policeman sometimes becomes an affirmation of justice rather than a crime," said Victor Gaviria, a film director who has studied the sicario phenomenon in Medellín for some time.

Sicarios like Alberto usually talk about killing policemen as if it were an act of triumph. They go fishing for an unsuspecting cop, then trap him in the labyrinths of the steep barrio roads of La Comuna. "My buddy on the street corner picks up on this cop passing by and cons him into chasing after him; they get to where I am and wham! All of a sudden, he's chasing me, too. So I set the cop up in a trap since I know where everybody is. I go running onto a dead-end street with him behind me and bang! we get him," says Alberto proudly, as if cop killing were an act of virtue.

For them robbing is "taking" and killing is "finishing off." And robbing a bank isn't a crime at all because "the bank isn't owned by anyone."

"What happens when you do a hit and there are innocent people who get caught in the middle and get killed?"

"Let's say there's a bank robbery. First you analyze the setup. But you know there's always somebody who gets in the middle of it all, trying to protect something that isn't his. A bank doesn't belong to anybody, you know what I mean? So, sometimes, innocent people get killed. But that's not your fault; it's fate. If you don't kill somebody who's making a lot of noise, the cops catch you and they kill you instead. You come first; as for the innocent guy, that's the way it goes."

"What about the guards that get in the way?"

"It's not like you're a fucking killing machine. But, for instance, if a guard is going to take a gun or something, then you kill him. And if the guy is quiet and doing nothing, why are you going to take his life, just like that? No way, man!"

The victims of the violence have no redress here; the justice system just doesn't work. There is no confidence in government institutions. The sicarios are controlling a state unto itself. In La Comuna, violence creates more violence. The only way for victims to respond to the law imposed on them by the sicarios is to fight back with the same methods. That's how vigilantism starts to appear in the barrios of the Medellín slums. Youth groups dedicated to wiping out the sicario bands are formed. They say their goal is to eradicate the crime and terror that exists in their barrios. But the militias build up just as much power as the sicarios and become just as terrifying for the rest of La Comuna. Here you respond to violence with violence.

They don't think about getting married or having a family—only about leaving some money to their mothers when they get killed: "I want them to remember me for having left my mother with a refrigerator," said one sicario who wasn't even twenty years old. The sicarios all pay supreme homage to their mothers. Fathers are, for the most part, symbolic; few are there at all. "You only have one mother, but any son of a bitch can be a father," goes the saying in La Comuna.

This is a crisis of family disintegration. If the father is even present, he exercises control by means of violence—there are many stories of fathers who beat and sexually abuse their children and their wives. But the sicarios bring their money from murder contracts to [their mothers], and the money opens doors, more than they ever could dream of before. The sicario becomes the provider, the surrogate father—the mother looks to the son as the dominant figure in her world. She accepts his life as a sicario and, with a certain banality, she talks matter-of-factly about the violence. "That boy was killed by a very nice-looking kid," they would tell you.

When mothers in La Comuna ask questions, there is always an easy explanation. "What did we do to have this kind of children? Why do they grow up twisted?"

The answer is always somewhere else; it's somebody else's fault. "It comes from outside; it's the neighborhood that makes them be like that; it's that bad friend of his that is a bad influence; well, you have to eat."

"Are you a man of your word?"

"Yes. I'm straight. If you give your word, you have to keep it. Like when I promised I would come to see you. How could I leave you waiting after having told you that I was going to come? I would have said to myself: I didn't keep my word! And even worse than that, I did it to a woman; . . . I didn't keep my word to a woman and that's worse than death!"

"Why?"

"Because I respect women a lot. I would say that I respect them too much, you know what I mean? I would say that a woman is the most beautiful thing that exists in life. It's because of a woman that you are here; your mother is a woman. So breaking a promise to a woman is a serious thing, you know what I mean?"

"So what you do, you do for your mother?"

"If it were for my father I wouldn't do anything. But I love my mother a lot, you get what I mean? And let me tell you something. The day my mother dies, she'd better die a natural death. It better not be from somebody doing something to her . . . because the day somebody hurts my mom, I'll kill whoever killed her with my own hands. If you don't love your own mother, who else are you gonna love?"

Even though he admits his first killing was a woman, Alberto says he has changed the rules, and insists that the drug Mafia knows that he won't kill women. He doesn't recognize the contradiction. He says that if somebody's ripping off a woman in his barrio, he's the first to go help her out.

"They offered me good bread to knock off women and I've turned it down. It's like an abuse. Women are more defenseless, more fragile. I don't know."

The truth is that the sicarios kill women all the time; the proof is that women are frequently found among the innumerable victims of hit teams. Among them are judges, journalists, and leaders of the Patriotic Union, not to mention countless others killed in domestic quarrels.

Father Tobón is concerned about the disintegration of the role of young women in the barrios. According to him, the woman's role has become the same as that of Manuelita Saenz, the companion of the Great Liberator, Simón Bolívar: keeping an eye on their men's weapons, serving as connections and for sexual satisfaction. He contends that the jealousy factor does seem to be a motive for murder. "You love your girlfriend and give her a lot of presents. If she betrays you, you kill her. They say that the worst cases of harassment and battering are against women.

"The sicario hates himself; he knows he is the lowest of the low. He's always trying to enhance his ability to destroy, his capacity for pure evil. He ends up being exactly what he expects himself to be. He hates everything, the outside world, the upper class, the rich. He just rejects the values of society."

Sicarios like Alberto are no recent novelty but have existed since the times of the Roman emperors. The word *sicario* comes from the Latin *sicarius*—hired killer. In Rome the sicarios murdered emperors and were part of the underpinnings of major conspiracies. In the Middle Ages they became known as *condotieris*. They were paid by the great feudal lords to murder their enemies. They are also related to today's most sophisticated version of mercenaries, like the Israelis hired by the drug bosses to train teenagers like Alberto in the art of killing, or as in the case of the British mercenaries who murder the members of the Medellín cartel.

They all live from the spoils of death, and they all deny their status in life.

The sicario doesn't think of himself as a murderer. He likes to be what he is but being called a sicario is considered an insult. He doesn't use that name; the society around him brands him with it.

The same thing happens to mercenaries or to arms traffickers who hide their activities under the flashy name of security companies. "I'm not a mercenary," Yair Klein would say whenever he was called that.

There is little difference between Alberto, boss of the Magníficos, and the top leader of the gangs of South Central Los Angeles, where it is said 25 out of every 100 young black men are likely to be killed by gunfire before they reach the age of twenty. And how different are they from the Chicago gangs, or from the "Palestinians," the assassins who protect the Colombian Mafia in the poor outskirts of New York? Or from the "Loubards" who live in the "HLMS," the slums on the outskirts of Paris? They all live in the same desperate reality: They are the marginalized, the unemployed members of society. They live where there is no social security, only crack and basuco and death. They are the damned in a society that condemns them to purgatory, hidden away in the ghettos.

"We are winning the war against drugs," William Bennett, the former U.S. drug czar, often pronounced. He said it one last time as he announced his departure from office in 1990, as he held up graphs and surveys showing a decrease in cocaine consumption. The statistics were based on questions posed to white middle-class youths in white American middle-class cities.

In Los Angeles or in Medellín, the only war that has been won is the war over who kills whom. "If I don't do it, somebody else will," Alberto told Sylvia.

THE ELECTIONS: A RACE AGAINST DEATH

The year 1989 was finally over. The only positive thing that happened was that Colombia won the Americas Soccer Cup, but even that triumph was fraught with contradictions because of the drug-trafficking problem. Soccer is Colombia's most popular sport, and the country had become world-renowned for its virtuosity in it, reminiscent of the glory years of Brazilian soccer when Pele was in his prime. But there was drug money behind the illustrious achievements of the Colombian soccer teams, the majority of which were owned by the drug traffickers in 1989. Our great soccer stars, the role models for Colombian youths, were paid with drug money. Violence had reached the soccer field. In an attempt to control the outcome of the matches, several soccer referees were kidnapped by the same terrorist squads that the drug traffickers used against the government. After one referee was killed, the national soccer championship was canceled.

Several weeks before the murder of Galán, Colombia won the Libertadores de America Soccer Cup. The same people who poured into the streets to weep for Galán came out en masse, wildly celebrating the Colombian soccer victory.

The coming year was likely to be tough, above all because it was an election year; congressional and mayoral balloting was in March, and the presidential election was in May. Little analysis was necessary to predict that the 1990 elections would bring not only more violence than we were experiencing, but also further attempts by the drug traffickers to destabilize the country. Voting itself had become a test of the nation's survival; exhausted as we were, we didn't know whether we would have sufficient strength, decisiveness, and courage to overcome our fears and vote.

In the midst of the pessimism, there was some good news. Rodriguez Gacha's death seriously reduced, though not eliminated, the threat from the paramilitary–drug dealers' alliance. Many of the anti-Communist paramilitary groups, all financed by the drug dealers, began to fall apart. This process coincided with the news that the M-19 guerrilla movement was about to be legalized—a signal that doors were opening and that political battles could be waged by peaceful, rather than violent, means.

On the other hand, the very act of legitimating M-19 might bring retaliation from the armed right. "They're going to kill Pizarro," was the common refrain even before members of M-19 began to return to civilian life. Pizarro was Carlos Pizarro, the M-19 guerrilla-turned-politician. (He was in fact killed in 1990.) One had the premonition that things could get worse as the election period grew near. "If they keep on killing candidates, it is possible there could be a political vacuum, and that would do away with the little democracy that this country has left," an academic told me at one of the many seminars on violence that were being held around the country.

The threats and other attempts to muzzle political opinion were such that we expected the call to vote to be louder and more urgent than ever in Colombian history.

It was in the midst of such precarious political conditions that Colombia rang in the new year. I went with my mother, Julia; my sister, Sylvia; and Sylvia's husband, Salomón Kalmonovitz, to the house of my cousin Carlos Angulo for New Year's Eve celebrations. It was the usual family gathering: pleasant, relaxed, and filled with talk of politics, the topic that always ended up dominating our get-togethers. We felt the weight of history upon us, but this still did not diminish our ability to enjoy a few moments together. Partying and rumba have always been the best way for Colombians to drive out bad omens and tensions. That night we danced salsa, sang romantic boleros accompanied by a guitar, and—for an instant—forgot about the bombs, the threats, and the fears.

I recently had seen little of Sylvia. She had been working on an investigative report on the gangs of sicario assassins in the outlying barrios of Medellín. At the party, she grew serious only when she spoke about the gangs and the sicarios she had interviewed in the course of her work. What she told us left the family speechless; no one could understand how my mother and Salomón could let her go to such dens of crime and danger. She was twenty-nine years old, but she had never voted; like many Colombians, she had thought that voting would not change things much. But such were the times we were living in that even the most skeptical among us, like my sister, had decided to give it a try. "How can we have gotten to the point where even I am going to vote?" she asked me.

Although Sylvia had been reticent to accept work on the British television documentary *The Veto Power of the Drug Dealers in 1990 Elections* because she was in the midst of her investigation of the sicarios, she could not help being interested in it. After seeking advice from her friends and consulting with me and Salomón, Sylvia agreed to do research and write the script. At that time many analysts thought the elections would not take place, that the country was going to sink into a bottomless abyss in an absurd, fratricidal struggle. The veto power of the drug bosses in elections had been felt dramatically with the assassination of Luis Carlos Galán. Drug terrorism had been shown to have the power to change the nation's destiny. It was known that the 1990 elections would be, above all else, a race against death and that any one of the candidates could be eliminated if the drug bosses decided to issue the death warrant.

The possibility of registering the dimensions of this historic juncture in a documentary was just the type of journalistic challenge that attracted my sister and me. We had never expressed it in words, but we shared an inexplicable attraction to risk, to the danger that is often second nature to reporters.

The documentary was filmed in an area that was chosen because it was a microcosm of the complexities of the country: Magdalena Medio, the chaotic region that Diego Viafara had fled one year earlier, seeking refuge under the auspices of *El Espectador*. The drug dealers were using it as the launching point for the "government takeover" that Barco had spoken of. There the Medellín cartel, through Rodriguez Gacha and Escobar, had fine-tuned their private armies, hiring British and Israeli mercenaries to train them to be bloodthirsty assassins of both peasants and presidential candidates.

Things seemed to have changed in Magdalena Medio, especially since the death of Rodriguez Gacha. But there was no practical way of knowing whether the veto power of the drug militias could be broken at the ballot box. What happened in Magdalena Medio in these elections would give us an idea of the magnitude of the threat the country was facing.

What impressed me most as a journalist was that when a popular leader in Magdalena Medio who proposed nonviolent options was brought down, he was immediately replaced by another. There seemed to be an inexhaustible supply of leaders who were willing to take up the cudgel of whoever of their colleagues might be murdered next.

"I can't understand how it's possible that there are still people who are willing not only to be president of Colombia but to face the veto power of the drug traffickers," said Sonia Goldenberg, a Peruvian colleague of mine who had come to cover the violence in Colombia, which seemed similar to the violence in her own country.

But the political struggle in Magdalena Medio reflected the confusion of all forms of violence: guerrillas and the union organizations they had penetrated and unionists who opposed the guerrillas. There were groups that wanted to maintain control with the power of their weapons, and there were campesino associations, like the Association of Campesinos of Carare, that sought peace in the region, attempting to negotiate with their violent enemies on both the Right and the Left. Everything was complicated; nothing was clear. It was Colombia.

The central theme of the documentary was an optimistic one, focusing on the peace experiment conducted since 1987 by the Association of Campesinos of Carare. These people were victims of ongoing violence whose lives reflected the difficult reality that had always marked campesino life in Colombia: Besieged by the drug militias on one side and the guerrillas on the other, they had ended up being victims caught in the cross fire.

Peace in these environs had always been unattainable. So when the peasants' group attempted to seek accords with the various armed factions, few people believed in them. Nevertheless, for three years, the campesinos had managed to maintain their isolation from the violent forces around them. They made peace agreements with the guerrillas and with the army. As part of these agreements, the guerrillas were to avoid coming into local towns for sanctuary, as they were wont to do. Because the peasants were usually forced to give food and shelter to the guerrillas, they were presumed by the army to be collaborators. For three years, the guerrillas went along with the pact, which in turn gave the peasants a measure of neutrality in the eyes of the military. The deal took the peasants out of the cross fire between the combatants, and little by little, the murder of peasants decreased. After having been in one of Colombia's most violent regions, Cimitarra's campesinos were able to return to their lands and begin an impressive economic resurgence. In answer to those who believed that waging war was easier and less expensive than achieving peace, they adopted the motto: "Peace is more feasible than war."

Yet the hard-won peace of the campesinos of Cimitarra was still fragile and viewed with great suspicion by almost all the players around them. Neither the army, nor the guerrillas, nor the central government trusted the campesinos' commitment and motives. The conflict in the region was reactivated by the presence of the drug traffickers, who began operating in Colombia in the late 1970s. As happened throughout the country, the drug dealers used their cocaine profits to buy up land all around, on which they built laboratories and bases for their trafficking operations. The land purchases were gradual and when they arrived in Cimitarra, they dramatically altered the balance of power.

As had occurred in other parts of Magdalena Medio, the drug traffickers' influence brought a fundamental change in the essential makeup of the paramilitary groups. These militias had become armies of the drug dealers in a process that seriously threatened the peace process in Cimitarra.

I had the good fortune to meet Josue Vargas and Miguel Angel Barajas, two leaders of the campesinos' association, in 1987, soon after they organized their peace crusade. There was no guile in the way they spoke, and they did not mince words.

"We went to see the guerrillas and met with Braulio Herrera, commander of the FARC squad in Cimitarra, and we told him not to use us anymore, that we weren't going to protect them anymore and that we weren't afraid any longer to say so," Barajas told me. They also spoke with the army, telling the high command that they, the campesinos, would no longer provide sanctuary to the guerrillas, that they were fed up with them.

"Why don't you speak directly with the paramilitary groups," I asked them once. Vargas answered with a cynicism that revealed my naive question for what it was: "The army and the paramilitary squads are the same thing; if we talk to the army, why should we bother talking to the paramilitaries?"

By 1990 the leaders of the campesinos' association were certain that Rodriguez Gacha's death would give them the chance to play a role in politics. But they also knew it was too soon to declare the end of the paramilitary drug squads, whose structure remained intact, as did their political aspirations, under the new leadership of Henry de Jesús Pérez. The drug militias also sought involvement in the elections by winning slots on the Liberal party ballot. On the side of the campesinos' association, Barajas led the slate for city council. The two sides would face off in elections. In January 1990 the militias had begun a campaign to disparage the campesinos. "The campesinos provide a base for the guerrillas," a militia spokesman told the newspaper *El Tiempo* in an interview in Puerto Boyacá.

The economic power employed by the drug bosses was a new, tough-to-manage ingredient, and Barajas and Vargas thought they were losing control of the situation. Cimitarra was facing a virtual siege.

Sylvia's first visit to Magdalena Medio was on January 15, 1990, to attend the Great Dialogue for Peace in Cimitarra, a forum organized by the campesinos' organization. The forum allowed Sylvia to make her own appraisal of the group. "They suffer from one of the problems of democracy: They get too caught up in details. What is lacking is a rigorous analysis of the paramilitary groups and their relationship to the drug-trafficking business. And there is excessive fear."

Sylvia was also witness to the presence of the drug militias—which called themselves "self-defense" groups. "Even though the defense groups are being seriously questioned at the national level," Sylvia wrote in her notes for the documentary, which she sent by fax to London, "here they blatantly go about their business on the street, terrorizing the population as they roam about in their jeeps. They maintain their complicity with the military, with the police, and with the mayor."

The commander of the police in Cimitarra assured Sylvia that he had never heard of the self-defense groups. The mayor also said he knew nothing about that type of activity, which is curious because everyone in town knew that Vladimir—the assassin who appears prominently in Klein's video and was responsible for a massacre of judges in Magdalena Medio, among many other killings—stayed at the mayor's house en route to Campo Capote. The only person who confirmed the existence of the drug militias was the local parish priest.

Finally, Sylvia diagnosed the general status of affairs in Cimitarra, which she intended to portray in the documentary: "Cimitarra," she wrote to her producers, "represents the country. While the association makes use of democratic mechanisms to overcome violence—perhaps at times with too much fury and too little long-term analysis—the town is governed by the code of silence." She added: "It is unclear why neither the attorney general's office nor the Elite Corps have come to the region."

It was difficult to do filming openly on the street because the people were afraid that being recorded on film or tape might later be used by their enemies to identify them and exact revenge, something that had happened on innumerable occasions in the past. "The population and all the violent groups are clearly opposed to the presence of reporters and filmmakers who they don't know. All the armed groups have intelligence operations; they send out agents disguised as journalists, something that leads people to take great care with whom they are talking."

Sylvia came up with a plan to deal with the problem. "While the situation seems hot, it is manageable for us in our role as reporters hired by a foreign organization. That is clear. What we should do is carry ID cards, letters of recommendation, etc. It is difficult but not impossible. It is a problem of dealing straightforwardly," she wrote to her producers in London.

On Wednesday, January 31, Sylvia conducted an interview in Bogotá with Barajas, who had come to the city in search of political support for the group's peace efforts. The renewed strength of the death squads was already being felt.

As a result of his trip, a march was held on February 10, attended by Rafael Pardo and Ricardo Santamaria as representatives of the government in a show of support for the campesino association's policies. While they wanted to provide clear moral support for the group, the government representatives once again reiterated to the campesinos that the government would not endorse the process because government policy permitted peace agreements only with guerrilla groups and dialogue only with the guerrilla high command, in search of agreements that would be nationwide. They said that the government did not talk with drug militias because those groups could not claim any political basis for their actions.

The campesinos interpreted this response as a new step by the government to abandon them. Although they had presented "concrete efforts toward peace, these were neither taken into account nor supported because they were not considered a valid political position and were not within the scope of governmental policies." They concluded that "to be a participant in the peace process, one must have committed a crime, as in the case of the militias and the drug dealers, or must have operated outside the law, as in the case of the guerrillas."

In their meeting with the government representatives, the association's leaders asked the government to provide representatives from the attorney general's office and members of the Elite Corps to block the drug militias' attempt to attain legal status and to take control of the area. This request alerted the paramilitary groups, which from that point on began to prepare a detailed method for killing the association's leaders, as well as my sister.

Sylvia did manage to tell me that the campesinos were asking the government to send the Elite Corps into Cimitarra. "I want to be prepared because if the Elite Corps shows up, I'd like to take cameras along with me," she told me several days before she was killed.

On February 26, the day she had arranged to meet the three leaders of the campesinos' association—Vargas, Barajas, and Saul Castaneda—Sylvia was unable to arrange for the camera crew. And although she had told her producers she would go only "with cameras and everything and only if the parish priest from Barrancabermeja decides to go, because otherwise it would be risky and useless," she did not alter her travel plans.

She was late getting to the airport that day and missed the flight to Cimitarra. But she still did not give up. She phoned Carlos Atuesta, a member of the association, and informed him that she was taking a plane to Bucaramanga and from there a bus to Cimitarra, where she would be arriving at 9:20 P.M.

Vargas, Castaneda, and Barajas were waiting for her at the café La Tata, located right next to the police barracks. Although they never mentioned it to Sylvia when they spoke with her, friends later said that they had been worried all day. Early that morning, word had come to town that a paramilitary group was on its way to the banks of the Carare river. On hearing the news, Vargas, a religious man, decided that the only thing he could do was pray; the prayers lasted more than an hour. At 7 P.M., when a car came to pick them up to wait for Sylvia at the restaurant, the association's leaders caught a glimpse of three police agents posted in the plaza. With them were three others no one had seen before. All that was known about these other men was that they had come from Puerto Boyacá. But what surprised the leaders most was seeing Carlos Atuesta, a member of the association, standing with them, taking amiably. "What is he doing with those guys? Wasn't he the one who said they wouldn't talk at all?" asked Castaneda.

At 9:15 Atuesta left to meet Sylvia. In town there was practically a smell of impending death. The feeling that something was about to happen was so strong that one person at the restaurant actually telephoned the police and said, "Please, get here right away. They're going to kill the association leaders and the reporter!"

"How do you know?" the policeman at the other end of the line asked.

"Because I saw 'El Mojao' and the other sicarios sitting in strategic locations around La Tata."

"We'll see what we can do. . . . Right now everybody is busy," the policeman answered.

Some people at the restaurant actually told the association's leaders and my sister to get back in their cars and get out of there, that they were about to be killed. These same people were witnesses to the killing and provided information to the authorities on what happened at the restaurant. Sylvia tried to ease the tension. She joked with the person who took her to one side and pointed out the assassins outside the restaurant, saying that "they probably were there to protect her." But those who had warned her insisted so strongly that Vargas changed his mind about having the meeting there. "Let's finish our drink and leave," he told my sister.

Outside, the net was closing in on them. Witnesses said they saw Atuesta kiss Sylvia on the cheek before he left. The gunfire began three minutes later. Quickly, three armed men who were seated in the restaurant fired at the heads of the association's leaders and my sister. One of them was a policeman.

According to DAS, the intellectual authors of the crime were the self-defense groups of Puerto Boyacá, commanded by Pérez. "It is better that you all do not get involved in the investigation because it is possible that there could be reprisals against you and your family," was the advice that General Maza Márquez gave me in a meeting at his office. "Leave it to us and the attorney general's office."

Among Sylvia's writings, one of the last entries was an interview with a subject who she described like this: "He is tall and has an evil look about him. He has the appearance of being a murderer." Without knowing it, she was describing one of her executioners.

I saw Sylvia for the last time the day before she set out for Cimitarra. She had been trying to reach me the entire week so she could talk to me "because she wanted to discuss some things that were worrying her very much." But the rush of work and the fact that we were both equally negligent about keeping appointments made us put off our date until Sunday. The original idea was for me to go with her to Cimitarra, but since I was scheduled to travel to New York, I decided not to go. "When I get back, we can go there to see what happened after the elections," I told her, without thinking for an instant that something untoward could happen to her.

That Sunday she came to the house with Salomón at around eight, after spending the weekend in Puerto Boyacá for "a honeymoon," she had said with that mischievous expression of hers.

We spoke about her trip to Cimitarra, though not to the depths of the issue, especially since I was in the middle of the outline for this book. She seemed somewhat nervous, but content with what she was doing. It seemed to her and to me that she could end up with a good story that deserved to be told. She was the way she always was when she got involved in investigating something: completely wrapped up in the problems of that area. Yes, it seemed dangerous to me. But Magdalena Medio had always been like that, and there was no place in Colombia at that moment where a reporter was not facing potential danger. The risk was ever present, as the telephone threats that I still received made clear.

The only person who told her not to go to Cimitarra and to wait for things to calm down was Julia, my mother. "Sylvita," she said with some concern, "don't you think it would be better to see what happens after the elections are over? . . . I saw that just last week they killed a radio reporter in Barrancabermeja."

Sylvia grimaced the way she did when somebody told her something she knew was the truth but did not want to accept. "Listen, mom, I think that if things get more difficult, I'll have to stay away from there for a while. But right now, I can't just drop everything and forget about the campesinos. They're waiting for me."

She managed, despite it all, to read a copy of the outline for my book and to make some suggestions. It was around 11 P.M. when she and Salomón got up to leave. "Could you get me a book about gangs . . . over there in the Strand Bookstore in New York? . . . Don't forget," she said as she was leaving.

Salomón was the first person to find out about my sister's murder. A reporter from *Vanguardia Liberal,* a regional publication in Santander, called him from Cimitarra to say that a body with Sylvia's ID card had been found. Salo, as Sylvia and the rest of us in the family called him, suddenly felt as if the world had shattered and fallen on him. He called my mother, but could not summon the strength to tell her that Sylvia was dead.

When news of the attack was broadcast on the radio, it said only that there had been a shooting. Neighbors gathered at my mother's apartment so she would have company. My friends, knowing that neither I nor my brother were in the country, also began to arrive. Rafael Pardo, the presidential aide, visited her as well, but could not bring himself to tell her the truth. So until about midnight—when they could no longer keep the truth from her—all my friends kept up the lie that my sister was still alive and that she was undergoing emergency surgery at the hospital in Cimitarra. When she learned that my sister was dead, my mother, with her customary strength, sat down on the couch and put her head in her hands. She could not cry. She could not speak. Her daughter Sylvia had been killed.

I found out about Sylvia's death the following day, when my brother, who was living in Michigan at the time, called me in New York. He was straightforward and to the point: "Bad news. They killed Sylvia."

When I hung up the phone, I could think only about my mother. She was a tall, beautiful, olive-complexioned woman, who always stood out because of her elegant style of dress. We, her children, had inherited her strong character, her indomitable, independent spirit that on many occasions had made her seem tougher than we were. She was the youngest in a family of six brothers and sisters who had been victims of La Violencia during the 1950s and, like many families, had lost everything. She was forced to leave school and eventually found a job as a secretary at an advertising agency run by Lucio Duzán, a well-known journalist who had a reputation as a womanizer. Nobody thought that my mother would catch him so easily, but she did. I am the oldest of their children; Sylvia was born next, and my brother Juan Manuel is the youngest.

"What makes me saddest of all is that they killed her when she was at her peak," my mother told me when I called her after my brother gave me the news.

Salomón wanted to leave immediately for Cimitarra. My cousin, Carlos Angulo, asked him to wait so they could go together. The two of them caught a flight to Bucaramanga early the next morning. Presidential aide Rafael Pardo had arranged for a plane from the Santander state government to take them to Cimitarra.

Their pilot was hostile and annoyed. "I have to get back quickly!" he told them. "Don't worry. We're even more interested in getting back quickly," my cousin answered.

After an hour, the flight arrived at the Cimitarra military base, where Salomón and Carlos were met by soldiers. "The colonel will be right here to meet you," said one of the soldiers, asking the two men to sit in the hallway. The soldiers asked who they were, what they were doing, and how long they were planning to stay.

All of a sudden one soldier asked, "And María Jimena, she isn't coming?" The question surprised my cousin and my brother-in-law, since beyond journalistic circles it was not commonly known that Sylvia and I were sisters.

"No," Carlos answered. "She's not coming." "Well, the thing is, if she comes, my colonel wants to talk to her," the soldier insisted. I never contacted the man nor did I find out what he wanted.

Half an hour later, the colonel met with them. "I'll never forget what he looked like," my cousin recalled. "He was about five feet tall, and he spoke to us quite directly in a military tone. From the moment we arrived in Cimitarra to the moment we left with Sylvia's body, I had the impression that we were considered persona non grata, that we didn't deserve the least amount of respect."

The colonel said that he was going to lend them a truck to bring back Sylvia's body. The truck arrived within half an hour, and Carlos and Salomón set off in search of my sister's body.

"They told us that they had no material to prepare Sylvia's body, so we went to buy sheets to use as a shroud," Carlos recounted. "In all the establishments we stopped at to buy the things we needed, everyone knew who we were, but no one spoke to us."

They went to the municipal court to ask for Sylvia's personal effects but were told that they could not have these items. "This is criminal evidence," one bureaucrat told them, holding a fistful of cosmetics, some keys, and a notebook. Nor did the officials want to give them a death certificate, without which it would be impossible to take the body home. There was so little cooperation that Carlos and Salomón had to remind everyone that they had been sent by the office of the president. Finally, the bureaucrats relented and issued the death certificate, but they kept Sylvia's personal effects.

When Carlos and Salomón got to the hospital, people were milling about, staring at them as they went inside. These were blank faces, faces devoid of emotion, with no glimmer of life. Carlos remembered the inquisitive expression on the faces of two men posted at the hospital entrance, who did not stop looking at them. "We never knew who they were, but they followed us every place we went."

When the mortuary preparations were finished, Salomón and Carlos found a coffin to transport Sylvia's body to the truck and returned to the military base. The bodies of the campesinos killed along with my sister were taken out later that afternoon.

Back at the airstrip, the pilot told them that the coffin was too big for the plane, so Sylvia's body was removed. My cousin, Salomón, and several soldiers carried the corpse on board the plane. "Be careful with the plane, don't get it dirty!" shouted the pilot.

Thus, between my cousin and her husband, my sister, Sylvia, covered in a shroud, took her last ride on an airplane. The only thing visible was her face—a gentle face, just like she was.

Back in Bogotá, my cousin took a deep breath as if he had returned from the depths of the Inferno. Then he said, "In Cimitarra, no one gave us their condolences. No one approached us to lend a voice of comfort. We felt hostility but something worse, something that I will never forget. This was horrible for us, but for these people, it was business as usual: Nothing special had happened. There was an inhumanity to it all. I felt there was a communion with death in that place. They had become inured to death."

The burial was as Sylvia would have wanted it. With her own people, her friends, mine, Salomón's, and my parents'. It was the first time that Sylvia was not late for an appointment.

Two years later, in 1992, the Colombian justice system issued fourteen arrest warrants against the material and intellectual authors of the Cimitarra massacre. Nevertheless, to this day, these murders—like countless others—go unpunished, even though they took place in a restaurant in the middle of Cimitarra with no lack of witnesses. All who have come forward to testify, despite the fear and the threats that the campesinos of that region still must confront, have had to leave the country.

Of the fourteen suspects, only one was captured and two, Henry de Jesús Pérez and Gonzalo Pérez, fell victim to the only justice that is certain to be meted out on time in Colombia: pirate justice, the same system they initiated and that finally wiped out the leaders of the self-defense groups of Magdalena Medio.

After the death of Rodriguez Gacha, his successors in Puerto Boyacá fell one by one. Henry de Jesús Pérez was murdered as he presided over a public event in Puerto Boyacá; Gonzalo Pérez was killed several weeks later.

In October 1991, Ariel Otero, who had assumed the leadership of the self-defense groups, decided—after having escaped uninjured in an early attempt on his life—to surrender to authorities, taking advantage of the submission decrees that opened the door for the paramilitary groups. Ironically, he let the government know of his decision via a spokesman for M-19, who called Ricardo Santamaria, President Gaviria's security adviser.

Ricardo had worked with Rafael Pardo throughout the process of restoring M-19 to legitimacy and understood, as did few others, the paramilitary operations in Magdalena Medio. He knew that it was necessary to seize the initiative and immediately presented a plan to the minister of defense and the military command.

Otero was required to surrender his arms, and hence to inform the government where his caches were hidden so that the armed forces could recover them. Once this step was completed, they would pass on to the judicial phase.

Keeping in mind that those who surrendered and confessed to the crimes of illegal possession of arms and conspiracy would not be imprisoned, Otero surrendered to the authorities. Within two days, Santamaria received a sketch from Otero indicating the location of the arms caches. As was planned, the army and the Elite Corps moved into Puerto Boyacá. One of the caches was submerged beneath the swimming pool in the old house of Henry de Jesús Pérez. In it they found about two hundred weapons, among them rifles, shotguns, and revolvers. Santamaria was surprised to find that the R-15 rifles were still covered with grease, as if they had just been unpacked.

The same day, a special judge sent by the Colombian Judiciary Criminal Division stood ready at the police command center to receive Otero's declaration of guilt. Otero stepped forward after the first ten paramilitary members had turned themselves in. In a period of ten days, 250 men had surrendered.

A few months later, Otero's body was found on the outskirts of Puerto Boyacá. Following his surrender, Otero had gone to live in Cali, seeking protection from the Cali cartel, as did many government informants. There he reported for court appearances precisely as he was required to do under his sentencing guidelines. A few days before he was killed, he had escaped another attempt in which a bomb was planted near his house.

"Ariel Otero died because he ended up trying to play both sides at the same time," a campesino in Cimitarra told me.

Basically, the chiefs of the self-defense groups in Magdalena Medio ended up being victims of their own macabre game. Their old allies, like the Medellín cartel, had become their strongest enemies. "Ever since the self-defense groups—which always professed themselves to be deeply anti-Communist—found out that Escobar had contracted with the ELN guerrillas to plant bombs, relations between Puerto Boyacá and Medellín were tense. For the right-wing self-defense squads such an alliance was treason," said a DAS source who conducted intelligence operations in Magdalena Medio.

The leaders of the self-defense squads quickly switched sides and approached their archenemies; they provided information to DAS and to the government about Escobar's hidden stockpiles. That was why Otero chose Cali as his refuge, with the fervent hope that his life would be more secure there.

With the death of Rodriguez Gacha and the fall of his successors, the wings of the rapacious paramilitary groups were clipped. Yet these groups have still not been deactivated. They are out there, waiting to arise once more. At the very least, their ghosts continue to haunt the campesinos of Cimitarra, who despite everything have not shrunk from their attempts to bring peace one day to their area.

For Santamaria, Otero's information and the capture of the weapons caches, which had little relevance at the time, would grow in importance: "The value of having demobilized this self-defense group has never been fully appreciated. For us it was a great event in the midst of so much violence to remove from the war 250 people, weapons and all."

THE NEW COUNTRY

As I left my sister's funeral, anguished, I spotted Enrique Santos. "Gabo and Mercedes arrived last night and want to see you. I haven't said anything about it because they want to keep it a secret. I'll stop by to pick you up tonight," he said, whispering in my ear.

Gabo was Gabriel García Márquez, who I hadn't seen in four years, since the Havana Film Festival in December 1986 when he had inaugurated the Cinema Foundation at San Antonio de Los Baños, and Mercedes was his wife. During that time, Gabo had been completely taken up in his new project.

At the film festival, he said, "Now it's time to get to work!" He raised those thick eyebrows of his and spoke with the energy he always shows when he gets involved in some new endeavor. Dressed in overalls, he wandered about the Hotel Nacional in Havana, talking about movies with students, film directors, friends, and anyone else who gave him the opportunity to discuss his new plans and the future of Latin American filmmaking. Only when his spoke about Colombia did his expression change. Gabo had been living outside the country since 1979, when he had received a tip from friends saying that there was a military plot to kill him. García Márquez was a well-known leftist, a friend and confidante of Fidel Castro. The Colombian military was deeply anti-Communist and the cold war mentality made him a dangerous person, a man hated by right-wing groups in the country. He spent much of his time in Mexico City and frequently visited Havana, where he had his own house.

At the time, it seemed that the possibility of achieving peace in Colombia was slipping through our fingers. And Gabo, who had participated throughout the process, realized that the country was entering a period of chaos, when nobody would know anything, not even his longtime friend Belisario Betancur. "He is the most stubborn man I know, the most unreasonably optimistic, the most reckless in pursuit of a peace with social justice. The only thing I'm not sure about is that if, in the harsh years of his government, he was always a president who was well informed about what was going on," García Márquez wrote in the prologue to Enrique Santos's book, *The Wars of Peace*.

Since then, Gabo had not only avoided the country, but had stopped speaking about it. In Havana I told him that everyone was anxiously hoping he would attend a literary event in Cartagena. He told me he wasn't going. His resolve was such that I thought he really would never come back.

Yet not even in that moment of despair was Gabo able to disconnect himself from what was going on in Colombia. He received telexes every day telling him what the newspapers were saying back in Bogotá; he kept up to date with the latest rumors circulating in the political arena and the social world; he spoke with ministers, ex-presidents, film directors, and journalists; and his friend José Vicente Katarain notified him within minutes every time an assassination took place in Colombia. He continued to be well informed and was always proud of it.

"Back there they kill someone for having dinner at a restaurant," Gabo said in that rhythmic tone of voice he uses when he wants to fill a single sentence with everything he's thinking. I couldn't argue with him because what he said was true. Days earlier, my friend Carlos Alfredo Cabal had been gunned down in a restaurant by a crazed Colombian, a U.S. Army Vietnam veteran who began firing from his table at anything that moved.

I was in Cuba the day they assassinated Guillermo Cano. It was Gabo who broke the news to me, ten minutes after it happened. I was returning from the theater, having seen a film about Frida Kahlo. It must have been after 9 P.M. when we arrived at the Hotel Nacional. At the entrance, a Peruvian friend saw me and said, "Gabo is going around looking for you. I think it's urgent. Something about an attack on the publisher of your newspaper." I went up to my room, my heart racing, and called him. "They've killed Guillermo Cano. That's why I don't want to go back to Colombia, because they're killing my friends," he said with the conviction that everything was taking place just precisely as he had told me it would.

A driver came by and took me to the house the Cuban government kept for him in Havana. That night Gabo, immersed in a pessimism and a profound sorrow at the death of his friend Guillermo, told me, "That country is going to hell. Nobody knows who is killing whom anymore. It could be the guerrillas, the drug traffickers, the army, or some nut."

I tried to cheer him up, to tell him to come home, that the situation in Colombia seemed worse viewed from the outside. But with his reporter's instincts, he had sensed that bad times were on the way; he knew he was going to stay away from Colombia for a long time. And that possibility, which I saw so clearly as well, made him even more gloomy. Neither of us could have imagined that our next meeting would come after four years of warfare. The day that Gabo and Mercedes decided to come to Colombia I was burying my sister. The roles were reversed: I, obviously, was now the pessimist, and Gabo was the optimist. He was charged with positive energy, bringing with him projects and plans for what he was calling "The New Country."

"I come back to this country thinking that things were improving. And the first thing I see in the newspapers is Sylvia's murder," he said by way of condolence. Neither Mercedes—we called her "La Gaba," a woman with a commanding disposition and beautiful, almond-shaped eyes—nor Gabo offered condolences. We didn't even mention the subject the entire night. Instead, we talked about Colombia.

"You know, this country is the only one that is making progress in Latin America," he said. "In the midst of this chaos and this destabilizing violence that is unprecedented in our history, we have been capable not only of avoiding a fall into the economic crisis that the rest of the Latin American countries have succumbed to, but of being along with Chile the only two countries to achieve economic growth. We have managed to demobilize the country's five guerrilla groups; the paramilitary militias, previously an unaccepted reality, are now something that is real and is being fought; and after the death of the Mexican, the self-defense groups also want to demobilize to return to civil life. The drug traffickers seek the same thing. We are defeating drug terrorism and we are building a much more realistic Colombia than that fictional country we had before. The Colombia of today is composed not only of heroes but of drug dealers, militiamen, and guerrillas—people on the left, center, and right. And the Liberal candidate for president, Cesar Gaviria, is a fine arbiter for this new country. Moreover, if Colombia was once considered a country of barbarians and drug dealers, its world image is now changing."

At the outset, Enrique and I tried to respond to this wave of optimism with a certain nihilism nurtured in the midst of so much death and so many funerals. But Gabo, locked on his course, found a bright side to all the negative things we said. "You know, in this country things are beginning to clear up; we're beginning to find out who is trying to kill whom. The point is that we have a very violent country. But our form of violence is something that doesn't push us toward the brink of chaos but rather leads us toward change; we are thrust forward in a diabolical way, without our even realizing it."

On the day of congressional elections in 1990, I was remembering what Gabo had said. Fear was conjured away. Colombians did come out to vote, and in record numbers; events hurtled forward, as he had said, at a diabolical pace. The traditional political bosses and their cronies faced defeat. More than half the congressional seats being contested changed hands.

The terrorists sought to sink Colombia in a sea of violence, but something quite different was happening. For example, students who had been apathetic up until then started to participate with spirit and energy, seeking substantial political reforms. It was no longer unusual for any even marginally well-informed Colombian to hear discussions about the need to change the Constitution in line with the new realities of the country. "The Constitution is too small for such a big country" was the way Gabo put it.

The traditional parties, conceived as they were at the turn of the century, no longer responded to Colombian needs. As never before, it was evident that ours was a restricted democracy. If we did not broaden its base to make it more heterogeneous and tolerant, we could slide into the chaos into which the terrorists wanted us to fall. We had to strengthen our taciturn system of justice because we could no longer tolerate the impunity that fed the terrorism.

Change was in the wind as we moved toward presidential elections. Cesar Gaviria understood the situation and summed it up in his campaign slogan: "Reform in order to create peace."

"We have come to the point where extradition has been the only way to punish outlaws who systematically assassinate judges and leaders who oppose their evil ways," Gaviria declared in a speech. "But to trust extradition alone would be permanent recognition of our own impotence. We should be capable of creating our own laws and developing a judicial system that can confront terrorism and protect the lives of our judges. Thus we would have a penal model to combat this illicit activity so we can restore Colombians' faith in justice."

The crisis of credibility in our institutions was a palpable reality whose presence was felt constantly. There was nothing new about it, but it never had been taken as a starting point toward real proposals for change. President Barco, convinced that it was necessary to introduce profound changes in our society, had tried unsuccessfully on two occasions to reform the Constitution. His last attempt during the 1989 congressional session had practically entombed the possibility of constitutional reform. Seeing that some congressmen wanted to include a referendum on extradition as part of any such package, the government ditched the reform proposal.

When the chances for a new Constitution were practically nil, suddenly a new proposal came from outside the government and the traditional party system. It came from the student movement. Young Colombians—many of whom were not even of voting age— took to the streets, knocking at the doors of newspapers; calling on politicians, ex-presidents, the entire political community, and leading a student movement under the provocative banner: "We can still save Colombia." Constitutional reform had proved impossible for the Barco government; the students resolved it. They found a consensus for a referendum on a new Constitution to be held in the first round of elections for Congress and mayors. On election day we were voting not only for congressmen and mayors but for a new Colombia. The next president of Colombia, if we could actually elect one, would have to start from scratch and rebuild the nation.

On March 20, Bernardo Jaramillo, presidential candidate of the Patriotic Union, left his house at 7:30 A.M. with Mariela Barragan, a young woman from Barranquilla whom he had recently married. Two hours later Bernardo was assassinated at the Bogotá airport by a twenty-one-year-old sicario. He was the third presidential candidate assassinated in the ill-fated election campaign. Immediately, Colombia's most important trade union—El Central de Trabajadores Colombianos—called a national strike; fearing street disturbances, merchants shuttered their stores in most major cities. The assassination of Bernardo reminded us of the fragile nature of the political process we were fighting for. A sudden explosion, an attack, or the assassination of a candidate could change everything in a minute. "With these types of attacks and terrorist actions, we lose any hope of a national recovery," Jorge Carreno, president of the Supreme Court, said sadly upon hearing of Bernardo's murder. "I don't know what to think; confronted with this type of crime, there is nothing left to say."

Bernardo met Mariela in Eastern Europe during one of his many forced exiles. Mariela, who was studying there, returned to Colombia, married him, and suddenly found herself the wife of one of the most threatened and protected men in the country. "We don't go out, we don't have the life young people should have, we live closed up. And when we go out, we're surrounded by a haze of bodyguards," she had said in an interview with *El Espectador*. The security measures had increased even more since Bernardo had kicked off his presidential campaign for the leftist Patriotic Union movement; his campaign slogan was "Venga Esa Mano, Pais" (a colloquial expression, something between "Give me five" and "Let's all join hands"). For several months he had been tirelessly crisscrossing the country and frequently appearing on television. In a television interview conducted the day before he died, he confessed that his greatest wish was simply to live a normal life: "I'd like to have the chance to walk along the street without bodyguards, without people pointing at me; I want to be able to go into an ice cream parlor and have an ice cream cone, to sit down on a park bench, to feed the pigeons, to read a magazine or a newspaper, and to go to the movies," he said. "That is my greatest dream. I hope that I'll be able to realize it one day soon."

Since the assassination of the previous Patriotic Union leader, Jaime Pardo, the death threats had become part of his life. It was during that period that we became good friends. Despite the danger, he would often come over to my house. There, along with other friends—many of whom happened to be advisers to Barco—

we would talk endlessly. The discussions were tough, passionate, and off the record. Sometimes Bernardo would come on strong, as when we spent the night debating the guerrilla problem and the drug militias. His great political struggle was the fight for a modern left wing, independent of the guerrilla groups whose political arm had traditionally been the Communist party. "We have our own dynamic and our own form of politics," he would say whenever they accused him of being a "guerrillero" himself. Toward the end, his criticism of the guerrilla movement had become stronger; he had publicly condemned the methods of "persuasion" (kidnapping and extorting money from landowners and peasants) that they used on civilians. It was not only at these gatherings when we saw each other. We also stood side by side at the cemetery as many of our friends were buried. Without saying so, in some way we knew that either one of us could be next. Those moments we spent together were always intense and productive. At such times the thread of life seems so fragile. Bernardo was never evasive; he had a direct and proud way of saying things. And what he said at home in the heat of a couple of shots of aguardiente, he would also repeat without the least hesitation before the microphones. "They want to exterminate us because we are the only party that has managed to mount a challenge against the two-party system in Colombia," he said before the television cameras after one of the countless funerals of his murdered colleagues.

If anyone could decipher the problem of the paramilitary and its linkage with the drug traffickers, it was Bernardo. "The persecution and the annihilation that this party faces is unprecedented in world history," he said with the vehemence he had learned in his years as a union leader among the banana workers of Urabá. "The drug traffickers are no longer involved just in underground activities; they are now also entrenched among major landowners, industry, and commerce. These are the patrons of the militia squads. They may or may not be drug traffickers, but they are defending concrete interests, and to support their private form of justice, they have required the help of the armed forces," he said more than once in television interviews. "The government should let the full weight of justice come down not only upon those who wield the weapons, but upon those who sponsor and protect them. Society will find, as it unravels, that at the apex of the paramilitary groups there are major empressarios and well-known political figures."

Bernardo soon became an inexhaustible source of information for the press on the drug militias. "If they kill me, you'll already know who it was who did it," he told me each time I asked him to confirm a story I was working on.

Well groomed and a flirt by nature, Bernardo had a great impact on women. He was a *rumbero* when he could pull himself away to have some fun but serious and focused when he was involved in the workings of politics. His extended outings could last until the crack of dawn, drawing frequent complaints from his bodyguards that it was less exhausting looking after the president than after him. "He never gets home before 4 A.M.," one of his weary bodyguards once told me. This routine had changed, however, since he had fallen in love with Mariela. The night that I went for dinner at their home—it was the last time I saw Bernardo alive—I could see that he was really smitten with her. As always, he was filled with ideas and plans for his presidential campaign. For an instant I thought that Bernardo would survive and that he would serve his country for a long time.

The last time I spoke with him was just a few minutes before I left the country, following the assassination of my sister. "Go away a while and take care of yourself," Bernardo advised. I was in Paris the morning I received the news that he had been killed. It filled me with both fear and rage—fear because his foretold death had finally taken place and rage because even though it was like watching the same scene of a movie being repeated over and over again, the government forces still hadn't been able to prevent his murder from taking place.

I was surprised to hear that on the day he died, Bernardo was not carrying a weapon or wearing a bulletproof vest. I had been accustomed to seeing him arrive at meetings wearing such a vest, but he stopped wearing it because of the strain it caused on his lower back. Though he had never fired a pistol, he always wore one in his belt and didn't take it off, not even to dance. "They won't kill me like a dog, as they did with all my friends," was the excuse he would give his dancing partners when we noticed the gun in the middle of a salsa number. Yet in his final days, something made Bernardo change his fatalistic outlook. He thought that after the death of the Rodriguez Gacha, "the drug militias in Magdalena Medio had calmed down" and that they had decided not to kill him after all. This was what he had told Mariela.

They had been living under a great deal of tension in recent months, so Bernardo and Mariela had decided to take a vacation on the coast before he resumed his campaign. Their security entourage, one of the largest assigned to protect anyone—eleven men from DAS and two others assigned by the Patriotic Union—went with them to the airport. Surrounded by such a huddle of bodyguards, the Jaramillos got out of their car and went to the terminal as they were supposed to. While two of the bodyguards confirmed their tickets for Santa Marta, they stayed in the main part of the terminal, watched over by their other eleven guardians. Stationed at a comfortable distance from them was a young man, around twenty-one years old, sitting on a chair. He was well dressed, wore an expensive watch, and carried a bag. His real name was Andrés Arturo Gutiérrez, a native of Medellín, but he carried a false ID card, as is often the case with sicarios who are sent to carry out this type of "job." He had arrived in Bogotá the previous day overland from Medellín. His first appointment was at the Bogotá air terminal. Upon arriving at the agreed-upon location, he met with a bearded man accompanied by three others. One of the men gave him a submachine gun, a mini-Ingram (machine pistol) made in the United States, a 3.80 caliber pistol, and a photograph of Bernardo. The sicario never learned who had hired him; the only thing that mattered to him was he had received an advance of 300,000 pesos (about $600) for the job. That morning, the young sicario had arrived at the Bogotá Puente Aerea terminal at 6:45 with time for a cup of coffee. In his travel bag he was carrying a ticket for the same flight that the Patriotic Union leader was planning to take. The ticket had been purchased in cash the previous Saturday—which suggested that the assassins had advance warning about Bernardo's itinerary, something to which few people had access.

With the airplane ticket he had a copy of a book called *Legends and the Truth about the Mexican,* a handbook on the use of computer diskettes, and an air-navigation map from the Antioquia Aviation Academy.

If his attack failed, another plan was in motion for other sicarios—four to be exact—to do away with Bernardo when he got to Santa Marta. Seated just a few yards from his target Andrés took out a newspaper so he would appear to be reading. Coldly and in a matter of seconds, he shot his weapon through the newspaper, hitting Bernardo four times. The bullets lodged in Bernardo's thorax, wounding him fatally. The sicario might have managed to escape had his weapon not jammed as he prepared to reload. The eleven bodyguards returned fire, managing to wound and capture him. Bernardo had only seconds left to live, but it was long enough for him to realize how naive it had been to think that he would get out of the campaign alive. "I'm wounded . . . they've killed me," he managed to say to his young wife.

"I didn't see anything," Mariela told *El Espectador* a few hours after her husband's death. There were no tears in her eyes, but the desolate expression on her face said it all. "I only heard the shots. I didn't know what was happening because I had never heard machine-gun fire before. They call us violent, but the thing is that we can't even recognize the sound of a weapon." She only remembered having seen the body of her husband spread out on the floor. She threw herself on top of him to protect him, then tried to pick him up. Bernardo was taken to the hospital, where he died shortly thereafter. His was the 1,357th murder of a member of the Patriotic Union.

The Boeing 727 Avianca jet, serial number HK1400, took off from El Dorado Airport in Bogotá at 9:15 A.M. on April 27, 1990. It was carrying 120 people on its one-hour flight to Barranquilla. The captain, Fabio Munevar, was banking toward the area of Cota, eight minutes into the flight, at an altitude of 17,000 feet. Suddenly, two alarms sounded from the cabin. "A minute after we had turned off the fasten your seat belts sign, we heard a lot of noise, as if there were bursts of gunfire inside the plane. We thought that it might have been the front bathroom door because someone happened to go into the bathroom at that moment." But within seconds of hearing the booms, the flight steward came to the cockpit and told them it had been machine-gun fire.

The captain realized immediately that it had been an attack on Carlos Pizarro, the presidential candidate for M-19's nascent political movement. Pizarro had been last to board the aircraft, surrounded by eleven bodyguards. The candidate had traveled several times on planes flown by Munevar, who knew the inherent risks. "As soon as we knew for sure that it was gunfire, we realized that it had been an attack on Pizarro," said Munevar. "It took us eight minutes to get back to the airport. We asked the control tower for priority status and advised Civil Aviation and the police so they would be waiting for us." The plane landed without incident; the other passengers were safe. Pizarro had been killed by a lone assassin, who was shot by Pizarro's bodyguards in a hail of gunfire on the plane.

The murder movie was being played again. Carlos Pizarro was the fourth presidential candidate murdered in Colombia in fewer than six months. There was still a month and a half until the presidential elections. How many more candidates would fall?

Pizarro, as the leader of the M-19 movement, had been the architect of one of the greatest peace efforts in the country. After long years of talks with the government, his guerrilla movement had decided to lay down arms, ending twenty years of combat. The guerrillas were prepared to come down from the mountains and return to civilian life, thanks to an amnesty decreed by President Barco.

Along with several other journalists, I was given the opportunity to observe closely the first conversations between the guerrillas and Rafael Pardo, the presidential adviser in charge of the peace process. I knew many of the members of M-19 from long ago, when we were somewhat younger and more innocent. I found them weary of living in the mountains and fed up with the deprivation of their underground lives. "Armed struggle makes no sense in this country," Antonio Navarro Wolf told me in all sincerity. After the death of Pizarro, Navarro Wolf quickly took up the leadership of M-19. He was himself the victim of an assassination attempt, which almost succeeded. One of the bullets was still lodged in his throat, making his speech difficult. He also lost a leg in the attack; though crippled, he still was a good salsa dancer.

At Pizarro's burial, Navarro Wolf tried to settle the M-19 followers down, calling for calm, knowing that those who killed Pizarro indeed sought to torpedo the peace process. "All Colombians will bury Carlos Pizarro in the peace that he advocated, in the peace that he was building and for which he gave his life," he said on television, attempting to ease angry tempers.

Pizarro's death was a shattering assault on the peace plan sought by President Barco and promoted for so long by my good friend Rafael Pardo, a shy economist from the University of Los Andes. Pardo and his assistant, Ricardo Santamaria, another friend, held the first peace talks for the government with Pizarro at the M-19 enclave in the Cauca mountains, near Cali. Before Barco, other presidents also had sought peace, but had long been stymied by opposition from the military. Pardo, who had worked hard at maintaining good relations with the military, won the military over on the question of talking with the guerrillas. "This time the peace plan will be carried out with the commitment of the armed forces," he said.

Armed with assurances from both sides, he and Santamaria set up a meeting with M-19 on January 5, 1989. Only the president, a few aides, and the high-ranking military command knew about the meeting. Even though I was closer to both of them than any other journalist in Colombia, they managed to hide it from me by saying they were going to a seminar in Cali.

They drove to the outskirts of Cali, into the thicket of forest. There was a persistent, drizzling rain, the kind of bone-chilling rain that penetrates without mercy. The road became ever narrower, and the visibility constantly grew more obscure.

After several hours of travel, they managed to discern a dilapidated truck. As they approached, four men dressed in olive-drab guerrilla uniforms and carrying AK-47s jumped out of the van. The last to hop out was Carlos Pizarro. They recognized him from his Panama hat, which made him seem more like a well-to-do landowner or a Mexican movie star than a guerrilla chief. They rode into the mountains in the truck, which broke down several miles up the road. "I'm sorry to have to tell you that we'll have to go the rest of the way on foot," Pizarro told the weary peace envoys. "Peace is never an easy thing," he added jokingly. The slope was formidable, but Pardo and Santamaria climbed it all the same, even though they felt feverish. When they got to the campsite, it was already night, and despite their exhaustion and fever, they got right down to the reason for their journey. They talked all night; cognac and whiskey flowed freely, easing the cold and breaking the tension. At daybreak, the government representatives staggered off to the shack they had been given to sleep in. Despite Pizarro's willingness to abandon guerrilla warfare, they knew this was going to be a complex, difficult process. While placing a blanket over a wooden slab that would serve as his bed, Santamaria noticed a snake crawling over his pants cuff. "Watch out for the snakes," he warned Pardo. They both were thinking that this was quite different from what presidential aides were supposed to experience—cocktail parties and high-level diplomatic meetings in fancy hotels. Santamaria paused a minute and then turned to Pardo again: "You know, this job of ours is really fucked up."

For many people in and out of the government, forging a peace pact with the guerrillas was not crucial. Given the situation of the country and the threat of drug terrorism, "the guerrilla" seemed no more than a pebble in one's shoe. "I don't understand you reporters. Every time we come down from the mountains, we bring good news. We say, hey, we're almost ready to make peace with the guerrillas. And you tell us, How come so many meetings with a bunch of burned-out guerrillas? . . . The problem in Colombia isn't the guerrillas, its the drug traffickers," Pardo would say with a certain dose of cynicism.

Many forecasted that Pardo's call for peace would be torpedoed by the Right or by the military. Nevertheless, it seemed that in 1990 there was a possibility that M-19 would lay down its arms. Pardo and Pizarro had about twelve more carefully planned meetings in the Caucas. The date of the treaty and the place for signing it were also chosen with care, so carefully that the date was matched up with the best alignment of the stars.

The accord was signed with great fanfare on March 17, 1989, and Carlos Pizarro soon entered the presidential campaign. His arrival in Bogotá was celebrated as if a movie star had come to town. The warm reception given M-19 as a new political party demonstrated Colombia's need, as Pardo had said, "to open up a closed society and reconfigure the two-party state." Public opinion polls showed Pizarro competing with the Conservative party for second place in the national election. But the possibility that he might be killed always lingered in the background. "Pizarro has to be protected in the best way possible because if they kill him, the entire process comes tumbling down," Santamaria told me.

The presence of the guerrillas out in the open did awaken skepticism among certain sectors, since their crimes were still vividly remembered. Many people thought the government peace policies were really a surrender to the guerrillas. But there was also the recognition that peace was a universal responsibility and that society as a whole had to be indulgent. "Peace is forged by sitting at the same table with the enemy," Pizarro often said. This new political mood was reflected in the excellent reception to Carlos Pizarro's candidacy. Pizarro was seen as a distinct and invigorating alternative. In the midst of the pessimism and inertia in which the country was mired, his political discourse was uplifting. He was a fresh new face. "We have to overcome the arms crisis anchored to the 1960s, linked to old national security doctrines," he told *El Espectador* in an interview. "This must be a nation that emerges with optimism and is sure of itself, happy and confident that it can find its way through the death threats and advance in a different direction, reconstructing public morality, because the old values have been exhausted."

Born into a wealthy Cali family, Carlos Pizarro was the son of Admiral Juan Antonio Pizarro, a respected official in the navy. He attended elementary school in the United States and completed high school in Cali. He did not finish his law studies at the Javeriana University in Bogotá because he was expelled as an agitator and for participating in protest movements. Absorbed in the simmering 1960s and convinced of the validity of armed struggle, he entered the Communist party and later, FARC, the armed branch of the party. When Jaime Bateman, frustrated with FARC's orthodoxy, decided to abandon the movement, Pizarro followed him. Since then, he had been moving up the ladder in the organization, but in the military cadre not in the political ranks. When I went to the M-19 camp, Pizarro was one of several members serving time in jail after being captured. He spent three years in prison before being set free under an amnesty decreed by President Belisario Betancur in early 1983. Since then he had been ensconced in the Cauca mountains and he was little mentioned. From this underground vantage point, he watched events unfold: The M-19 leadership was being wiped out. After Jaime Bateman died in an apparently unrelated airplane accident in 1983, his successor, Ivan Marino Ospina, was killed in Cali. Marino's successor Alvaro Fayad was killed as well. Pizarro took control in the midst of one of M-19's worst crises, its leadership decimated, its urban sympathizers falling away.

A survivor, Pizarro watched and waited. And by the end of the Betancur government, the name "Comandante Pizarro" cropped up again in the battle of Corinto.

Hours before the battle with the army was to begin, I managed to get to the M-19 camp, accompanied by a colleague at *El Espectador,* Fabio Castillo. Someone had contacted me, saying that Comandante Pizarro wanted to tell the press how he was being surrounded by the army in the mountains. The possibility of a military confrontation was close at hand. It was an important story. We managed to cross the army's lines and reach the M-19 camp. Along the way, we saw that the army was preparing for a major operation.

With the battle impending, I found Pizarro aggressive and

ready to enter the fray. "If it's bullets they're looking for, this is where they're going to find them," he told me, showing me how the army was approaching them slowly but surely, as he grasped a bottle of cognac, his favorite drink. The guerrillas had been allowed to set up camp in the Caucas as part of the first phase of the peace agreement. But the army had started hemming them in from all sides, especially Pizarro's column at Corinto.

Wearing a drab-green military uniform and a black beret with a star on it, the same type that Ché Guevara wore, Pizarro was evidently more disposed for war than for peace. Since he never believed in the peace process, he was pleased to see that the army was no more interested in peace than he was. That night, expecting the worst, he recommended that we get away from the guerrilla camp. We left as everyone was taking his battle position, ready for combat. Pizarro had grown in stature, surrounded by his men. He looked confident. He was so certain that the peace process was tenuous that he had dug trenches into the mountain, knowing that the army would attack one day, despite the accord with the government. "As you can see, to get us out of here they'll have to come in and get us," Pizarro told me.

The battle took place the following day. Surrounded by the army, Pizarro had managed to resist its firepower, and what had been considered an easy military victory for the army quickly became a war of attrition. Well entrenched in the mountain, the army had not found a way to dislodge M-19 in its first attempt. A major war would have been needed to defeat them. Facing the possibility that such a move would unleash a bloodbath, the verification commission that was set up to monitor the peace treaty managed to halt the military operation. The guerrilla column was moved to another area. But the peace process was mortally wounded.

Pizarro's insistence on armed struggle later brought him to the point of organizing an international column called the America Battalion, which included guerrillas from other Latin America countries invoking the vision of Simón Bolívar. Although Pizarro was a Marxist, he always had a greater affinity for Bolívar's dream of Latin American integration. But the plan was an overwhelming failure. The idea of an international guerrilla force was out of proportion with Latin American realities. "They told us they were going to give us food, but we ended up dying of hunger," one Tupac Amaru (Peruvian) guerrilla told me; he was living in a shack in one of the barrios jovenes that surround Lima, after having managed to return to Peru.

Three long years had passed since then. During that time, Pizarro had gone through fundamental changes. He began to reflect seriously about the validity of the armed struggle. He traveled to Europe and soaked in new political currents there, as well as the changes going on in the rest of the world; he began to understand that the use of arms in Colombia didn't make sense. All the energies that I had seen him put into the war now were rechanneled toward peace.

Moments before he boarded the plane on which he would be killed he told reporters: "We offer something fundamental, plain, and simple: That life must not be murdered in the springtime."

Pizarro was sitting in the rear of the plane, close to the bathroom and surrounded by eleven bodyguards. After takeoff, the sicario, a teenager carrying a false ID, got up from his seat and went to the bathroom. When he came out, he committed an act of pure suicide—firing thirteen times—as he passed the row where Pizarro was sitting. The bodyguards immediately returned fire with twelve rounds, and the sicario died instantly.

From the manner in which the attacks on Jaramillo and Pizarro were carried out—sicarios participated in both cases and each carried the same type of weapon, a mini-Ingram, small and easy to use—everything seemed to indicate that the drug Mafia was behind these assassinations. The two sicarios also carried false IDs, came from Medellín a day before each attack, were duly trained, and clearly acted with premeditation.

Both had been sent by Pablo Escobar; official police reports confirmed it. The police reports said that the two sicarios knew each other and had worked together in a Medellín factory that made chalk for pool cues. But they were also in the employ of "El Zarco," one of Escobar's military chiefs who had recently been captured by DAS.

To confuse matters, Escobar sent out messages from hiding, all bearing his signature and fingerprint (so there would be no doubt it was him). He denied any connection to the deaths of the two leftist leaders. Such denials had become routine.

A week after Pizarro's murder, a communiqué issued by the Extraditables claimed their innocence as well: "Our military and political organization has always had the best relations with M-19 and affirms that it could hardly have ordered the death of Pizarro, considering the fact that he was an advocate of negotiations with us, an enemy of extradition, and a symbol of peace." In the communiqué, the Extraditables also made serious charges against high-ranking members of the police, who they said "were responsible for atrocities committed against us."

If indeed the two attacks followed the pattern used by the drug terrorists, many questions remained unanswered concerning the degree of complicity of the government forces. In both cases it was evident that the itineraries of the candidates, so zealously concealed, were known to the assassins several days ahead of time. In both cases the sicarios had been able to smuggle through their weapons despite the formidable security measures in effect at the airport. But, above all, in the case of Pizarro, the sicario had managed to carry his weapon onto the airplane in his undershorts. Yet none of these questions were answered by the security forces. If the contention of the police and the army was true—if the drug Mafia was really the instigator of these deaths, as it was for countless other assassinations, it was also true that these attacks depended on complicity among members of the security forces.

Despite the war of communiqués, none of them has helped solve the mystery surrounding the deaths of these two leftist candidates. The attacks provoked an emotional chain reaction that crossed the country from north to south and east to west. Whoever had initiated these crimes, it was evident that the intent was to draw the country toward chaos. Something quite dramatic must have been taking place in a country where an eighteen-year-old boy would agree to kill someone on an airplane for money he would never spend, knowing full well that he too would end up riddled with bullets.

"The way things are going during this election, the winner will be the last one left alive or, perhaps, the one who they let live," a colleague remarked. If there was any logic to what was going on in Colombia, terror would have already taken hold. But logic was not operating after the death of the two candidates. The terrorists found an impassioned country prepared to keep on its course no matter what happened to the electoral process. This reaction took many of us by surprise. We had suffered fifty years of violence, but the country had never responded in such a united way. It was a great moment.

All the remaining candidates announced that they would stand and, if need be, would conduct the campaign on television. President Barco quickly proclaimed that the elections would in no way be hampered and that the electoral process would carry on.

For many people, it was evident that the next likely assassination target was Cesar Gaviria, an ex-cabinet minister who had taken over as standard bearer for Luis Carlos Galán. Gaviria had just been chosen as the Liberal party candidate for president in the party's first primary election in history. (Previously, presidential candidates were chosen in Liberal party conventions.)

Owing to the vision of a seventeen-year-old boy, Gaviria launched his presidential campaign on the day Galán was buried. Though immersed in the pain of his father's murder, Juan Manuel Galán surprised all Colombians—including Gaviria himself—when, on the day of the funeral, he anointed Gaviria as the incontrovertible heir to his father's political legacy.

That day is ingrained in my memory. The Bogotá central cemetery was jammed with people crying for their fallen leader. On the platform Galán's colleagues were giving their final speeches of farewell. Bodyguards clutching machine guns surrounded all those under death threat while people pushed and shoved without knowing why. Juan Manuel was nervous. He had never spoken in public, much less before such a throng. For a moment, he thought that his voice would break and that he would be unable to speak the words of farewell to his father. No one, not even his mother, Gloria, nor his cousin, Juana, both of whom had helped him clean up his speech, knew his plan. Everything had been prepared so it would be a surprise. Without knowing that he could be changing the course of history, Juan Manuel rose and faced the microphone. Slowly his words began to come forth more clearly, emanating from that thread of a cracking, adolescent voice. There was silence all around.

"The people rise up and demand justice!" he exclaimed. "I pray to God that this sacrifice will serve finally to compel society to react, to unite in support of the government and our institutions, but at the same time to demand more efficient efforts, without allowing itself to be intimidated by the sicarios or by kidnappings. . . . In the name of my family, I want to give thanks for the solidarity that the government and authorities have shown us, and I want to say to Dr. Cesar Gaviria, in the name of Colombia and my family, that we hand over to him the standard borne by my father and that he can count on our support so he may be the president who Colombia wants and needs. . . . Salve Usted a Colombia—It is you who must save Colombia!"

When he was through, Gloria, surprised by what her son had said, managed to look at Gaviria. "I saw Gaviria's face as he stood below in the middle of the crowd," she recalled. "I saw how he hung his head and how the tears ran from his eyes. . . ."

It was not only Gaviria; all of us were crying. Gaviria responded as best he could, staggered by what Juan Manuel had said. He gave a signal of "thumbs up." Words were unnecessary. A massive cheer rang out, as if the country had been given a second breath of life.

The voice of a teenager had given the clarity that the country needed to emerge from a trying moment. "When Gaviria greeted me at the cemetery before I gave my speech, I . . . I nearly admitted to him what I planned to do, but I didn't," Juan Manuel told me with a certain mischievousness and innocence when I spoke to him some months afterward in Paris, where both of us had taken up exile.

Cesar Gaviria had never been a New Liberal, but his political trajectory—he was mayor of his hometown at twenty-six, Colombian senator at thirty, and cabinet minister at thirty-five—showed he was skilled in managing the affairs of state. I had known him at the University of Los Andes when he was working on a master's degree in political science. We would meet frequently at the home of a mutual friend, Mario Latorre, one of those rare characters who comes along only so often. Mario had been a member of the Council of State and the Supreme Court. He had dedicated his life to the study of law and to his books, but his real passion in life was teaching; his classes in political science at the university were unique. He was one of the first people to classify Colombian democracy as a restricted club that had to be opened up for fear of self-asphyxiation. The study in his home in northern Bogotá, replete with books and a Chagall painting he had bought during his days in Paris, was one of the most active gathering places for political conversation in the city. Politicians, journalists, professors, ministers, presidents—all would go there; Mario treated everyone with the same frankness. "Hola, maestro," was his universal greeting to the men and women alike who came to visit. At 6 P.M. they would start arriving. By 9:30 they would be gone. For me, as a young journalist, it was better than any classroom at the university. This was the real thing.

Mario had a big, bushy moustache that made him look like Albert Einstein, although García Márquez had said that if they ever made a movie version of *One Hundred Years of Solitude,* Mario would be perfect for the role of Aureliano Buendia. Virgilio Barco's presidential campaign recruited many of Mario's habitual guests. Gaviria would often show up at these gatherings, always wearing a jacket and tie. He must have been around thirty years old at the time because he had already been mayor of Pereira and was one of the young stand-out figures of Liberalism, although his name seldom appeared in print. "Provincial politicians like me rarely make our way into the newspapers," he told me by way of friendly criticism. In speeches he always zealously defended the role of politicians and the liberal ideas of his party. He took to politics as if it was the only thing he had done from the moment he was born.

During his tenure in Congress, he was considered a pragmatic politician, and the speeches that he delivered passionately and to the point had a strong Liberal ideological content. He had been one of the harshest critics of the way the army had stormed the Palace of Justice when it was taken over by M-19. Half the Supreme Court had been killed in the cross fire as a result of that operation. As a cabinet minister during the Barco government, it was he who denounced the existence of paramilitary squads; he was also the strongest supporter in the cabinet of the peace process with M-19. He combined the talents of an able politician with his training as an economist. As treasury minister in the early part of the Barco government, he devised a tax reform program that had been the object of criticism in some circles for being based too heavily on neo-Liberal doctrine. "Gaviria is very much a Liberal in politics, but he is a Conservative when it comes to economics," said my brother-in-law, a well-known economic analyst himself.

Gaviria served as acting president when Barco traveled, skillfully facing whatever crisis developed. His work earned him the title "minister par excellence." He was a moderate and knew how to compromise, but he never did so with his principles. For these reasons, Galán knew that Gaviria was perfect for the job of campaign manager.

Although Juan Manuel Galán had chosen Gaviria for emotional reasons, the move became a major political symbol. It also had the practical effect of averting a much more difficult succession process at a time when Colombia could ill afford it. As he told me later, Gaviria knew the impact of the moment: "I was assuming an enormous responsibility. Frankly, at that moment, I could think of nothing else. We were conducting politics purely as a means of survival. That was a period during which one could not even conceive of having a future."

On September 29, two weeks after the death of Galán, Gaviria opened one of the most dramatic election campaigns in Colombian history. His campaign slogan, "There Will Be a Future," symbolized what was at stake: Death itself had to be defeated. That day there was a photograph of Gaviria wearing a bulletproof vest and surrounded by bodyguards who carried small Uzi submachine guns on the front page of *El Tiempo*. That was how he looked when he spoke to the thousands of people who jammed the Barranquilla stadium. His speech was long and intense, full of passion and sorrow. "Today, Luis Carlos would be celebrating his forty-sixth birthday. Let us mark the occasion the way we should: embarking on the road toward restoring the political agenda of Luis Carlos Galán. Let us serve that commitment that Juan Manuel Galán placed on our shoulders . . . his was the greatest of gestures, one that can emanate only from a heart tempered by adversity and molded by an unflagging optimism," Gaviria said. "Faced with the assassination of his father, the fact that Juan Manuel Galán could conceive of a response to his death and make sense of his martyrdom by seeking a democratic, civilian response was a supreme act of confidence in Colombia and its institutions. Juan Manuel Galán's actions embody the country's rejection of violence."

Five months were left until nationwide elections, and Gaviria simply didn't know if he would be alive at the end of the campaign. His first objective was to survive to the March 11 primary election in which the Liberal party candidate was to be chosen. He reflected on that period sometime afterward, when he was already president. At that time, he told me: "There were moments in which we were just living from day to day. We were in a fight for survival. No one saw things in the medium or long term. The country was thinking about how to preserve democracy because we respect democracy in this country. That is why we chose my campaign slogan, 'There will be a future.'. . . At that moment no one thought we would have the chance."

Gaviria's five-month campaign was unprecedented. He avoided public rallies; when he did participate in one, he did so wrapped in his bulletproof vest. And when he flashed the V for victory sign at the end of his speech, his arm could be seen from behind the rifles wielded by his bodyguards. His participation in such public events was announced only moments before his arrival to avoid publicizing his itinerary. Despite all these precautions, campaign swings were often canceled because of the death threats he was receiving. Nevertheless, when Gaviria went out in public, people tried to touch him, and the forsaken glances of his followers sought last-minute encouragement from him. Murder plots against him were foiled time and again. "I haven't been able to do anything besides devote myself to protecting the candidates, especially Gaviria," General Maza Márquez told me at the time.

When Gaviria was still alive for the March 11 primaries after so many threats from the drug traffickers, Colombians started to believe that they might be able to ward off the death sentences. "That was the most important day of our campaign," Gaviria recalled, not without a certain melancholy. "When we won the primary, the feeling was of having disproved expectations and that the sacrifices we had made were worth the effort."

But it was still too soon to start singing victory songs. The presidential election would be on May 27. The two months between the two elections seemed like years. Every moment that went by was a moment in which he had cheated death. There was a feeling that his victory in the primaries was still fragile, that we were still in mid-course. While all the other candidates and political leaders spoke about the need to negotiate with the drug traffickers, Gaviria kept insisting on clearly defined policies in which there could be no room for concessions. "Some leaders propose a dialogue with the drug traffickers; I don't know whether they do so out of weakness or out of a conviction of the need to legalize drugs or because they believe that if they show themselves complaisant in facing the terrorists, they will reach a change in attitude toward collaboration in re-establishing order," Gaviria said, speaking against certain political leaders who were proposing such a dialogue. "The terrorists don't work like that. Terrorism must be fought from a position of strength, by reiterating one's principles, with a defense of legitimacy, certainly not by offering concessions to the terrorists. All societies that have gone through this have come to the same conclusion. We shall not be the exception."

254 ☐ DEATH BEAT

His public declarations were delivered amid tremendous security measures and at times seemed suicidal and reckless. Every time the terrorists struck a blow at the country, Gaviria stood up and answered them. After the death of Jaramillo, a communiqué issued by a group calling itself the Rodriguez Gacha command announced that "the next victim will be presidential candidate Cesar Gaviria." This threat came just after an attack against him had been thwarted several days after his return to Colombia from Miami. "He got away from us by a tenth of a second," said the caller, who phoned the Associated Press bureau in Bogotá, adding that Gaviria "could have one hundred bodyguards, or wear a bulletproof vest up to his head, but he'll still be next." The anonymous caller claimed that the Medellín cartel had reorganized its military apparatus with the assistance of fifteen British, Irish, German, Peruvian, and Libyan mercenaries to "destroy half the country" now that its peace proposals had not been accepted by the government. "We'll surrender when you kill us, but before that this country will be torn in half because as of tomorrow we will resume our terrorist attacks, especially on government and leftist targets. And you journalists, before getting a chance to see our dead bodies, will see the bodies of this nation's leadership."

Somehow Gaviria was able to say what many Colombians did not dare to say, and the mere fact that he would do so was a sign of fearlessness and of the profundity of his democratic convictions. "Colombianos, during these months of national tragedy, we have been trampled time and again by events. The violence strikes at the heart of our institutions, our values, our democracy, and our best people. The ultimate goal of these violent men is to halt the workings of democracy," he said after the murders of Jaramillo and Pizarro. "For this reason, they have unleashed their evil against those who opt for changes that might fortify our democracy and build a Colombia that has no room for violence. So it is no coincidence that during the current electoral process four presidential candidates have been assassinated. The country has lost Rodrigo Lara Bonilla and Guillermo Cano, and we lost Luis Carlos Galán just eight months ago. Bernardo Jaramillo fought for a democratic and peaceful left and Carlos Pizarro, the last in this macabre chain of so many other fallen players, represented the possibility that the guerrilla groups might lay down their arms and join institutional political life. The death of our colleagues must not be in vain. And their murderers believed that quenching their voices would intimidate those who defend freedom of opinion. But we will not be deterred!"

On May 27, in one of the bloodiest presidential campaigns in Colombian history—in which four of the six candidates were killed—Cesar Gaviria was elected to a four-year term as president. He was the first president elected on a platform to undertake constitutional reforms, reforms that would eventually reshape the closed Colombian system with the notion that it was necessary to "reform for peace."

"What I felt that day was a sense of relief for the country . . . having been able to survive the two elections," Gaviria told me eight months later.

The truth is that all of us who were still living felt like survivors of a bloody war in which we lost the most important members of an entire political generation. The majority of Colombian households had experienced death close at hand. Mothers lost their children, brothers lost their cousins, and cousins lost their best friends. No matter how hard we tried, we could never be the same. There was a sense that we had returned from the brink of chaos and that from here on there was a tomorrow on the horizon. There were great expectations for the future as Cesar Gaviria, surrounded by his wife, Ana Milena, and their two small children, María Paz and Simón, dedicated the triumph to one of the many who had died. "This is also his victory," he said, recalling Galán, "the victory of his ideals, the victory of his faith in Colombia."

Basically, we had voted for those who had died. For Galán, for Jaramillo, for Pizarro, for countless others. "Colombia has concluded today the most difficult, destructive political campaign in all its history. Never before have all its values, democracy, and basic liberty been so much in jeopardy. Never before as in this span of time have the purveyors of violence from all quarters tried to topple our institutions. However, Colombians as never before have risen to the historic moment. The powerful democratic will of the Colombian people prevailed. All those who sought to threaten our democracy hear this: The people have spoken today, courageously, clearly: We shall prevail!"

If solving the drug-trafficking problem is far from being the exclusive responsibility of the Colombian government, these dramatic elections signified the greatest defeat that a developing country has ever dealt the evil countenance of drug trafficking, which is nourished on terror and on the disdain for human life, democracy, and justice.

The great achievement was to have reclaimed confidence in democracy and hope for the future. "I think that the institutions and democracy in Colombia were much stronger than we supposed and than people believed," Gaviria said, recalling those days of war. "That was finally what we demonstrated: That the respect for democracy among the citizenry was much greater than expected. And beyond that, the country was capable of finding civilized and democratic solutions. The country did not become radicalized, and there were no authoritarian tendencies such as usually develop when there is a violent crisis of that magnitude."

Two months after taking office, President Gaviria issued a series of decrees that sought to subject the drug traffickers to the Colombian justice system, using to that end a legal means broadly employed by the U.S. justice system: the plea bargain. On February 3, 1991, almost seven months after Gaviria issued these decrees, the youngest of the three Ochoa brothers, Fabio, was the first to surrender to Colombian justice. His two brothers, Jorge Luis and Juan David, were soon to follow. On July 25, Pablo Escobar, together with six of his bodyguards, also acquiesced to the decrees and surrendered to Colombian authorities.

In that same month Colombia ratified a new Constitution that would abolish extradition forever, introducing a profound judicial reform that confronted the drug-trafficking problem head-on. The Napoleonic code was abandoned, and a U.S.–style criminal justice system took its place. In addition, new positions were created: a general prosecutors office and "invisible judges," who were to be duly protected and endowed with the power to investigate and collect evidence with the help of the police forces. These judges would also decide who might be tried for the crimes for which reduced sentencing applied.

The most important members of the feared Medellín cartel were in jail, awaiting judgment. But the flush of success would not last for long.

SURRENDER

On July 14, 1991, the National Constituent Assembly, responsible for writing Colombia's new Constitution, removed the bitter chapter on extradition from the text of the draft document. One day later, the head of the DEA in Miami, Tom Cash, said, "Colombia has surrendered to the drug dealers."

The U.S. Department of State, slightly more circumspect, called it a decision of the Colombian people that would have to be respected. Nevertheless, a State Department spokesman made it clear privately that the United States disapproved of the decision, which, he said, showed Colombia's shaky commitment to the war on drugs.

The *New York Times* and the *Washington Post* published editorials opposing the Colombian decision. A pundit on Cable News Network used the term "narco-state" in referring to Colombia.

In Colombia, there were some doubts even among high-ranking police officials, including General Maza Márquez. He told me, "You could see this coming. The assembly was being threatened. The DEA has a videotape showing one of Pablo Escobar's lawyers giving money to a member of the Constitutional assembly. I investigated the story extensively but never found the videotape. A Colombian government source told me it was a DEA invention intended to show that the decision on extradition was not freely taken but forced by pressure from the drug dealers. Only a small number of Colombians opposed the ban, among them *El Especta-dor* and Luis Carlos Galán's brother, charging that the unseen video showed that the traffickers were successfully controlling the outcome. *El Espectador* argued that banning extradition was a defeat for the country and a surrender to the drug dealers.

Yet a poll conducted by the news magazine *Semana* showed that 92 percent of those questioned supported the abolition of extradition. In their eyes, it was a response to the fact that war was not the only possible political recourse. This ban was not the result of fear or cowardice, as the DEA chief in Miami insinuated. It was the consequence of the very war itself and of the bloodshed from three years of terror. "It is easy to decide from the sidelines what the people at the battle front have to do," said Miguel Silva, President Gaviria's personal secretary, in an interview on ABC's "Nightline."

In January 1991, the Extraditables kidnapped twenty businessmen in Medellín, along with Alvaro Montoya, the son of German Montoya, President Barco's chief of staff. It was an act of desperation, but it also was a clear indication that the war strategy needed to be rethought. The Extraditables, besieged and hunted as they were, wanted to force the government to submit to their demands for negotiation. The kidnapping victims were well-known business figures, members of prominent families. This brazen act was strongly felt among the high political circles of Medellín. Former President Alfonso Lopez Michelsen was called upon to negotiate their release. He agreed and formed a "Prominent Citizens Committee," whose members included a member of the Catholic church, a leftist leader, and two ex-presidents. The goal was to save the lives of the kidnapping victims. "I received a call from Medellín," Lopez Michelsen told me, "proposing that we meet . . . right away; they said they had come to talk about the kidnapping of [Alvaro] Montoya and that the drug dealers want to make a proposal for their own surrender," Lopez Michelsen said.

The Prominent Citizens Committee wrote the first draft of a letter to be sent to the Extraditables, which was published in the press. In the letter, they called for the liberation of the twenty-one prisoners and proposed that the Extraditables suspend their criminal activities and cocaine shipments in return for "less harsh" treatment in the Colombian justice system.

The episode laid on the table a thorny subject for domestic and foreign consumption: negotiating with the drug dealers.

As opposed to previous negotiation proposals, rejected by popular opinion, this one was immediately embraced by the Conservatives, the Liberals, and the Left. Within two days of the publication of this letter, an anonymous caller told the news media that the kidnappimg victims would be set free in the Medellín Without Slums neighborhood, the project built by Pablo Escobar. The drug dealers also sent an answer to the letter with two of their kidnapping victims, Patricia Echavarria Olozaga and her daughter, Diana, who were relatives of President Barco. The two women were discovered unharmed in a van.

For the first time, the Extraditables—after three years of outright war—proposed their own surrender. Their language was replete with pledges of respect for the rule of law and government institutions, words that did not seem to come from people who had threatened Colombian democracy for so long.

"We accept the triumph of the State, of its institutions and of the legitimately established government, and we are prepared to lay down our arms and the materials of war at the altar of the nation's welfare," the document said.

"We accept the existing rule of law with the hope of receiving from the government and society respect for our rights and the reintegration of our families."

As proof of their desire for peace, they offered to release all those they had kidnapped; to serve as mediators in the dispute between the emerald miners and the paramilitary squads; and to intercede with the sicario hit squads "with the sole aim of putting an end to the violence that wounds and troubles our Colombian homeland."

At the same time, the document said they had decided to halt the shipment of drugs, the delivery of arms and explosives, the operation of cocaine laboratories, the seizure of hostages, the establishment of clandestine airstrips, and the other activities as soon as they received "legal constitutional guarantees."

Also for the first time, the Extraditables called themselves "an organization and a group of people outside the law." Nevertheless, they used the term "political criminals" in hopes of falling under the category of the law that decreed a pardon for guerrilla activities.

Two other significant pledges were that there would be "no bomb attacks in any part of the country" and that they would halt "all forms of execution of political leaders, government and union officials, justice employees, journalists, police, and the military."

These pledges meant that they were confessing to having participated in such activities in the past.

The document ended with their renewed repudiation of extradition: "The essential cause of our struggle has been, and always will be, our family, our liberty, our people, our lives, and our rights of citizenship and homeland."

The communiqué caused a commotion throughout the country. Who, finally, were the Extraditables—two, five, or six drug traffickers? "Everybody knows that the Extraditables are Pablo Escobar and the Ochoa brothers," one of my sources in Medellín told me.

Despite the ambiguities of their declaration, it was certain that the drug traffickers had accepted defeat and were prepared to face the Colombian justice system.

President Barco, interviewed by reporters on the possibility of seeking a formula for the drug traffickers to face the Colombian criminal justice system, left the door open, saying "the government is not inflexible in the study of the nation's problems."

Carlos Lemos Simmonds, the interior minister, agreed, saying that "if the drug traffickers want to turn themselves in, the only thing the government can do is wait to see if they live up to what they propose."

Although the government asked the country not to have "hasty expectations," the drug dealers actually began to do what they had promised. Shortly after the release of the two women, another one of the kidnapping victims was set free in Medellín, also carrying a communiqué that asked, "To President Bush and the men of the DEA we say that if they don't accept the word of the drug dealers, then why are they negotiating with them and why do they put them on the stand to testify against their own?" This was a reference to a declaration by Bush that he did not trust the word of the drug dealers.

Eventually the remaining hostages were also set free. For a moment, the possibility of a truce began to take shape. The terrorist attacks ceased. And, on February 15, 1990, when the presidents of the United States, Colombia, Bolivia, and Peru were posing for photographs at the Cartagena drug summit, the drug dealers turned over three cocaine laboratories.

However, the drug traffickers' proposal never reached fruition. The window of opportunity closed for good two months later with the assassination of Bernardo Jaramillo, the Patriotic Union's presidential candidate. Following this new assassination, a wave of bombings was unleashed, many focusing on commercial districts, killing a number of innocent victims. The truce had been broken.

Although Pablo Escobar denied any connection to the death of Jaramillo, as well as to other acts of violence, the renewed attacks were taken by Barco as an obvious demonstration that drug trafficking was still alive and that the continued goal of the drug bosses was to destabilize the country. "If Barco would have acceded to the drug traffickers' proposal at the moment it was released, many deaths would have been avoided," said Lopez Michelsen months later.

Other deeper reasons also impeded a political change. One was the calamitous episode that *Semana* called "Montoya's dialogues," referring to German Montoya, Barco's chief of staff.

Coming from the private sector, Montoya managed the affairs of government with the force of his personality. He was respected, feared, and hated all at the same time. Along with former justice minister Low Murtra, he had been one of those responsible for the attempts to reinstitute extradition. So it was now a surprise to see that he favored talks with the drug traffickers.

According to news reports, the dialogues had been conducted at the presidential palace itself, with a prominent go-between. The image of the Barco government suddenly had become clouded. It was hard to understand how Barco publicly could call himself an enemy of drug trafficking while negotiating with the drug bosses behind closed doors. We were putting ourselves in danger in this war: Which of the two policies was the real one?

Montoya said that the news reports contained "disinformation." He confirmed that the conversations had taken place but said that they had been conversations and nothing more. He insisted that they had not been negotiating sessions.

According to Montoya, everything started when Joaquin Vallejo Arbelaez, his friend and a former cabinet minister, visited him at the palace. Vallejo said he was acting as a representative of Pablo Escobar, who, along with his allies, wanted to negotiate the extradition treaty. According to Montoya, he simply listened to Vallejo, but promised him nothing. However, the drug traffickers had a different version. As a result of the conversations, they presented the government a negotiation offer: In exchange for handing over their weapons, explosives, laboratories, and clandestine airstrips, the extradition treaty would be lifted and they would be granted a pardon. They even discussed contacting Henry Kissinger's consulting firm to develop a lobbying campaign.

The final dialogue took place thirty-six hours before the assassination of Galán. Afterward it was halted for good. President Barco never knew about it, Montoya said. "We thought that Mr. Montoya was acting in accord with what the president wanted," said Guido Parra, one of the lawyers who helped edit the draft proposal delivered to Montoya. (Parra was another eventual victim of assassination.)

The episode reinforced the impression that affairs at the palace were not managed by the president but by people like Montoya. That concern grew when Barco decided not to ask him to resign.

The dialogues were costly for Montoya. In one tape intercept, whose text was published in *Semana,* a voice that DAS said was Pablo Escobar's tells Guido Parra: "that guy made a fool of us."

Montoya's insurance company was the target of a bomb attack. Meanwhile, one of the twenty-one people seized by the Extraditables in Medellín was his son, Alvaro Diego, who was set free on January 23, 1990, following the declaration of surrender by the Extraditables. A year and a half later, Marina Montoya, German's sister, was kidnapped by the Extraditables and later brutally murdered in reprisal for the death of a member of the hit squad Los Priscos at the hands of the police.

There were other impediments to overcome in the short term. The police forces neither understood nor accepted a change in policy. After all, Barco had started the war. And DAS and the police kept insisting that the capture of the bosses of the Medellín cartel was imminent. Barco, facing a broken truce as a consequence of Jaramillo's death and the continuing attacks, chose to believe them. Barco would thus avoid defending an internationally unpopular about-face, especially with President Bush preparing to travel to Colombia to participate in the drug summit in Cartagena. The offer of surrender was left dead and buried.

Drug trafficking was responsible for more than fifteen hundred deaths in 1989 and 1990. The impact on economic growth was acute. In 1989 the growth in the gross national product was 3 percent, despite early predictions of 4.5 percent. Industry, commerce, and agriculture all suffered. Insurance companies had to cover multimillion-dollar losses.

On the other hand, the demand for bodyguards grew by leaps

and bounds. In 1988 the industry was worth an estimated 3 billion pesos ($6 million). The next year, Colombians paid 5.5 billion pesos ($11 million) for protection. In 1968 there were 30 private security companies operating in Colombia, whereas in 1989 there were 551.

The bombs and the terrorism scared away foreign tourists. Colombia was listed among the most dangerous places to visit in the world.

The war was an economic bloodletting for Colombia. There was both a feeling of exhaustion and sincere hope for peace on the street. Even the Barco administration officials who had worked to revive extradition ended up accepting the fact that it hadn't worked. "Why, instead of fighting about extradition, can't we just dedicate ourselves to rebuilding our justice system?" asked Eduardo Diaz, the minister of health.

Between April and June 1990, the corpses of policemen began showing up in the barrios of Medellín. At the beginning there was a daily murder; later two, and then three. By June, two hundred policemen had been killed. These policemen were not killed in shoot-outs or ambushes. They were shot point-blank as they left their homes. From the manner in which they were killed and by the quantity, it was evident that this was a mission directed by the Medellín cartel. It was quickly learned that the orders came from on high, and, according to General Maza Márquez, they had been handed down by Pablo Escobar himself.

The killers collected five thousand dollars a head. "These policemen would have had to work two and a half years to earn that much money," said *Semana*.

This was the first demonstration in the aftermath of the Barco government that the battlefield between the drug traffickers and authorities would be Medellín itself.

Never before in Colombian history had the security forces paid so high a price for fighting violence. The chief of the antinarcotics police, Colonel Jaime Ramirez, had been assassinated in 1986. The commander of the Medellín metropolitan police, Waldemar Franklin Quintero, had been executed by sicarios. General Maza Márquez, the DAS chief, had escaped four attacks. Police deactivated a car bomb timed to blow up the exact moment that General Gomez Padilla, the police commander, drove by.

In their decision to take on Escobar, high-ranking police officials were being driven into the same clandestine life in which

Escobar had taken refuge. Their offices had become bunkers. They could not go out to have lunch in a restaurant or go to a café with their friends. And they could not see their children, all of whom had been taken out of the country for fear that the drug traffickers would murder them or—even worse—kidnap them and force the police to yield. They lived like prisoners.

"For me the thing I long for is to be able to go out and have coffee some place without bodyguards," General Maza Márquez told me with a touch of melancholy.

In the final months of the Barco government, the security forces lashed back vigorously against important members of the Medellín cartel. Strangely, the extradition agreement that had been established as a weapon against the cartel members was rarely applicable, since the majority of cartel members were killed in shoot-outs.

In May 1990, the police cut down Pinina, Escobar's military chief. Gustavo Gaviria (no relation to the president), Escobar's cousin and best field lieutenant, perhaps the most important man in his organization, was gunned down in a Medellín barrio as he visited one of his girlfriends in August 1990.

The police operation let Escobar know that if he attacked the family members of any official, they would do the same thing in return. Although Escobar managed to escape from them, the police campaign against the Medellín cartel in the final months of the Barco government pounded the military and economic structure of the cartel as never before. For the first time, Escobar's empire began to falter.

In their attempt to wipe out Escobar, the police and DAS built strategic alliances with Escobar's enemies, who were their own enemies as well. The Cali cartel, at war with Escobar, provided them with valuable intelligence information. Members of the drug militias of Magdalena Medio—the private army of the deceased Rodriguez Gacha—who they had fought so often in the past, having been the source of peasant massacres and attacks on notable personalities—now accompanied them on their operations to catch Escobar. But above all there was a reversion to the same private justice that they had fought.

In Bogotá and Medellín, death squads, known as the "Urracas," began to execute the supposed culprits of terrorist attacks. The bodies of these terrorists appeared on the outskirts of the cities, their heads hooded and their hands tied. Inscriptions like

"For being an assassin" and "For being a son of a bitch" were written on their backs.

In the slums of Medellín, the sicarios took their revenge for their dead, killing still more police and, in the wealthy districts, the oligarchy's children in the discotheques they frequented. One such attack took place on May 26, 1990, when fifteen children from Medellín high society were shot down in retaliation for a police massacre carried out in the barrios. Groups called "militias"—behind which, it was said, were the police—committed massacres in the barrios that wiped out families, leaving slogans on the walls such as "eliminating vice in the barrios," which sought to justify their acts.

"Who are the people carrying out these killings?" I asked a DAS agent. "I don't know who they are. But they're doing a good job, don't you think?" was his answer.

The first to take advantage of this situation, as always, was Pablo Escobar. He sent letters to the news media condemning atrocities by the police and DAS, whom he referred to as "official assassins."

If the results seemed favorable, the war of vengeance nevertheless damaged the prestige of the police and DAS around Medellín as the police first became victims and finally gang members in their own right. It will be a long time before society can accept them as the authority that should be protecting it and safeguarding it's rights under the law. Whenever there is a robbery or an accident, many people hesitate to call the police. "We always think that there's a policeman somewhere behind every theft or attack," a mother living in the comunas of Medellín told me.

Gaviria's new judicial policy for dealing with the drug traffickers was announced on September 5, 1991. Six months later it was endorsed by President Bush, after many reservations were expressed by the U.S. agencies charged with fighting drug trafficking. During the Persian Gulf War, Bush took a moment to express open support for Gaviria's policies: "I support the policy of having them face justice, since in that way the drug traffickers will be judged for their crimes."

In a brief visit to the United States in January 1991, President Gaviria touched all the necessary bases in stating his intent and the scope of his policies. "No country can be expected to maintain a permanent policy of war," he said at a meeting at the *Miami Herald.*

Actually, Gaviria had begun to develop this new strategy as a member of the Barco administration, when the leaders of the cartel had first brought up their proposal for surrender. On that occasion, he had said that the "declaration of the Extraditables includes statements that, once established, could be considered in the best interest of Colombian society" and that "the only thing the state can expect is that if they really suspended their illicit activities, they will come to be judged according to the sentences intended by law." Furthermore, if the traffickers actually deactivated their criminal activities, he said, "the state could give them constitutional guarantees in return." Those guarantees were suspended following the death of Galán when antiterrorism decrees were promulgated. He was emphatic, however, in stating that "these decisions should be unilaterally developed by the government and issued exclusively by it once the criminals have ceased their illicit activities."

During an official visit to Europe in the final days of his administration, Barco raised the possibility that if the drug traffickers were to surrender, extradition would not be employed. His minister of government, Carlos Lemos Simmonds, was the first to propose an additional enticement—the reduction of sentences.

Finally, Rafael Pardo, a Barco aide who was also chosen by Gaviria, was designated to merge all the various proposals into a single policy. Pardo had been thinking about the matter ever since the traffickers offered to surrender. "What we learned at that point was that if it was not yet the right moment for various reasons, it was nevertheless necessary to begin planning a policy in which the drug dealers would be brought to Colombian justice," he told me several months later.

Pardo came up with an idea that was not new. Industrialized and democratic countries, including the United States, already had measures, such as plea bargaining, in which reduced sentences are negotiated with criminals in return for their cooperation with the government. Colombia's problem was that the security forces were unable to catch the criminals; thus, they had to find a way for the drug traffickers to surrender voluntarily, to get them into custody in the first place. To achieve that goal, Pardo proposed that a sentence-reduction plan would be offered only to those who turned themselves in. His experience in peace negotiations with guerrilla leaders had shown him the distinction between the two groups; it was clear to him that the drug dealers could not be dealt with as political prisoners.

Such a surrender would have to be linked to two conditions, without which there would be no reduction of sentences. First, the drug traffickers would have to call a halt to their illicit activities; second, they would have to confess to their crimes, a step that would eliminate the possibility that they would intimidate judges to find them not guilty. Anyone complying with these two requirements would not be subject to extradition to the United States. Anyone entering the program who committed some other crime or who tried to escape would no longer be eligible.

The criminals would be tried by a special division of anonymous judges similar to the Italian system. Thus, the Colombian justice system would be abandoning the Napoleonic Code and approximating the U.S. system of criminal prosecution.

The accused would be housed in special high-security prisons, as was done in Britain with members of the Irish Republican Army. The problem was that there was no such prison in the country; without high-security prisons, the entire exercise would be little more than an illusion. To date, the maximum-security prison at Itagüí, outside Medellín, is the only such institution in Colombia.

Gaviria agreed with Pardo that there was no time to lose. If a plan for the drug traffickers' surrender was to be devised, it should be developed by the government alone, not in concert with the criminals or their negotiators. The drug traffickers should be treated as common criminals and, above all, the strategy should be carried out publicly for the whole country to see.

For the government, this was the right moment to formulate this type of policy. The terrorist attacks by the drug dealers had stopped since Gaviria was elected. For the first time, the government, without any pressure and fully on top of the situation, would be able to impose conditions for the drug dealers to face justice.

Gaviria quickly presented the plan to his ministers and aides, all of whom approved it—even General Maza Márquez. Thus the Policy for Facing Justice was born. The recently appointed minister of justice, Jaime Giraldo Angel, a veteran Conservative jurist, was designated to write the policy into law. On September 5, when there had been no terrorist attacks for three months, the government promulgated Decree 2047. To prove that the policy did not constitute a surrender to the traffickers, Gaviria ordered that day the extradition of five people who were sought by foreign jurisdictions.

But the truce did not last long. Three days before Gaviria announced the new policy, Diana Turbay, the daughter of ex-president Julio Cesar Turbay Ayala, was kidnapped by the Extraditables, along with six other journalists. A month later, Francisco Santos, the news editor of *El Tiempo* and a good friend of mine, was taken. In December, Maruja Pachón, a television producer and relative of the long-suffering family of Luis Carlos Galán, and her sister-in-law Beatriz Villamizar were abducted, and Marina Montoya, the sister of Barco's ex-chief of staff, German Montoya, was kidnapped and brutally murdered.

The Extraditables had known where to strike; they had lashed out at the Liberal establishment; at the press; and at those who, in their way of thinking, had been their most dedicated enemies—the government of Barco and the supporters of Galán. With the kidnappings, the Extraditables wanted to show that they had not been defeated. They also were able to use their hostages as bargaining chips to try to force the Gaviria government to make concessions.

In December, after the kidnappings, the government announced Decree 3030, in which it declared that the special sentencing measures would not apply to anyone who had committed crimes after September 5, the day the measures were announced. But a tragic event would change things.

Diana Turbay, who had been kidnapped in September, was killed on January 24, 1991, in a rescue attempt orchestrated by the police. Caught in the cross fire, Diana, who had declared a hunger strike, was too weak to run when the shooting started. When her body was brought back to Bogotá, she weighed only ninety-two pounds. Her death was a blow felt throughout the country. The drug traffickers again had lashed out at one of the most prominent Liberal families in Colombia.

I had met Diana three years earlier while she was involved in efforts to demobilize the M-19 guerrillas. It was her interest in demobilizing the other guerrilla groups that led her to be lured out of Bogotá with the promise of an interview with Father Pésarez, the leader of the ELN guerrillas. The invitation was a pretext for her kidnapping and had been contrived by the drug traffickers.

Her death brought pressure on the government to offer concessions. A new decree was announced, retracting the earlier decree and saying that criminals would be accepted into the amnesty plan even if they had committed crimes up until the day of their capture. Although Diana's mother criticized the government for having done nothing to save her daughter's life, others insisted that the new decree was too much of a concession. Every time the government issued a new decree—there were eight in all—lawyers for the Extraditables said it was a new declaration of war. In any case, the journalists were gradually released, except for Marina Montoya, who was killed in revenge for the death a member of Los Priscos. By January 1991, only two journalists were still imprisoned—Francisco Santos and Maruja Pachón—and were being used as hostages by the Extraditables. Both were released on May 20, 1991. On December 18, when Fabio Ochoa took advantage of Decree 3030 and surrendered at the Itagüí prison, General Maza Márquez—despite his support for the sentence-reduction plan—told me his strong reservations: "Things are now backwards. We're turning the state over to its enemies."

He was right in a way: Things had changed. And he did not participate in the new policy. His influence in the Gaviria government was less than it was under Barco. He had lost his ability to persuade the president on policy matters, perhaps because of his unfulfilled promise that he would capture the big drug bosses. In the final analysis, his drug-trafficking investigations did not bring concrete court cases and convictions; the majority were merely accusations without proof. The most dramatic example of such accusations was the case of the suspects in the killing of Galán. After three years of investigation, it was concluded that these suspects were innocent of the crime.

On June 19, at 5:10 P.M., a helicopter left the headquarters of the Antioquia State interior ministry. Among those on board were a representative of the attorney general's office, Father Rafael García Herreros, and Alberto Villamizar, a former member of Congress and member of Galán's New Liberal movement. Father García Herreros had been an important player in the tense, drawn-out negotiations with the Extraditables since the kidnapping of the eight journalists. But the one who had played the pivotal role in these negotiations had been Alberto Villamizar. This forceful man with a penetrating gaze would be the unheralded craftsman of the surrender of one of the most sought after criminals in the world.

Villamizar had started his political career alongside Galán. Like many New Liberals, he had been firm in his statements about drug trafficking. In 1986 he had miraculously escaped from a terrorist attack right after he had challenged Jairo Ortega's group for the chairmanship of the First Constitutional Committee in the Senate. "These guys want to become the bosses of the committee to block approval of extradition via the legislative route," he told me at the time, when he had called to tell me about the infighting before he finally was elected chairman. Galán, his brother-in-law, political confidant, and friend, had been murdered by the drug traffickers. "The drug traffickers killed my friend Rodrigo Lara Bonilla after trying to kill me, and then they killed Luis Carlos Galán. Now they kidnap my wife and my sister, and it's up to me to defend the drug dealers' human rights in order to save them," Villamizar told me.

The day that Diana Turbay's death was reported, he understood that if he wanted to see his sister and wife alive again, he would have to resort to every means of persuasion possible. He would thereby be the right person to save the rest of the hostages as well, since he could establish contacts that the government couldn't.

He hadn't slept ever since Maruja and his sister were kidnapped. He dedicated himself to negotiating with their kidnappers face to face, like the good son of Santander he was, where people are known for their tenacity. There were moments when he thought that all was lost, but he remained optimistic, drawing on his inner strength. He quickly lost his sense of fear and focused on a single obsession. "Look, I give you my word that as soon as Maruja and Francisco (referring to Maruja Pachón and Francisco Santos, the two kidnapped journalists) are freed, I'm going to do everything I can for Pablo Escobar to surrender," he said on one occasion. "What better service can New Liberalism give to the country, after having fought so hard against the drug traffickers, than to help put Pablo Escobar behind bars?"

Villamizar became secretive in his movements and trusted no one. By the same token, all his actions were known to the government. He never acquiesced to Escobar's demands for surrender because he considered them outrageous. The traffickers accepted surrender, but they said they would confess to no crimes; they sought status as political prisoners, contending that drug trafficking was a societal crime. They would not accept being sent to jail, demanding instead that they be sent to confinement camps, as had been done with M-19. They demanded that General Maza Márquez and Carlos Eduardo Mejia, the director of criminal investigations, be fired. Mejia, who had opposed all their demands, was responsible for formalizing the surrender. Slowly but surely, as the police kept lashing out at him and with continued pressure from Villamizar, Escobar gave up his demands, finally holding out only for guarantees of his own safety.

The only thing that was negotiable, in Villamizar's view, was the most obvious—that the state would offer Escobar the guarantee that his rights would be respected. At that point, that small guarantee boiled down to one thing: the duty of the state to ensure that Escobar would not be killed.

So the government agreed to meet any demands having to do with protecting Escobar's life. It accepted the proposal that the guards at the prison in Envigado—near where Escobar's family lived—would be locals and it would sign a controversial agreement with the municipality in that regard. It also agreed that the jail would be guarded by an army cordon rather than by the police. "The great paradox in all of this is that the state had to protect Escobar to prevent his enemies inside and outside the government from killing him," an aide to Gaviria told me.

For those like Villamizar who had been involved in the process, the result was a political triumph for the state over the drug traffickers. But others had a different view: Any concession, no matter how small, was capitulation.

In reality, considering everything that Escobar sought, the government gave very little. But for a country without a prison policy and without time to construct maximum-security jails, those few concessions allowed Escobar to live in a five-star prison, where he could continue to manage his illicit business.

Having sought treatment as a political prisoner, Escobar ended up accepting treatment as a criminal and a drug trafficker. From having insisted on surrender without self-incrimination, he went along with confessing to at least one crime. From seeking a detention camp instead of a jail, he had to accept being placed in a penitentiary, although it was not a maximum-security jail.

"The problem wasn't so much what we went along with but rather the development of events afterward and the way in which policies were carried out," acknowledged Ricardo Santamaria.

Villamizar, who had no relationship with the government, did agree to petition for one of the most insistent demands of the Extraditables, a demand that they had set as the prime condition for freeing the hostages: giving air to their charges of unwarranted assaults by the police forces. Villamizar considered this demand not only reasonable but as something that should not be hidden from public view. The charges included an attempt to murder Escobar's brother, as well as murders committed by the police in the barrios of Medellín.

Villamizar tried to have these charges published in the news media, but he had little success. He also sought investigations by the attorney general's office. More than once, he clashed with Juan Manuel Santos, assistant publisher of *El Tiempo* and one of the most adamant opponents of accepting any demands by the traffickers. "If this is true, it is part of the newspaper's reporting, but it can't be reported based on their demands," Santos told Villamizar, openly irritated. Tension between the two came to such a point that, in a moment of desperation, Villamizar accused Santos of not wanting to save his cousin Francisco, who was one of the hostages.

Villamizar's role as mediator had led him more than once to speak with the Ochoa family at the Itagüí prison. It was through them that he was able to establish contacts with Escobar. He never spoke with Escobar himself, but communicated with him via clandestine mail.

A day after his wife, his sister, and Francisco Santos were released, Villamizar boarded a plane for Medellín and met with the Ochoas at Itagüí. It was on that occasion that Father Rafael García Herreros's name was mentioned. What was needed was a person who could deal with Escobar, whom Escobar could trust, a person who would be the guarantor of Escobar's life. "Who better than Father García Herreros?" Villamizar thought.

Few people in the government knew what was about to unfold. There was a sense that Escobar's military chieftains would turn themselves in, but there was no expectation that Escobar himself would surrender so quickly or so easily, as he finally did.

Seconds before the helicopter left the interior ministry in Medellín, Villamizar arrived with "the man," a confidant of Escobar's, who would keep the secret of where his boss could be found until the last minute.

"Let's go to El Poblado," the man told Villamizar, who passed the instructions on to the pilot. Exactly five minutes later— Villamizar was timing it—the helicopter landed at a soccer field in back of a house. From the helicopter window, Villamizar saw at least thirty well-armed men standing between the bushes. The door of the helicopter opened, and a man wearing a cap and a sports jacket got on board, followed by one of his bodyguards. A long beard hid a face that was burned by the inclement weather.

While the helicopter took off, the two men got settled. For the first time, Villamizar was face-to-face with Escobar. "A very good afternoon, padre," Escobar said to García Herreros. Villamizar and Escobar shook hands. Escobar avoided so much as a look in the direction of the representative from the attorney general's office. For the ten minutes they were airborne en route to the Envigado prison, not another word was spoken.

When the helicopter landed on one of the hills that surround Envigado, it was 5:20 P.M. "So far, so good; it's going like clockwork," thought Villamizar.

It was windy, and the helicopter's rotors raised a cloud of dust that made it impossible to see. The first to emerge from the helicopter were Villamizar and "the man," Escobar's confidant. Escobar came out next, alongside Father García Herreros. Suddenly, one could hear the sound of submachine guns clicking ready, all aimed at Escobar. Escobar got nervous. Quickly, he was brought into the prison's reception area, where Carlos Gustavo Arrieta, the attorney general, was waiting for him. The two men sat down at a square table in the center of the room. All at once, Escobar bent down and started to pull a gun out of his left boot. Before he could put it on the table, the guards protecting the attorney general reached for and cocked their own weapons. "Stay calm," Arrieta said. As if in slow motion, Escobar placed the gun he was holding on the table. It was a Sig Sawer 9-mm pistol with fourteen rounds.

I watched the surrender ceremony on television in Miami, along with two colleagues, Francisco Santos and Mauricio Gomez. Santos, recently freed by Escobar, had arrived in Miami enthused with the prospects of spending time with his wife and two children far from the tumult of Bogotá. Mauricio had gone into exile after publication of the joint news media project following a failed kidnapping attempt. He had returned to Bogotá only for several days, when his father had been kidnapped by M-19.

The three of us had been victims of the violence of the drug traffickers, the guerrillas, and the paramilitary groups. And each of us had seen our lives changed forever. We had the sad conviction that all Colombia had changed and that despite our suffering and tears, the drug-trafficking business was still thriving.

It was deeply moving to see the helicopter landing in the hills at the Envigado prison. We didn't know what to say. I had running through my mind all the people who were no longer with us. The only sound was a heavy sigh from Francisco, something that came deep from within, a gulp of relief.

EPILOGUE

On July 22, 1992, Pablo Escobar fled from a jail that never was a jail at all, just as he was about to be transferred to the headquarters of the Fourth Army Brigade in Medellín. Actually, it was nothing like a prison escape. He walked right past the guards, taking advantage of the fragility that has always distinguished the Colombian prison system. Jaime Eduardo Rueda Rocha, one of those responsible for the murder of Luis Carlos Galán, had done exactly the same on September 19, 1990, escaping through the main entrance of La Picota prison, carrying the false identification of a lawyer. Years earlier, Juan Ramon Matta Ballesteros, the Honduran drug trafficker, walked out the front door of Modelo Prison in Bogotá.

Violence and force were the only two forms of justice for Rueda Rocha, who was killed by the police in 1992, and for Matta Ballesteros, who was kidnapped illegally by a U.S. Marshals Service commando team in Honduras.

On December 2, 1993, after sixteen months of intensive search, Pablo Escobar, the most sought-after drug dealer in the world—certainly the most dangerous and most violent—was shot to death in a Medellín suburb by members of an eight-man team created especially to recapture him. Curiously, when I heard the news, I felt sadness rather than relief, remembering all the people

I loved who'd been killed in the violence generated by this single, profoundly corrupt man. When I got to the office later that morning, I was surprised to find out Ana Maria de Cano was also sad, even though Escobar had killed her husband. "When I heard the news," she told me, "the only thing I did was start to cry; I was thinking that perhaps, if this had happened several years earlier, Guillermo would still be alive. Escobar's death seems the only solution to the violence." But Fernando Cano told me with a furrowed brow that a threatening call had come into our switchboard earlier that morning, warning that "they were going to spoil our party." Who knew what kind of reprisals might take place?

From the day of his flight to the day of his death, Colombia faced an increasing wave of violence. The more time passed, the more Escobar was able to reorganize his operatives and resume attacks. Soon the streets of Medellín were plagued again with car bombings and other acts of terrorism. But for the first time there began to be a backlash against the man behind the violence—even in the barrios where he had once been an idol. A group calling itself the "Pepes"—People Persecuted by Pablo Escobar—set out to harass and terrorize Escobar's family, while at the same time providing information to the search group looking for him. Escobar did not hesitate to strike back, focusing his attention on Bogotá now.

About ten o'clock one night, just a few yards from my mother's apartment and a block from my own, a car bomb exploded near a pizzeria. The impact shook my bed and knocked out the lights. I ran barefoot out of the building and down the hill while debris and broken glass rained down. I could see a huge cloud at the end of the street; I got to my mother's house, and the building's facade was damaged badly. The building's glass door was stuck, and I could hear people shouting that they were trapped in the elevator. I broke the door in and pounded on my mother's door. To my great relief, she opened it, anguished but unharmed. Nothing had happened to her. Five minutes later, my brother arrived with his girlfriend, pale and trembling. They had been on the street near the car bomb and had missed being caught in the explosion by an instant—had a red light been green they would have been right next to the car. Fortunately, no one was killed, though a child was blinded.

The next week another, stronger bomb went off in the center

of Bogotá at 6 P.M., next to a school bookstore filled with parents and children. This time, two hundred pounds of dynamite killed twenty people and wounded sixty. Similar bombings continued: from January to April, Escobar's attacks had killed forty people and injured eight hundred; entire families had been wiped out, and the economic losses were staggering.

Though the devastation was horrifying, the attacks began to occur with decreasing frequency and strength. It began to be clear that Escobar was running out of money and ammunition, and that his once impermeable military organization was collapsing. The Pepes continued their assault, burning ranches and laying bombs in Escobar's lieutenants' properties. They also stalked and, in many cases, gunned down Escobar's chief lieutenants and their families. More violence, unfortunately, but unhappiness with Escobar was so strong—and the efforts of the police so weak— that many people in the barrios supported the Pepes' actions. And though few Colombians would say this openly, all believed that the only way to begin to stop the violence for good was to wipe out Escobar. The attorney general himself said to me, "The best thing that could happen for the country would be for Escobar to die of a heart attack." But the months passed and Escobar remained just out of reach of the security forces.

The police had begun their search operations the day after Escobar's escape. The army, which had been responsible for security at the jail, was eager to join in the effort, and Minister of Defense Rafael Pardo quickly decided to create a special joint task force drawing on the police and the military. The Bloque de Busqueda (Search Squad) encompassed fifteen hundred men trained and dedicated to the single task of tracking down Escobar. They tried every new and old method, including search profiles, personality analyses, and—most fruitful in the end—innovative techniques in radio tracking and transmission monitoring.

Operatives from the Delta Force, a top-secret specialized U.S. Army unit, came down with new tracking devices that they had used successfully in the Gulf War (though with less success in the 1989 attempts to track Manuel Antonio Noriega). Delta Force claimed they would find Escobar within forty-eight hours, but soon discovered that the signals from their triangulation devices were hopelessly distorted by the mountain ranges near Medellín. They tried from airborne sites, but after several unfortunate incidents with commercial airlines, they gave up and went home. A few remained to train Colombian personnel with the trackers, and they eventually proved useful in producing precise aerial maps which showed the topography of the regions where they suspected Escobar might be hiding.

In the end, the Bloque succeeded with a canny combination of toughness, instinct, technical know-how and sheer human intelligence. Zeroing in on the frequencies from Escobar's cellular phones, they managed to track him down to Aguas Frias, in the northeastern state of Antioquia. The prosecutor's office had operatives watching Escobar's family in Medellín and determined that his son, Juan Pablo, spoke with his father between 5:30 and 6:00 every night. They were able to pinpoint Escobar's general location through the frequency of the phone he was using, and in the late fall, after monitoring him for three days, the Bloque prepared to move in. The timing was tight—the calls provided only a thirty-minute window in which to determine his location, and the zone indicated was large, covering a series of houses a mile or so apart from each other.

The on-site forces decided to raid the home of Reverend García Herreros, who had in fact been given his house by Escobar, first. The helicopters landed; they surrounded the house—no Escobar. Then they tried three other likely locations, and in the fourth, it was clear that Escobar had just left. They found his radio, as well as a young girl he was known to have had sexual relations with in the past. But Escobar himself was gone; he spent the night in the mountains and, in the morning, crossed over to the other side of the hills and into the nearby countryside.

Two months after the incident in Aguas Frias, another opportunity presented itself. While Escobar was safe, he was increasingly concerned for his family's safety. His wife, Victoria, and children, Juan Pablo and Manuela, had decided to leave Colombia for Germany, but when they arrived at the Frankfurt airport on November 28, the German government refused them entry. They were forced to return to Colombia and checked into the Tequendema Residence, a large hotel in Bogotá. The Bloque knew Escobar would call his family, and he did—six calls, between Monday, November 29, and Thursday, December 2—enough to give them his exact location in a house in a suburb of Medellín. Within five minutes of placing the sixth call, their eight-man force stormed the two-story house. Five minutes after they entered, Escobar was gunned down in three shots as he attempted to flee across the roof.

"The criminal considered one of the richest men in the world was finished even before they gunned him down," wrote a reporter for *Semana*. Escobar, who once traveled protected by a virtual army of sicarios, was found hiding out with a single bodyguard. Twenty thousand people attended his funeral at a cemetery on the outskirts of Medellín, but the Bloque (and the Pepes) had decimated his entire criminal enterprise, killing any number of his lieutenants and family members. The Medellín cartel's machinery was in ruins. There were rumors of millions of dollars stashed in overseas bank accounts, but Escobar's own family were international pariahs without refuge.

Never in the history of Colombia had one person provoked so much misery or consumed so much of the attention and resources of a government. With him died ten years of terror that left its mark on all of Colombia and all Colombians. We all felt as if we had been living in a police state for a decade. Because of this one man, Colombia had been stigmatized throughout the world, his name more well known than that of any president or other hero.

Yet if the death of Escobar signals for Colombia the end of one criminal organization and its trademark violence, it is far from the end of the drug-trafficking enterprise. The Medellín cartel has been dismantled, and the Ochoa brothers are in prison awaiting trial; negotiations are under way to bring the first members of the Cali cartel to justice, too. But the drug-trafficking business continues unabated, adapting to and taking advantage of new opportunities in the international markets. Every time one route is closed or one supplier is apprehended, the drug traffickers find a new place to operate and expand. Although there may be more cocaine seizures, new markets are opening in Eastern Europe and Japan. While the Medellín cartel's bosses are surrounded and stopped, an international network of drug traffickers is consolidating forces. And despite increasing efforts to halt cocaine traffic in the United States, a new heroin epidemic is spreading through the same distribution networks used first by the marijuana and then by the cocaine trades.

After the death of more than 60,000 people in Colombia in the past five years, among them more than 1,000 policemen, 60 judges,

70 journalists, 1,500 leftist union and political leaders, an attorney general, two cabinet ministers, four presidential candidates, a governor, and several police chiefs, Colombia has finally managed to dismantle the most virulent and vicious drug cartel in the world. But nothing will really change until the world understands that the problem involves not just drug trafficking but drug consumption, and that it reaches to the core of the industrial world, not just the relatively poor producer nations; it touches on international banking practices and the activities of multinational commerce. If the world does not grasp this crucial connection, Colombia will suffer the fate forecast by Gabriel García Márquez: "We will rot alive, in a war that cannot be won"—and the rest of the world will rot with it.

María Jimena Duzán
Bogotá, Colombia
January 20, 1994

A NOTE ON THE SOURCES

The following are the principal people interviewed in the course of preparing this book. There are many others who I do not name, including those who asked not to be identified, and I am grateful to all for their time.

Carlos Gustavo Arrieta, Bruce Bagley, Virgilio Barco Vargas, Fernando Britto, Ana Maria de Cano, Fernando Cano, Juan Guillermo Cano, Tom Cash, Fernando Cepeda Ulloa, Hernando Corral, Eduardo Diaz, Peter Eisner, Gloria Pachón de Galán, Juan Manuel Galán, Luis Carlos Galán, Gabriel García Márquez, Reinaldo Gary, Cesar Gaviria Trujillo, Mauricio Gomez, Richard Gregorie, Michael Izikoff, Carlos Eduardo Jaramillo, Bernardo Jaramillo, Salomón Kalmonovitz, Mark Kleiman, Julio Londoño, Felipe Lopez Caballero, Alfonso Lopez Michelsen, Miguel Maza Márquez, Maria Emma Mejia, Ethan Nadelmann, Rafael Pardo, Andrés Pastrana, Otti Patino, Alejandro Reyes, Ricardo Santamaria, Enrique Santos Calderón, Juan Manuel Santos, Francisco Santos, Gabriel Silva, Mauricio Vargas, Juan Tokatlian, Joseph Treister, Alvaro Uribe Velez, and Alberto Villamizar.

I consulted the files of the following newspapers and magazines: in Colombia, *El Espectador, El Tiempo, Semana, El Siglo,* and *La Prensa*; in the United States, *Newsday,* the *New York Times,* the *Miami Herald, Time, Newsweek,* and *New Times.* I also had access to the files of the Department of Administrative Security and the Attorney General's office in Bogotá. I made use of documents from Banco de la Republica and the Plan Nacional de Rehabilicion, both in Colombia, and had access to U.S. Senate committee documents and U.S. Justice Department documents on drug trafficking. For the section on Israeli arms shipments, I used material from a report prepared for the government of Antigua, in addition to investigations conducted by Peter Eisner and myself.

The following articles were especially useful:

Barco Vargas, Virgilio, "En defensa de la democracia: la lucha contra el narcotrafico y el terrorismo." Bogotá: Presidencia de la Republica, 1990.

Kalmonovitz, Salomón, "La economia del narcotrafico en Colombia," *Economia Colombiano* (March 1990).

Nadelmann, Ethan A., "The DEA in Latin America: Dealing with Institutionalized Corruption," *Journal of Inter-American Studies and World Affairs* 29, no. 4 (1987–1988), 1–39.

Tokatlian, Juan Gabriel, "The Political Economy of Colombian–U.S. Narco-Diplomacy: Case Study of Colombian Foreign Policy Decision Making, 1978–1990."

Among the many books written about Colombia and drug trafficking, I found these particularly helpful: Carlos Gustavo Arrieta et al, *Narcotrafico en Colombia, Dimensiones politicas, economicas, juridicas e internacionales;* Paul Eddy, Hugo Sabogal, and Sara Walden, *The Cocaine Wars: Murder, Money, Corruption and the World's Most Valuable Commodity;* Guy Gugliotta and Jeff Leen, *Kings of Cocaine;* Ciro Krauthausen and Luis Fernando Sarmiento, *Cocaina & Co.: Un mercado ilegal por dentro;* Alfonso Lopez Michelsen, *Parabola del retorno;* Carlos Medina Gallego, *Autodefensas, paramilitares y narcotrafico en Colombia: Origen, desarrollo y consolidacion, el caso de Puerto Boyaca;* Alfredo Molano, *Selva adentro: Una historia oral de la colonizacion del Guaviare;* Elaine Shannon, *Desperadoes: Latin Drug Lords, U.S. Lawmen, and the War America Can't Win;* Jean Ziegler, *Suiza lava mas blanco.*

An earlier version of this book was published in Spanish in Colombia in 1992. Since then, we have taken into account subsequent events in Colombia and the United States. The present book reflects considerable revisions, editing, and additions to the Colombian edition, and I have worked closely with the author to render her colloquial Spanish into equivalent American English while still retaining the very personal flair of her writing and reporting.

Peter Eisner